THE
GYM OF
LEADERSHIP

ADVANCE PRAISE FOR THE BOOK

'Leaders need muscles of courage, knowledge and vision, and strength to stand firm in adverse/hostile situations and face bullets of team failure and still lead and guide them to goals. Four decades of leadership in a disciplined/regimented organization spurs me to recommend leadership expert Anil Khandelwal's recipe for building eighteen gym-style foundational skills. A game-changing book every senior leader can gift to their colleagues, team members and managers'
—A.N. Roy, former police commissioner,
Mumbai, and DGP, Maharashtra

'*The Gym of Leadership* is an exceptionally readable and insightful book, ideal for leaders at all levels and from all corners of the globe. Anil Khandelwal, a highly respected practitioner and professor of leadership, uses the metaphor of a gym to compellingly illustrate how leaders can develop and enhance their skills. Enriched with stories, personal experiences and anecdotes, this book not only imparts valuable lessons but also allows readers to connect deeply with the subject matter. I wholeheartedly endorse *The Gym of Leadership* as a monumental contribution to leadership development. It is a must-read for anyone aspiring to lead effectively'
—Anup K. Singh, director general,
Nirma University, Ahmedabad

'Anil Khandelwal has once again, in his inimitable style, brought together both aspects and crisply condensed his decades of experience into practical and actionable solutions. The "how" is distinct from the "what". The gym analogy could not be more apt, more so with the young generation of leaders. As I've often said, the key job of a leader is to produce leaders. Anil's willingness to candidly share personal anecdotes is a clear demonstration of his commitment to this mantra'
—Ajay Nanavati, former chairman, Syndicate Bank,
former managing director, 3M, and chairman,
Quantum Advisors

'Anil Khandelwal has written a stimulating and thought-provoking book that will enable you to leverage your strengths to become a better version of yourself. He uses the analogy of the "gym" to enable us to start a practice of tapping into our capacity for leadership. By developing habits of setting goals, reflecting, seeking feedback and practising new steps, he inspires us to raise our game. The four aspects of understanding self, emotional regulation, managing relationships and communication are the ones that convert our capacities to learn, think, relate and act into effective leadership behaviours that are sure to create a greater impact. An outstanding book that is both practical and eye-opening!'

—Anil Sachdev, founder and chairman,
SOIL Institute of Management

'Based on the author's leadership experiences, the book aims to provide insightful lessons to improve leadership skills and abilities. Leadership is not a mere skill acquisition, but a transformative journey of personal growth. In the author's characteristically lucid style, the book provides a detailed road map to develop one's leadership capabilities. With eighteen chapters, this is truly a Bhagavad Gita of leadership development—a must-read for anyone seriously committed to leadership development'

—Arvind N. Agrawal, leadership coach
and organization consultant

In *The Gym of Leadership*, Anil Khandelwal has distilled eighteen simple sutras representing the quintessential soft skills of leadership. What I find most appealing about each chapter is the discussion of theory coupled with practical insights . . . a unique and insightful way to prod readers to delve into self-reflection, reaction and refinement of themselves. Understood as a disciplined act, akin to going to a gym, Anil posits leadership development as a lifelong journey. I hope this book, like his other contributions, inspires us to become better versions of ourselves in the service of others'

—Chetan Joshi, professor, organizational
behaviour group, IIM Calcutta

'The Gym of Leadership* is a fascinating guide for managers to build their leadership fitness. Packed with insights, Anil, with decades of experience as a successful business and HR leader, presents a game plan to build eighteen critical leadership skills. No cliches, no sermons, no jargon—just simple workouts to help you become a successful leader in these disruptive times. Bolstered by the latest research, stories and case studies of success from battle-hardened leaders, this is a must-read for all those who want to make a difference in their profession'

—Professor Jagdish N. Sheth, Charles Kellstadt
Professor of Business, Goizueta Business School,
Emory University, Atlanta, USA, and Padma Bhushan awardee

'The Gym of Leadership* uses the gym metaphor to provide practical steps—things that people can do to become more effective leaders. Written by someone with enormous amounts of real-world experience and rooted in the realities of contemporary organizations, this book provides a fantastic road map for people seeking to both understand and improve their leadership capabilities'

—Jeffrey Pfeffer, Thomas D. Dee II Professor of
Organizational Behaviour, Graduate School of Business,
Stanford University, and author of *Leadership BS*

'The German philosopher Immanuel Kant once said, "Experience without theory is blind, but theory without experience is mere intellectual play." Among the many contributions to leadership, it is very refreshing to read Anil Khandelwal's book *The Gym of Leadership*. As a highly experienced executive, he uses his deep knowledge of organizational life to help the reader understand what it means to be an effective leader. Anybody aspiring to be a leader would do well to take note of this book'
—Manfred F.R. Kets de Vries,
distinguished clinical professor of leadership
development and organizational change, INSEAD, France

'*The Gym of Leadership* is a masterful exploration of leadership, combining deep personal insights with practical wisdom. This book distils decades of experience into actionable strategies that are both inspiring and transformative. Anil Khandelwal emphasizes the importance of resilience, emotional intelligence and continuous learning, which are crucial for anyone aspiring to lead effectively in today's complex world. His candid reflections on his own leadership journey provide a compelling blueprint for growth and development. *The Gym of Leadership* is a must-read for leaders at all levels who are committed to honing their skills and making a meaningful impact'
—Marshall Goldsmith, *Thinkers50* #1 Executive Coach
and *New York Times* bestselling author of *The Earned Life*,
Triggers and *What Got You Here Won't Get You There*

'Can leadership be learnt and if so, how can an aspiring manager best do so? The answer is unequivocally "yes" in the persuasive guidance here from the former managing director of one of India's leading financial institutions, the Bank of Baroda. Drawing on his own experience, university research, and the leadership of others, Anil Khandelwal has provided *the* primer on how to become more resilient, more credible and more authentic. If exercising at a fitness venue is foundational for your muscle tone, exercising in Khandelwal's "gym of leadership" is essential for your tone at the top'
—Michael Useem, faculty director of the
McNulty leadership programme, Wharton School,
University of Pennsylvania, and author of
The Edge: How Ten CEOs Learned to Lead

'*The Gym of Leadership* is a standout guide for anyone aiming to strengthen their leadership skills. Written by a seasoned former bank chairman, this book delves deeply into the essential soft skills needed for effective leadership. What makes this book truly remarkable are the personal anecdotes and real-life stories that Anil Khandelwal shares, bringing the concepts to life in a relatable and engaging manner. The author's clear and straightforward writing style ensures that the insights are easily accessible

and immediately applicable. By seamlessly weaving together Western and Indian management principles, the author provides a unique and holistic perspective on leadership. This book is an invaluable resource for aspiring managers, offering practical wisdom and actionable advice to build and refine their leadership capabilities. *The Gym of Leadership* is a must-read for anyone committed to becoming a more effective and enlightened leader'
—P. Dwarakanath, former chairman,
GSK Consumer Healthcare, India

'I have known Anil Khandelwal in many capacities—a friend and a board member of Bank of Baroda where he was the CMD. In every capacity, I have learnt from him. His leadership and the enthusiastic followership he created led to Bank of Baroda strikingly improving its performance. In this latest book of his, he has bared his heart and mind so that every manager can learn from his vast experience and expertise as an apex manager. The eighteen skills he has described are worth imbibing by every manager who aspires to rise and make a worthwhile contribution to his organization and society. As he puts it eloquently, "Leadership is about using your authority and position to work towards a higher purpose, a goal that is far above your own." That commitment to something higher than one's self-interest purifies the mind to seek solutions that are creative, compassionate and competent. I wish the book outstanding success'
—Pradip Khandwalla, former director, IIM Ahmedabad

'There are not too many people who can write about leadership with the authority that Anil Khandelwal can. Presented in an easy-to-use manner, the ideas in the book clearly bring out the author's personal experiences and insights, and the force of his conviction shines through. A must-read for everyone—practitioners and scholars of leadership, wannabe leaders and students'
—Pramod Solanki, leadership coach and founder,
Performance Enablers—The Growth Catalysts

'*The Gym of Leadership* is a remarkable book that deeply resonates with my journey in leadership and personal development. Anil K. Khandelwal brilliantly weaves practical insights and profound wisdom, focusing on self-awareness, emotional regulation, relationship management and communication. This book offers a comprehensive workout for the leadership muscles, guiding readers through a disciplined regimen of continuous improvement. It is an invaluable resource for anyone dedicated to enhancing their leadership effectiveness and creating a lasting impact in their organizations. I highly recommend it to aspiring leaders committed to making a difference'
—Prasad Kaipa, co-founder, Institute of
Indic Wisdom, and co-author of *From Smart to Wise*

'My work involves interactions with thousands of people managers, assessing their effectiveness, researching and reporting successful stories. All managers eventually want to move up to bigger roles and shine. The defining factor for career growth and success is leadership. Anil Khandelwal's book *The Gym of Leadership* brings hope for managers to build their critical soft skills of leadership in a manner akin to building one's physical fitness. This book must find a place on every manager's shelf to act as a multivitamin to build their leadership muscle'

—Prasenjit Bhattacharya, co-founder, Great Place to Work® Institute, India, and CEO and co-founder, Great Manager Institute®

'*The Gym of Leadership* is a must-read for aspiring leaders, seasoned executives and anyone seeking to unlock their full leadership potential. With its engaging narrative, thought-provoking reflections and step-by-step exercises, this book serves as a comprehensive guide for those committed to embarking on a journey of self-discovery and leadership excellence. *The Gym of Leadership* is a testimony of Anil's profound understanding of the art and science of leadership, making it an invaluable resource for anyone seeking to inspire, empower and leave a long-lasting legacy'

—Prem Singh, group CHRO, JK Organization, and president, National HRD Network

'Anil Khandelwal is a well-established and proven CEO with distinct leadership skills. When he writes a book on the "gymnasium" of leadership, he should be read seriously'

—R. Gopalakrishnan, former executive director, Tata Sons, author and corporate commentator

'*The Gym of Leadership* unfolds a refreshing approach to help individuals in any sector build key critical skills and improve their leadership muscles. Anil Khandelwal, a transformational leader himself, has offered many insightful lessons for the new generation of leaders. Unputdownable and a must for any aspiring leader'

—Rajnish Kumar, chairman, BharatPe, and former chairman, SBI

'*The Gym of Leadership: Insights to Help You Build Your Leadership Muscles* is an insightful, compelling and elegantly written book abounding with pragmatic wisdom. It will introduce the readers to eighteen all-important leadership muscles needed to transform into an esteemed leader. Every person who aspires to be a leader—and that includes most of us— should read this book to transform into a distinguished leader and take the world by storm'

—Rajesh Srivastava, former president, J.K. Helene Curtis Ltd, educator and author

'Just like building physical fitness, leadership development requires dedication and consistent effort. *The Gym of Leadership* provides the perfect training programme, equipping you with the tools and exercises to strengthen your leadership muscles. This book is valuable for anyone who wants to become a more impactful leader'

—Ravi Venkatesan, former chairman,
Microsoft India, and co-chairman, Infosys

'Anil Khandelwal has looked at the important subject of leadership through an interesting and novel lens. He has so aptly compared building strength of leadership with developing muscle in gym training. Drawing upon his own rich experience as well as from other relevant examples, he has weaved together a road map in a succinct manner which can be practised in real life to achieve greater success'

—Ravi Kant, former vice-chairman, Tata Motors,
and co-author, *Leading from the Back*

'*The Gym of Leadership* is a playbook for the passionate seeker that spells out the essential (and universal) building blocks for becoming skilled at leadership. The amazing quality of this book is its immediate relevance for both the novice starting on this journey and the expert wanting to up his game, and everyone between these two markers. For everyone on this continuum, the book answers the often-heard question: "Why didn't anyone tell me this earlier?" Well, now someone has, and it may still not be late!'

—Raj Bowen, executive coach and leadership adviser

'A profound, well-researched, simple to understand and actionable book on the science and art of leadership from an outstanding business and HR leader. Its fundamental message is that leaders become leaders primarily from their actions and the learnings therefrom. Leadership is not a 100-metre dash but an ongoing journey of action-reflection-learning-action requiring dedication, practice and continual improvement "just like being trained in a gym, often under the expert guidance of a coach". Also, leadership roles do not reside only at the top level but are required at all levels right through the organizational structures and processes. I have no doubt that Anil Khandelwal's priceless contribution to the world of leadership will add huge value to practitioners and academics alike. This book, which is like a personal trainer guiding you to build your leadership muscles, is a must-read which will definitely occupy pride of place on my bookshelf'

—Rajeev Dubey, former group president,
Mahindra & Mahindra, and member of the
governing body, International Labour Organization, Geneva

"In this era when we are facing a shortage of genuine and holistic leaders, Anil Khandelwal's *The Gym of Leadership* provides a welcome framework to shape the leaders of tomorrow. By breaking down a sometimes-elusive concept like leadership into a set of constituent skills, this book provides a practical yet insightful guide to building leadership capabilities. Though I initially wondered whether we need another book on leadership, this book carved a niche by providing a distinctive approach'
—Rishikesha T. Krishnan, Ram Charan Chair
Professor in Innovation and Leadership, and director, IIM Bangalore

'*The Gym of Leadership* is not merely a book but a leadership gymnasium for all, especially the youth in every sector, who would like to initiate themselves and practise and hone their leadership skills to make a difference to other people in their workplace and society. This is an amazing book based on Khandelwal's own rich experiences, reflections, insights and also readings. I find the book practical and absorbing. It is well articulated, and the research and quotes from the global geniuses of leadership are very appropriately placed. I wish every reader a happy practice in this gym and I am sure this book from an experienced Indian leader and reflective practitioner will be a global bestseller'
—T.V. Rao, chairman, TV Rao Learning System, former professor,
IIM Ahmedabad, and founder president, National HRD Network

'As organizations increasingly grapple with deficit leadership, *The Gym of Leadership* arrives as a timely and transformative guide. Through a rich tapestry of theory, research, real-world stories, and actionable 'workouts', Anil Khandelwal, a seasoned leader, presents a holistic approach to leadership development. It is not just a book but a blueprint for cultivating leadership excellence in today's complex world. As John Quincy Adams, a former US President, wisely noted, "If your actions inspire others to dream more, learn more, do more and become more, you are a leader." This book is a testament to that enduring truth, equipping managers with the tools to inspire and lead with unwavering efficacy'
—Ullhas Pagey, OD and HR professional,
mentor, coach, author, management teacher and consultant

'*The Gym of Leadership* details Anil's active approach to bulking leadership muscle. Best of all, it doesn't demand a time-consuming trip to Soldiers Field or the services of a costly coach. All the gym equipment needed is this slim book, an open mind and lots of energy. As Anil puts it: "Only those who are willing to put in the work by dedicating time to it beyond regular office work can eventually experience the pains and thrills of the journey of leadership, help build great institutions, and leave a legacy for posterity"'
—Visty Banaji, CEO, Banner Global Consulting

'Anil Khandelwal has the remarkable capability of converting effective result-oriented management practices, producing transformational results. The concept of building leadership capability in an individual being analogous to body toning in a gymnasium is an exceptionally appealing comparison. The ease and appeal with which the author explains the conceptual framework of each skill and narrates the action steps to imbibe it, is amazing. Having drawn heavily from his own experiences in utilizing these practically implementable traits through deft calisthenics, Khandelwal has created a path-breaking innovation. In his inimitably lucid style, the author explains each foundational skill, and then with persuasive logic, tutors every aspiring leader to condition their mind to imbibe the trait. This feature is the underlying appeal of the book which renders it as a sure crucible for leadership creation. The book is a must-read as it expounds on the power of mind and body training to create a unique generation of high-performing leaders of whom we can never have enough'

—Vinod Rai, former secretary,
Ministry of Finance, Government of India,
and former comptroller and accountant general of India

'Mr Khandelwal covers in his new book the importance of learning and practising a set of non-cognitive skills for successful leadership. He emphasizes that leadership is the result of regular practice, and inculcating a cluster of leadership behaviours curated from his experience and readings is akin to building one's mental muscles in a gym, normally associated with physical isometric exercises. The bedrock for learning the elements of successful leadership behaviour lies in deep self-reflection and discipline. For more on his leadership mantra, watch this space . . .'

—Yogi Sriram, former senior vice president,
Corporate Human Resources, L&T,
and strategic HR consultant

THE
GYM OF
LEADERSHIP

Insights to help you build
your leadership
muscles

Anil K. Khandelwal

PENGUIN
BUSINESS

An imprint of Penguin Random House

PENGUIN BUSINESS

Penguin Business is an imprint of the Penguin Random House group of companies whose addresses can be found at global.penguinrandomhouse.com

Published by Penguin Random House India Pvt. Ltd
4th Floor, Capital Tower 1, MG Road,
Gurugram 122 002, Haryana, India

Penguin
Random House
India

First published in Penguin Business by Penguin Random House India 2024

Title illustrations used in the workout section of each chapter have been designed by macrovector/Freepik.

10 9 8 7 6 5 4 3 2 1

The views and opinions expressed in this book are the author's own and the facts are as reported by him which have been verified to the extent possible, and the publishers are not in any way liable for the same.

Please note that no part of this book may be used or reproduced in any manner for the purpose of training artificial intelligence technologies or systems.

ISBN 9780143470571

Typeset in Adobe Caslon Pro by MAP Systems, Bengaluru, India
Printed at Thomson Press India Ltd, New Delhi

www.penguin.co.in

MIX
Paper | Supporting
responsible forestry
FSC® C010615

To my late brother Krishna Gopal Khandelwal,
whose support and nourishment
helped me shape my career and life

Contents

Section 4: Communication and Conversation

Preface

My Odyssey of Leadership

How do things spark your interest? I would say it's when you feel its impact, whether it's the profound absence of a thing or the sheer force of its presence. Ironically, both sparked my interest in leadership.

It was 1971, the first day of my job. Back in those days, getting a job was a far bigger milestone than it is today. It signalled the first day of your adult life, one full of responsibilities but also rich with possibilities—independence, money and the freedom to steer your life in the directions you desired.

I turned up to work, excitement and trepidation coursing through, only to have them knocked out of me. I tapped on the door of the manager's office to report to duty and heard a 'come in'. Stepping inside, I introduced myself. My manager looked at me silently. Then, without a word to me, he picked up the phone and dialled a number. The conversation went something like this.

'Sir, I asked for a capable officer, someone who has experience, not a rank greenhorn! What use will this rank newbie be? So what if he is an officer? How can I get work done if I am to babysit him through his duties?'

Throughout this half-hour 'meeting', he didn't address me once or offer me a seat. In the end, I was told to hang around, while they decided on my placement. And that's how I came to occupy the role of savings bank officer without any prior training, coaching or guidance. A few staff members and officers helped me out in discharging my duties, but it was my clerk who trained me on the job.

Thanks to the manager's (lack of) leadership, the entire branch was in chaos: customer service, professionalism and employee motivation were at their lowest; indiscipline and a lack of productivity were at their peak, mostly on account of the union–management environment prevailing in the bank, and our branch was the epicentre of such activities. Six months later, we got a new manager. A.A. Raval from Gujarat was experienced, talented and known for his administrative skills. Raval was like a breath of fresh air in a closed room. He had a strong people orientation; he interviewed every single staff member, aligned the right man for the right job (there were few women in the field in those days) and enforced discipline and processes, notwithstanding massive union problems at the branch. He encouraged me and met me at least twice a week to check on how I was doing. Such an approach endeared Raval to his employees, while his insistence on discipline and protocols made for a smooth workday. The result—our branch began to run smoothly internally and with customers as well.

In my very first year, I experienced two distinct leadership styles. And ever since, over and over, I have experienced how leadership is an 'act of making a difference' and can play a pivotal role in changing 'a failed strategy or revamping a languishing organization'.[1]

In my case, my leaders were my reporting managers. They both held the same post with the exact same job description. Did his post make Raval a good leader? No. It was his tough mental make-up and his humaneness—the value he placed on employees and customers—that defined his responsibilities in his role. To paraphrase the famous quote by John F. Kennedy, he asked what he could do for the people and the bank, not what they could do for him.

In essence, **I realized that leadership is not about power and perquisites; rather, it is about being responsible or accountable**—for the company's goals, for the team's well-being and success, and for customers' satisfaction. How they use it and for what purpose is what differentiates leaders from bosses. Leadership is a position of trust—like being asked to pilot an aircraft because there's confidence in your ability to navigate the skies and land your vehicle safely.

My own rise to the top has been rather unconventional. To be frank, I didn't set my sights on getting to the top; I've always believed that if you hanker for the next position, you're not able to fulfil the role you occupy to the fullest. Rather, you must explore the responsibilities of your rank and position to their utmost limits. Wherever you are, do your absolute best and honour the position that you hold. I realize that this goes against conventional wisdom, which advocates aiming for the top. Then again, much of my own career has been unusual.

I believe that sharing my journey with you will answer the questions I am often asked: What makes a leader? Was I born a leader? Did I go to some hallowed and exclusive school to learn the etiquette and mannerisms essential for leadership? Did I receive leadership training at a prestigious management school? Or was it some course at an Ivy League school that taught me about leadership? Did I work with some great leaders? Did I experience leadership roles in top positions alone? What is it that made me a leader? Is it because I became a CEO?

First, I was not born a leader. I did not have a privileged background. I come from a middle-class family, and I did not attend any exclusive schools or colleges. What I did have were my father's insistence on discipline and my mother, who lived her beliefs every day—being genuine, kind and compassionate, doing her best to keep her word—and these attributes, along with other early experiences, shaped my own personality and beliefs, leaving a strong desire to be fair and compassionate.

Over the years, I have seen many others who came from circumstances like mine rise to the highest positions. So, no, privilege—social or economic—doesn't make a leader. Neither is leadership hereditary. Rather, leadership needs to be nurtured within the family and organization.

Of course, intelligence and hard work certainly pave the way, as they do in all walks of life. After completing my engineering studies, and while pursuing my MBA, I joined a bank as a direct officer. I found the job experience quite unsatisfactory on account of the challenging work environment due to massive human problems and lack of any induction training. The MBA and my experience on the job sparked my lifelong interest in human resources—how people can make or break organizations—and later in my career, motivated me to work on my PhD in this area. As I developed mastery in human resources (HR), I began writing articles and books, participated in conferences, and received recognition at the national and international level.

I realized that, unlike in the medical and legal professions, there is no formal training for managerial or leadership roles as you rise through the ranks. Success in these roles is left to chance. Many succeed without any formal exposure or preparation, like an MBA, and just as many fail despite professional qualifications.

Your success as a leader depends on certain basic human qualities that are necessary for leadership. Educational qualifications and experience are helpful, but not essential. Over the years, I have seen all kinds of work styles, from the autocratic to the very friendly. Both styles produced results, but the latter style demonstrated the value of gaining cooperation through collaboration. These leaders created trust by being authentic, straightforward, accessible, fair, hands-on and humane. They were charismatic and persuasive. Everyone loved working with them. They were also tough; they did not tolerate indiscipline. There were occasions when they took strict action against wrongdoers. The point is, they knew when to come down hard—which is only when the situation requires it and generally as a last recourse. They were smart communicators, so they worked towards their goals with their teams, choosing to focus on the problem and offering opportunities for improvement. I also learnt the value of an empathetic attitude in speedy problem-solving. All this reinforced my belief that the two are not contradictory; it exposed the myth that one cannot be compassionate and tough. This was of particular significance, as compassion is often considered a sign of weakness.

Do you need to be an extrovert to become a leader? Not necessarily. This logic assumes that extroverts always make good leaders. That isn't the case; introverts have their strengths. But as leadership is a people-forward role, it may discomfit introverts more. Every role puts a limit on your usual style, and you need to adopt a style to suit your role. By nature, I am more comfortable in small groups of peers. Over the years, however, I have very consciously developed my communication skills, which have greatly helped me build connections with people. That is to say, becoming fixated on a style can be problematic. There's no need for a sword when a knife will do the job. Aspiring leaders would do well to read the situation correctly and adopt a context-specific style—a skill that is neither introvert- nor extrovert-specific.

Another myth is that only experienced executives can be effective leaders. This one is only partly true. Experience alone doesn't count; you need the right attitude and spirit. In my case, my late induction into business roles could have been a handicap, as my background was in HR. But I was able to build a symbiotic relationship between my line managers and myself, and I did not hesitate to learn from them. In some cases, the experience can be a burden, creating inhibitions such as a lack of adaptability, whether to a new business environment, disruptions caused by technology, or even the induction of highly talented people.

My growth through the ranks and in leadership came about through several tough experiences, or what Bennis and Thomas call 'crucible experiences', which led me to examine my values and in many ways strengthened my conviction and principles.[2] From such experiences, I learnt many lessons in managing difficult situations through a relentless process of reflection and action. They also helped me in learning while performing my roles. Robert Thomas notes that these crucible moments or experiences trigger a search for meaning, and if handled properly can lead to a deeper self-understanding and an enhanced performance.[3] Reflecting back on my own crucible moments, especially during 2000–03 in my tenure as executive director of Bank of Baroda, I couldn't agree more with Robert's observation. These experiences sharpened my perspective, bolstered my confidence and reinforced my mental toughness to deal with crises. I have described all of these events in *Dare to Lead: The Transformation of the Bank of Baroda*.[4]

In my career of forty-odd years, I have experienced many twists and turns, periods of rejection and humiliation as well as success and good luck. All these have shaped my vision of leadership: credibility, personal discipline, responsiveness, compassion, courage, result orientation and a policy of tough love: insisting on quality performance while remaining compassionate. Such values may sound impractical, esoteric and peripheral to achieving the business objectives of a commercial organization. Only commercial acumen, howsoever deep, can be short-sighted and possibly counterproductive in the absence of a culture for sustainable performance.

My achievements in my business role were largely driven by my deep focus on building an architecture of intangibles—culture, human processes, leadership, accountability and governance—to get the best business outcomes. As CEO of one of the largest public-sector banks, I initiated interventions to develop an internal culture that was more open, transparent, meritocratic, accountability-based and intensively people-focused. I firmly believe that all these steps helped my bank bounce back to the top within the shortest possible time. But that story is for another day and has already been described in *Dare to Lead*. In this one, I have tried to distil the lessons I learnt and communicate them simply and directly, without all the academic jargon.

Paramount for any leader, are some basic beliefs, conviction, competence and a personal style that influence people (colleagues, reportees and others) to work towards a common goal. It is human skills—in communication, relationship management and qualities such as positive behaviour and self-management—that are key to success in leadership roles, apart from job competence. Bear in mind that my idea of leadership is distinct from occupying a CXO or CEO position. Not all those who wear the crown are real leaders. Rather, my idea of a leader is one who believes in that rather iconic line from *Spider-Man* that captures the idea succinctly: 'With great power comes great responsibility.' And only those who use that power for the good of the people and the company are leaders.

So how do you build leadership? I believe that nothing teaches you leadership like the school of life. There's a powerful saying that 'a thorn of experience is worth a whole wilderness of warning'. Experience, reflection, trial and error—no amount of theory can be an equal substitute.

You need to be aware and alert to review your actions and experiences with objectivity, to be able to examine them without bias and to consider other ways to proceed. You will make mistakes along the way, but they too will teach you. In short, anyone can become a leader—so long as they put in the work. As the late Warren Bennis, a global icon on leadership, has observed, 'As weather shapes mountains, problems shape leaders. Difficult bosses, lack of vision and virtue in the executive suite, circumstances beyond their control, and their own mistakes have been the leaders' basic curriculum.'[5] An essential element in the making of leaders is the **crucible experiences** that prepare them to find meaning and learn, even from negative events and the most trying circumstances. It is a personal journey that requires preparation, passion and relentless practice.

At its core, behind every problem lies a lack of connections. I believe that all leadership skills must build and reinforce connection. This is the essence of good leadership. You can achieve this by laying down a strong foundation, brick by brick, with all the skills examined in the chapters that follow. One that will stand resilient through all kinds of trouble, whether time, tornadoes or tsunamis.

Introduction

Why Has This Book Been Written?

A couple of years ago, I taught a course on leadership in various programmes for working executives at the Shailesh J. Mehta Institute of Management, IIT Bombay. I was struck by the participants' enthusiasm to learn about leadership as well as their confusion about the whole concept. In subsequent programmes, in the corporate space and at management institutes, my experience was no different. The questions remained the same: How do you become a leader? How is it different from managing? Can all managers be leaders? These experiences sowed the seeds for this book.

A Leader Is Not Merely a High-Ranking Manager

To start, let's look at the concept of leadership. Who is a leader? Very often, a leader is confused with a high-ranking manager. Someone with the power and authority to make grand, sweeping changes that affect employees across levels. Someone who sets the direction and pace of the organization. Someone who can, with one signature, elevate your career or cause it to plummet. But these ideas only reflect the power that comes with such a position. Leadership is not about holding on to a position of power and using it for self-aggrandizement.

Leadership is about using your authority and position to work towards a higher purpose, a goal that is far above your own self.

A leader is a visionary who designs the future of the company, sets the tone for its culture and ensures its overall health through decisive initiatives and sometimes tough, even unpopular, decisions. Leadership is about creating a legacy that benefits the organization, its employees, and all other stakeholders. It is a supererogatory effort to bring something of lasting value and realize a vision that benefits all. Leadership roles do not reside exclusively at the top level but exist across different tiers of management.

Of course, policy and future-forward decisions are made at the top. But equally, the effectiveness of leadership roles at other levels down the hierarchy contributes to a facilitative business culture, engagement of people and effective implementation of corporate vision. Leadership action largely means a quest to align your company/unit/division/vertical with the competitive reality, to create a thriving people culture and to seek excellence in all aspects of business. These are, of course, the bigger, more obvious areas. Equally, leadership must also leave its stamp on the smallest things, from courteous communication and responsiveness to the upkeep of the premises.

Broadly speaking, a manager at the junior and middle levels is expected to fulfil short-term performance targets for their function. Leadership roles are typically higher up the ladder. Thus, all leaders also need to be effective managers. All managers may not possess leadership qualities—to move up with greater responsibilities, they need to build their leadership skills.

Leadership Is a Choice

In addition to meeting their business responsibilities, leaders are expected to set priorities for action, mobilize people's efforts and find creative solutions to problems. They need to possess a transformational mindset to catalyse changes—short-term goals as well as longer-term objectives of the organization—by passionately engaging people. This requires a serious and sustained effort, and it is often an exercise in restraint—to be judicious in exercising choices, to be objective and meritocratic, and to still be empathetic. Such behaviour sets off a chain of goodwill and payback. You become a seeker of excellence, a creative thinker with an entrepreneurial drive. Your behaviour and actions inspire and win the trust of your people, creating a desire in them to give their best.

To be able to inspire others, leaders need to manage themselves well. Leadership, thus, requires an investment of the 'Self into the Self' in the quest for becoming what leadership expert Warren Bennis calls 'an integrated human being'.[1] This represents the ultimate goal of leadership. Such a notion of leadership implies that it is a matter of choice. You can choose to be a high-ranking manager, or you could choose to be a leader.

So how does one become a leader? Does it require a certain mindset, attitudes and skills? Is it necessary to attend a prestigious management school? Does an individual inherit leadership? These are all important questions. It is an established fact that (barring certain cases) leadership is cultivated; it is also hierarchy-neutral: leadership can exist at any level of management. It requires a growth mindset, focusing on learning and building on one's strengths.[2] In other words, it depends on whether an individual is willing to learn, experiment, innovate and create a new paradigm for their life based on hard work, preparation, courage and integrity.

Jeffrey Pfeffer, a professor at Stanford Graduate School of Business, in his book, *Leadership BS*, mentions that there is ample research to suggest that traditional training programmes for leadership development have not been found to be effective and articulates the 'failure of the leadership industry'.[3] Pfeffer laments that on the one hand, there is an ever-growing, enormous leadership industry consisting of an almost limitless number of books, articles, speeches, workshops, blogs, conferences, training sessions and corporate leadership development efforts, and on the other, there is abundant evidence to support that 'an overwhelming number of disengaged and dissatisfied employees who do not trust their leaders do exist'.

Other experts have also observed that leadership development interventions, in terms of both design and facilitation, do not offer participants space and context to reflect, making such interventions highly conceptual and saturated with theoretical insights. Additionally, organizations also fail to translate their company's strategy into an enduring leadership philosophy. They typically provide leadership training as quick-fix solutions to groom 'instant leaders'. Mere participation in leadership development programmes, with an overdose of classroom-based cognitive or theoretical input, rarely makes competent leaders.[4] Barring some marquee companies, such as the Tata Group, HUL, L&T, ABG Group and others, very few companies have the institutional capacity or a long-term strategy in place to build leadership in a focused or sustained manner. Most organizations, even progressive ones, use ad hoc strategies by delegating senior executives to advanced management programmes abroad or inviting prestigious management institutes to undertake leadership development programmes in-house. In any case, such exposure has limited value as building leadership requires an organizational learning culture along with great and sustained personal effort, disciplined practice, reflection and mentoring.

So what should aspiring leaders do? Should they wait for selection for such programmes, or should they prioritize skill development early in their career? An Irish proverb captures the idea well: **'You have to do your own growing, no matter how tall your grandfather is.'**[5] There is inherent wisdom in this idea. You can't become a leader by reading books or attending programmes, no matter what insights they provide. You will have to develop your leadership skills through your own efforts and dedication, learning from experience. High-performance expectations make this particularly challenging.

The Pressing Need for a New Genre of Leaders in the Twenty-First Century

Leadership becomes all the more relevant and valuable in times of instability and upheaval—what with climate change, epidemics, political turmoil and polarization, in addition to all the technological advances and the attendant competition—and is set to stay that way. However, new contexts demand new skills from leaders.

While digital disruptions and AI have indubitably streamlined processes and enhanced ease of use, they have also effected many adverse changes. They have increased the intensity of competition; thus, the pressure to perform and achieve targets is greater for employees and their managers. In such a high-pressure environment, even the best-intentioned managers/leaders fail to control their emotional impulses in charged situations. Personal problems are often ignored, dismissed or sacrificed at the altar of business exigencies and delivering quality work on or ahead of time. In this scenario, where there is pressure all around and disruptions abound (and thus skills and knowledge need constant updating), it is no longer the person with the deepest knowledge or longest tenure who is most valuable to the organization. Rather, it is the person who can stay calm in turbulent situations, diffuse stress and strain amicably and achieve results. As a result, these changes have a significant impact on the chain of command.

Managers' work has considerably changed in flavour; they are now required to design more innovative and creative solutions. Working in such volatile and disruptive environments, often with people with higher technical skills or other specialized qualifications, requires operating with greater sensitivity, emotional regulation and compassion. Only this can ensure team effectiveness and derive good results.

The need of the hour is to expand the boundaries of the human imagination and the capacity to bring it to life. This demands a new kind of leadership, one that works through partnership and group processes. And the current hierarchical structures (based on command and control and operating through bureaucracy), are completely out of sync and ill-equipped to facilitate this.[6]

The new genre of leaders need to act as psychological anchors in a tough environment, mobilize and help their staff realize their full potential, and facilitate collaborative problem-solving through smart communication, group processes, team building and self-management.

A number of surveys and reports also reflect this trend—whether the World Economic Forum's Future of Jobs 2023 report or LinkedIn's 2024 survey on the most in-demand skills—leadership appears among the top ten critical skills. The 2023 Global Leadership Development Study by Harvard Business Publishing also lists leadership among the top ten in-demand skills for the future of work. Interestingly, in that list are skills such as empathetic communication, emotional and social intelligence, persuasion and influence, which are all components of leadership skills. In sum, it is evident that in this new environment, leadership skills are considered the most critical and strategic to running a successful business.

As noted earlier, while leadership may be enhanced or boosted by organizational training, it cannot be cultivated in such programmes. It is the responsibility of individuals to develop their leadership skills out on the field in their everyday work lives; no amount of theory is enough. Leadership is an action science, one that requires constant and mindful practice. You must do the work to learn about your strengths and weaknesses, reflect on your actions and decisions, and learn from all the situations that life throws at you. Doing this will help you grow, increasing and improving your skills, as well as your effectiveness as a leader.

To return to our question of what makes a leader, a leading organizational psychologist McCall suggests that 'Experience—not genetics, not training programmes, not business schools—is the primary source of learning to lead.'[7]

David Day, professor of psychology at Claremont, further elaborates, 'Instead of recasting leadership development entirely in terms of experience, it might be productive to think of ways to encourage more deliberate practice.' What would this mean? Professional excellence and expertise in various disciplines, whether music, sports, surgery, driving, software design, professional writing or chess, require deliberate and disciplined practice. As Day suggests, 'If experience is the primary driver of leadership development, then learning surely must play an important mediating role. For that reason, more attention needs to be given to the role of deliberate practice both on and off the job. Executives should practise leadership in various ways, such as giving and eliciting feedback, managing negative emotions, projecting a positive and optimistic tone in the face of adversity and engaging in active listening.'[8] Therefore, the deliberate practice of leadership should be given greater attention in the development of leadership.

In my own journey of leadership, I learnt from my experiences at work—from excellent, good, bad and terrible bosses, colleagues and reports. More than this, I learnt from disciplined practice through daily reflection, soliciting feedback on my performance, through mistakes of judgement and actions, but also from reading and learning from excellent books and research studies. I also learnt from a mentor, a leading academic and a friend, who helped me with new paradigms of organizations, research and books, and helped me see reality through new lenses. These were far more invaluable than any theory I learnt during my MBA.

Why Another Book on Leadership?

I debated for a long time whether there was a need for yet another leadership book, especially considering the market's constant influx of new ones each year. Except for the odd book on leadership authored by working executives or CEOs, the majority of these books are either academic, featuring multiple theories on leadership, or self-help, offering numerous dos and don'ts. There are, however, very few books for aspiring managers to help them build the foundational skills of leadership through in-depth discussions of those concepts as well as practical and actionable steps to develop those skills; thus, there is a need for such a book. As a reader and practitioner, you must bring curiosity, a willingness to learn and reflect, as well as wholehearted and sustained effort.

Why the 'Gym' of Leadership?

Leadership requires **dedication**, **practice** and **continual improvement**, just like we train in a gym, often under the expert guidance of a coach, to boost our physical fitness. To excel in their roles, leaders must continuously develop their skills and find mentors from among bosses or friends to help them along the way.

The focus of this book is therefore on building the foundational skills of leadership that can help you face all sorts of new and different contexts, circumstances, challenges, and crises in the same way that a fit and healthy body will create a strong immune system that can combat ill health or disease. I have envisioned this book as a personal trainer guiding you to build your leadership muscles.

There are several reasons why this analogy with a gym holds true, as seen in the table below.

1. Progressive growth	In the gym, individuals gradually increase the intensity of exercises to build muscles.	Leadership requires continuous growth and improvement. New challenges and experiences help individuals review and develop their skills and abilities over time.
2. Consistent practice	To build muscles effectively, consistent and disciplined practice is essential.	Leadership is not a one-time effort but requires continuous practice through real-life experiences, feedback and self-reflection.
3. Focused training	In the gym, individuals can target specific muscle groups to build strength and improve overall fitness.	Individuals can target training and practice in specific areas, such as communication, decision-making or emotional intelligence, to enhance their overall leadership capabilities.

4. Adaptation and flexibility	The gym routine helps your body be more agile, pliable and resilient.	Leaders need to work on their emotional resilience, keep aside their emotions and work effectively towards their larger goals.
5. Overcoming obstacles	In the gym, individuals may encounter physical challenges they need to overcome and push through towards the goal.	In leadership, one faces various organizational and interpersonal hurdles that need to be overcome.
6. Mentorship and guidance	Many people seek guidance from personal trainers or fitness coaches in the gym.	Individuals benefit immensely from seeking mentorship, where experienced leaders provide guidance and support to help them improve their leadership abilities.
7. Lifelong journey	Fitness is a lifelong pursuit.	Leadership development is an ongoing journey.

In both areas, there is always room for improvement and growth. In essence, leadership building is working on your mental and emotional muscles, akin to maintaining physical fitness. Again, you will not see the results overnight but gradually over time through disciplined practice. There are no shortcuts, whether it's physical fitness or becoming a leader.

Only those who are willing to put in the work by dedicating time to it beyond regular office work can eventually experience the pains and thrills of the journey of leadership, help build great institutions and leave a legacy for posterity.

How to Use This Book

In writing this book, the challenge was to identify the skills that form the very bedrock of leadership. I tapped into my own experience in leadership roles and consulted academics and practitioners, senior managers across industries, as well as the participants in my training programmes, to carefully select these eighteen key skills. The idea was that they should be universal and foundational across roles in corporate functions, and social or non-governmental organizations. Since leadership is an interconnected and integrated concept, working on these skills will help you build and scaffold many others, as well as facilitate collateral learning.

Broadly, these eighteen foundational skills have been grouped as:

1. Understanding the Self
2. Emotional Regulation
3. Managing Relationships
4. Communication and Conversation

Before we go further, let me explain the logic behind this grouping.

Section 1: Understanding the Self

Most key responsibility areas (KRAs) for managers deal with supervising others—telling them what to do and how to do it. While a great deal of training goes into this, there is little emphasis on self-management. This section addresses that gap.

The self is the foundation for growth. As we interact with the world, we get opportunities to act, react, learn and reflect. A self that is aware can build on its strengths. By learning to understand themselves, reflecting on their strengths and weaknesses, and working on improving themselves, aspiring leaders are better able to direct their team's output, quality of work and interpersonal dynamics without any biases or hang-ups. Unaware people, particularly in leadership positions, are like unguided missiles and can wreak untold damage. Thus, our focus is on these aspects of the self:

Self-Awareness: Knowing Thyself Is the First Step
Reflection: Diving Deep into the Self
Self-Management: Building Your Strengths
Self-Discipline: Fuel for Personal Growth
Time Management: How to Work Smarter with Your Time
Resilience: Bouncing Back from Setbacks

Section 2: Emotional Regulation

Our emotional impulses in different circumstances determine our effectiveness. Reining in our impulses, acting with compassion and demonstrating courage will win cooperation. But if we are dysfunctional by being reactive, short-tempered or unable to manage our emotions, we damage our relationships, thereby closing the doors for any effective collaboration or understanding with the other party.

Staying composed allows you to objectively assess situations and think creatively. Thus, you are able to achieve your purpose. Similarly, being compassionate will help you extract better performance from your team. An absence of compassion and insistence on results begets a toxic environment in which people feel exploited and thus demotivated. Emotional regulation also means overcoming your fears and acting courageously to take initiative and risks in the greater interest of the organization.

> Emotional Regulation and Anger Management: Taming Your Temper
> Compassion: Empathy in Action
> Courage: Conquering Your Fears

Section 3: Managing Relationships

It is the leader's responsibility to help build rapport among the team and nurture an environment that encourages collaboration and passion. They must lead by example and set the tone by demonstrating their own authenticity, credibility and humility within a framework of fair processes. Such a relationship-focused leadership strategy drives success by creating a united, motivated and resilient team. Intelligence can only take you so far without the ability to nurture relationships. This section examines the following aspects of managing relationships:

> Relationships: Making Meaningful Connections
> Authenticity: Being Your Real Self
> Credibility: Building Trust and Reputation
> Humility: A Differentiator for Leadership Effectiveness
> Fairness: Exercising Sensitivity in Delivering Organizational Justice

Section 4: Communication and Conversation

A leader's job demands constant interactions across the board—with individuals, teams, and across teams—internally and with external stakeholders. Most leadership traits find expression through communication—the way leaders articulate their vision, inspire others or engage and motivate. Thus, impactful communication helps deliver impactful leadership; it is what drives operations and effects change. This section examines the following aspects of communication:

> Communication: A Keystone for Impactful Leadership
> Listening to Attend, Absorb and Act
> Detoxifying Communication: Being Accountable for Your Behaviour
> Dialogue: The Most Effective Tool for Problem-Solving

How to Get the Best Out of This Book

Though we have grouped those eighteen skills under four sections, you can start reading from any section or chapter that you choose. The themes in leadership are interconnected, and strengthening one skill will strengthen others.

The individual chapters exhaustively examine various critical aspects of those sections. The first part of each chapter is an intensive examination and analysis of the concept, its relevance, the benefits and the consequences of its absence for the leader, the team and the organization. It also has accounts from successful practitioners and discusses available research on the topic.

The second part of the chapter takes you to the gym of leadership and helps you develop and enhance that leadership skill through simple, practical and actionable steps.

In the end, there are some questions for reflection to build your awareness of the theme and to draw up a personal action plan.

A word of caution before you begin: though this book gives you strategies to develop the essential skills for a leader, leadership, let me state once more, is action science and needs sustained effort. This book doesn't offer quick hacks for leadership but will facilitate your understanding of the concept and work towards your gradual and eventual transformation. You will have to develop these leadership 'muscles' through a strict and disciplined regimen, as in a gym, and keep at it even when you see progress. Remember that even after you work on a muscle, you must keep practising to remain at that level of fitness. But once you enter this leadership gym and start these circuits to facilitate your overall growth, you will have created a stable foundation on which you can build other valuable qualities.

Finally, I believe that each one of you has the potential to enhance your leadership effectiveness and become more impactful through the principles outlined in this book. Embark on your leadership journey with passion, focus and discipline.

People develop leadership qualities by practising them, by acting them out and rehearsing them until they become natural and part of the individual.[9]

—Jeffrey Pfeffer—

Section 1

Understanding the Self

Chapter 1

Self-Awareness: Knowing Thyself Is the First Step

To know others is intelligence, to know oneself is wisdom.[1]

—Lao Tzu—

Self-awareness, in its most simple form, is knowing yourself at a deep level. What sort of person am I? What do I believe in? What values do I pursue? What are my shortcomings, and how do they affect my life goals? Engaging with such questions will offer you insight into yourself, a fundamental aspect of personal growth and self-awareness. While this exercise is meaningful on its own, it is also a crucial first step for effectively dealing with real-world problems.

Self-awareness is among the most crucial qualities of a leader. This is because it gives you self-knowledge—information and insight about yourself—that you can use to become aware of the conscious and unconscious tendencies that impact you and your interactions with others. You can then work on them to get better results in your personal and professional lives.

Self-knowledge will reveal the following aspects about your 'self':

- **Personal Strengths:** Knowing what you are good at, such as effective communication or problem-solving.
- **Personal Weaknesses:** Recognizing areas for improvement, for example, time management and the tendency to procrastinate.
- **Values:** Understanding what is most important to you—honesty, family or independence.
- **Emotional Triggers:** Being aware of what makes you feel happy, sad, angry or anxious.
- **Learning Style:** Knowing whether you learn best through visuals, reading, writing, listening or hands-on activities.
- **Motivations:** Understanding what drives you, such as achievement, helping others or personal growth.
- **Stressors and Coping Mechanisms:** Identifying what causes you stress or discomfort, and how you cope with them.
- **Confidence:** Being aware of how confident you feel in different situations.
- **Communication Style:** Knowing whether you're assertive, passive, aggressive or passive-aggressive in your interactions.

My Experience of Deeper Self-Awareness

In 1982, I attended a Basic Human Process Lab workshop organized by the Indian Society for Applied Behavioural Science, where participants (typically between eight and fifteen people) learnt about themselves and small group processes in general through their interactions with one another. The workshop used the T-Group methodology for feedback and problem-solving to help participants develop insights into themselves, others and groups.[2]

The programme methodology centred on examining members' behaviour in a here-and-now situation, where both participants and facilitators freely gave feedback to other participants about their behaviour based on their experience in the group. Towards the end of a week-long programme, I received some eye-opening feedback about myself that, among other things, included my tendency to become impulsive and emotional with my viewpoint, almost to the point of avoiding listening to others. Although I always pursued a passionate articulation of my viewpoint, I was not aware that I had unconsciously stopped appreciating others' viewpoints. Although initially, I was quite perturbed by this feedback, I began to reflect on it. Since then, I've done my best to pause, reflect and decide if that impulse of mine will be helpful to the matter at hand. This restraint has helped me tremendously in my career.

Self-awareness is at the heart of building personal effectiveness and leadership skills. It helps you map out your desires and needs in the present, develop a vision for the future and work towards it while factoring in your shortcomings. Self-aware individuals have clarity and confidence about where they are headed and the reasons behind it, and they ensure that their decisions are aligned with their values. Thus, they make sounder decisions, build stronger relationships and communicate more effectively. For such people, work can be energizing and uplifting.

Successful leaders are self-aware. They pay attention to their inner voice. They understand the defining moments of their lives and thereby know their inherent strengths, psyche, behaviour and biases. They play to their strengths and work on their limitations. They speak accurately and openly, although not necessarily about their emotions. And that understanding provides them with a deep well of energy and passion that they draw on throughout their lives.[3]

Why Is Self-Awareness Critical?

Through self-awareness, leaders can exercise their responsibilities through their best selves.

Table 1.1: Advantages of Being Self-Aware

Self-Aware Leaders Can	Leaders Lacking Self-Awareness
• Exercise choices with wise judgement • Build emotional agility and moderate their responses when dealing with difficult people and situations • Be open to constructive criticism • Be aware of priorities and allocate time more productively for themselves and their team • Inspire their team and build cohesion	• Cannot exercise good judgement • Are emotionally rigid • Behave with a sense of positional power and entitlement • Discourage feedback and are unable to make decisions through collaborative thinking • Fail to inspire their teams and, in fact, cause conflict among team members

People with a high degree of self-awareness, empathy and social sensitivity are extremely effective in building rapport with others, moving them in the desired direction and thus proving themselves as good leaders. This would require having both internal and external self-awareness, as suggested by organizational psychologist Tasha Eurich.[4]

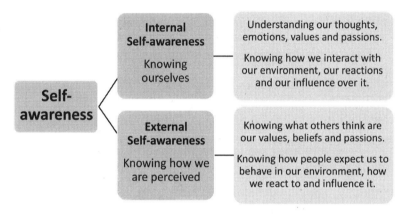

Figure 1.1: Levels of Self-Awareness

While one may tend to give prominence to one over the other, both internal and external self-awareness are equally important for effective leadership. If our understanding matches others' perceptions of us, then the relationships are more meaningful.

Derailers of Self-Awareness

Tasha Eurich has compiled several research findings in her article, 'What Self-Awareness Really Is (and How to Cultivate It)'. She says that experience, hierarchical position and power can hinder self-awareness, making a leader overestimate their skills and abilities. She quotes business professor James O'Toole, who observes that as their power grows, leaders become less willing to listen, 'either because they think they know more than their employees or because seeking feedback will come at a cost'. Eurich's analysis shows that most successful leaders, as rated by 360-degree reviews of leadership effectiveness, counteract this tendency by taking frequent critical feedback (from bosses, peers, employees, their board and so on). They become more self-aware in the process and are seen as more effective by others. It is evident, then, that those who assess themselves honestly and are more self-aware are likely to be more effective in conducting their personal and professional lives.[5]

A Workout for Developing Self-Awareness

Developing self-awareness can be a one-time affair, but that would be of little use. Even when we experience growth, there is always room for improvement. The challenge is to remain self-aware and keep updating your self-knowledge to address emerging and older issues. For this, you need to practise self-awareness consistently. I find that slotting it as a non-negotiable activity into my daily schedule works best.

1. **Develop the Practice of Reflection**
   Reflection helps us review our experiences and behaviours, and learn how to act in the future. We cannot challenge ourselves without reflection. And there are no changes without challenges. Reflection is such a crucial part of self-work that we have dedicated a full chapter to the topic (see Chapter 2 on Reflection).

2. Practise Mindfulness

To achieve a higher level of self-awareness, it is critical to seek complete mental focus. Practising mindfulness helps you become aware of your deeper self. Leadership consultant and author Michael Bunting has explained the concept rather succinctly:

> Mindfulness is maintaining open-hearted awareness of our thoughts, emotions, bodily sensations and environment in the present moment. It is paying attention in the present moment, purposefully, warm-heartedly and non-judgmentally.[6]

Mindfulness meditations help build mental awareness and quietness (a chicken-and-egg kind of situation). There are several forms of mindfulness you could try. You may refer to *A Miracle of Mindfulness* by Thích Nhất Hạnh, or *Mindful Manifestation* by Neville Goddard to learn more. Whichever method you choose, several thoughts and feelings will surface through the practice; acknowledge them and continue. In the beginning, it may feel like you're zoning out. But do persevere—and dwell on the thoughts that emerge.

You may want to isolate yourself initially while starting a mindfulness practice, but with regularity, you can do it effortlessly anywhere or at any time; for example, while commuting, waiting in a queue, listening to music, etc.

3. Build Emotional Agility

This is the ability to use your emotions, especially the negative ones, to give direction to your decisions—ones that align with your values. This means that rather than reacting to or suppressing your emotions, you become capable of responding in a manner that can be more helpful to your goal.

You can build emotional agility through the following steps:[7]

a. Recognize your emotional patterns, especially the rigid and repetitive ones.
b. Label your thoughts, feelings and emotions.
c. Notice them and accept them with openness.
d. Act on your values (ethical guidelines) to come unstuck from patterns that don't serve you.

For example, when your boss admonishes you for a mistake, emotional agility can help you recognize and identify your pattern of response and the emerging emotions and thoughts: 'I am angry' and 'I made a mistake'. It will help you focus on the content of the reprimand (mistake) rather than the delivery style (loud or harsh). You will thus be able to accept your anger and consider your next steps calmly based on your values rather than reacting emotionally or in a knee-jerk manner. If your values are 'responsibility' and 'knowledge', you can identify why the mistake happened. You can then take ownership, rectify it and take steps to avoid making similar mistakes in the future. This would be the best response that serves you, your boss and your organization.

4. **Seek Feedback from People You Respect**
In the Mahabharata, Krishna's counsel on the battlefield helped Arjuna own up to his delusions and develop clarity in thinking. By asking for and considering Krishna's advice, Arjuna developed deeper self-awareness and confidence.

No matter how intensely we reflect, there will inevitably be aspects that we won't consider and thus cannot improve on. This is why asking for feedback is valuable (see Johari Window in Point 6). One way would be to ask a trusted colleague or mentor: 'I know I lack expertise in this area and I am working on improving myself. How do you suggest I go about it? Are there other areas that you feel I am weak in?' Another way is to consult professional counsellors or firms who can scrutinize, analyse and interpret the results as well. Reflect on the feedback and develop a plan of action for those areas.

A friend of mine shared an experience that rather acutely illustrates the value of reflection and feedback. He's a warm, sensitive and intelligent person but somewhat reserved. Some decades ago, he was at a faculty meeting—he was teaching at one of the prestigious IIMs—when he felt that the director was trying to manipulate an issue. 'I am normally not one for confrontations, but something about the whole affair worked me up. I was angry enough to raise my voice and express my discomfort and anguish about it. To his credit, the director didn't hold it against me. However, this behaviour was so unusual for me that I went over it repeatedly. While I was confident that I disagreed with the director, I was anxious about how I had communicated it. I consulted my colleagues, who told me that they supported my outburst and, in fact, appreciated me all the more for it. I'd go back to this incident over the years to come—it made me realize that I could confront issues and people that I disagreed with if I found that they were not in the best interest of the institution we served.'

In his case, reflection and feedback helped my friend take action that was in consonance with his beliefs and values. In my case, where I received feedback about my impulsiveness,

I learnt to exercise restraint. Thus, reflection and feedback can help you create desirable outcomes in a variety of ways.

5. Use Auto-Analytics

This means using technology to observe, record and analyse data about ourselves to work on self-improvement. Today, there are plenty of opportunities to apply auto-analytics to track personal health and productivity.

There are two broad categories of auto-analytics tools available. Trackers record and reveal patterns about our work (such as productive hours, time spent on emails, phone calls, preparing reports, etc.) and our health (such as sleep patterns, blood-glucose readings, heart rate, etc.). Like with any analytical tool, the analysis and pattern recognition get more accurate over a longer period of time. Nudgers go a step further to prompt or 'nudge' users to push forward towards their goals. For this, users need to feed in their goals/objectives and plans to achieve them.

James Wilson, a leadership and technology researcher, suggests that auto-analytics areas of operations are rather sweeping and can track your physical, emotional and intellectual states:[8]

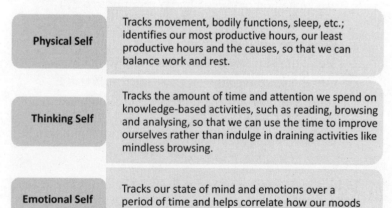

Physical Self	Tracks movement, bodily functions, sleep, etc.; identifies our most productive hours, our least productive hours and the causes, so that we can balance work and rest.
Thinking Self	Tracks the amount of time and attention we spend on knowledge-based activities, such as reading, browsing and analysing, so that we can use the time to improve ourselves rather than indulge in draining activities like mindless browsing.
Emotional Self	Tracks our state of mind and emotions over a period of time and helps correlate how our moods affect our decisions and productivity.

Figure 1.2: Tracking of Self with Auto-Analytics

6. **Use Psychometric Tests and Tools**

Several aspects of our personality—our thoughts, emotions and behaviours—are hidden from us, while we actively hide and suppress some. Thus, we often have an unclear and incomplete picture of our 'self', which can hinder our goal of developing self-awareness. To overcome this hurdle, psychologists have created several psychometric tests and tools to achieve a clearer and more complete assessment of ourselves. Of course, these applications will have their own biases and blind spots.

a. **The Johari Window** is a simple tool developed by American psychologists Joseph Luft and Harry Ingham (the name Johari comes from their first names). It identifies the conscious and subconscious aspects of our personality (our emotions, thoughts, behaviour and biases) and is also useful to assess our interpersonal dynamics (one-to-one, in groups and at work) and even knowledge (soft skills, competencies and experience).[9]

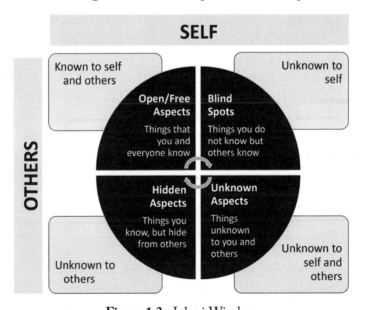

Figure 1.3: Johari Window
(Source: Selfawareness.org and MindTools)

b. **FIRO-B (Fundamental Interpersonal Relations Orientation-Behaviour)** is a psychometric test developed by William Schutz of Stanford University in the late 1950s and is still among the most preferred tools for self-assessment.[10] It uses three dimensions of human behaviour (inclusion, control and affection) and two factors (what we express and what we want) that affect it.

c. **360-degree Feedback** helps gather anonymous feedback from various people with whom we have working relationships, including managers, peers, subordinates, etc.[11] The name comes from the well-rounded feedback taken from various people in different relational positions and functions with respect to the test taker and gives insight into their work, behaviour, relationships and competencies.

All these exercises will help you examine your actions, reactions, flaws and strengths, and will be the crucial first step in improving your performance and therefore your leadership skills. Only self-aware people are truly confident in their abilities and can express them in their words and actions, and that is how they are able to exercise leadership.

Self-awareness is a process and should be practised lifelong as it motivates us to transform not just our behaviour (through self-management) but also drives us to make a difference to others and build a better culture that facilitates transformation for others. As we evolve, others around us evolve, thus shaping the evolution and growth of our skills.

Questions for Reflection

1. What are your key learnings from this chapter?
2. Create an action plan to develop and improve your self-awareness using the questions below.

3. How has reflecting on yourself helped you learn about your own instinctive responses, biases and prejudices?
4. How do you react when you receive negative feedback?
    a. I tend to reject it in the moment and then reflect on it.
    b. I accept it immediately but later decide it is not valid.
    c. I tend to agree intellectually, but I have trouble changing my behaviour/attitude.
5. What do you do when you feel unclear about your goals or get anxious about the future? Do you respond in a similar manner as you do for question 3?
6. Have you set up any personal and professional goals for becoming a better leader?

Chapter 2

Reflection: Diving Deep into the Self

Follow effective action with quiet reflection.
From the quiet reflection will come even more effective action.[1]

—Peter Drucker—

One of Harvard Business School's most oversubscribed courses was titled 'How Will You Measure Your Life'. Designed for outgoing batches of MBA students by Clayton Christensen, a senior professor at Harvard Business School, it was also published as a book in 2012. In the book, Christensen mentions his dedication to shaping the purpose of his life:

> For me, a clear purpose in life has been essential. When I was a Rhodes Scholar, I was in a very demanding academic program, trying to cram an extra year's worth of work into my time at Oxford. I decided to spend an hour every night reading, thinking, and praying about why God put me on this earth. That was a very challenging commitment to keep because every hour I spent doing that, I was not studying applied econometrics. I was conflicted about whether I could really afford to take that time away from my studies,

but I stuck with it and ultimately figured out the purpose of my life. It is the single most useful thing I have ever learnt.[2]

Closer to home, we have people like Sarathbabu Elumalai, an engineer who graduated from BITS Pilani and went on to do an MBA from IIMA. He refused high-paying jobs during campus interviews and chose to start a food chain selling idlis to the poor at a reasonable cost.[3] Elumalai sacrificed the prestige and glamour of a job to pursue his purpose, about which he had great clarity.

This is where Christensen's question to outgoing students becomes relevant. Standing at the threshold of the business world, it pushed them to articulate their dreams and consider the distance from the present. Should they start with a purpose or make it up as they go? What bridges would they design and build to reach their goals? All of these questions can be answered through reflection. Reflection helps us shape our life's **purpose** and develop our **character** and **willpower** to achieve it.

What Is Reflection?

Reflection is a process of careful self-scrutiny through conscious introspection. It is the key to self-awareness—it helps us examine our experiences and can either confirm or transform our perspective, thereby deepening our understanding of ourselves.

Jennifer Porter, a leadership and team development expert, suggests that those who practise regular reflection, both inward and outward, are happier, more productive and reap many other benefits. She notes in her article, 'Why You Should Make Time for Self-Reflection (Even If You Hate Doing It)', that 'Reflection gives the brain an opportunity to pause amid the chaos, untangle and sort through observations and experiences, consider multiple possible interpretations, and create meaning.'[4] This meaning becomes learning, which can then inform future mindsets and actions. For leaders, this 'meaning-making' is crucial to their ongoing growth and development.

While it may not be possible to stay ahead of time to handle every situation that may arise in one's work or family life, one can **reflect** and **learn from past experiences**, ensuring a more seasoned and balanced response to issues.

Reflective Practice for Continuous Learning

Donald Schon, a well-known expert in organizational learning and professor at MIT who conceptualized the idea of 'Reflective Practice', notes that **'Reflective practice is the ability to reflect on one's actions so as to engage in a process of continuous learning.'**[5] It involves asking ourselves:

- What did I do well? What did I do wrong?
- Why did I do things in that particular manner?
- What can I do to improve my performance or correct my mistakes?

Your vision will become clear only when you can look into your own heart. Who looks outside, dreams; who looks inside, awakens.[6]

—Carl Jung—

For example, a cricketer can reflect on the mistakes made during the training session and figure out ways to avoid those in the future. A human resource manager can engage in reflective practice by thinking about the recent discussions with the trade unions and learning about the employees' response to a new promotion policy.

Research by professors James R. Bailey and Scheherazade Rehman has revealed that executives can benefit immensely from their professional development through reflection when they experience situations of surprise, frustration and failure (see Table 2.1).[7] However, learning can only take place when people create meaning from these experiences through reflection.

Table 2.1: Emotions Evoked in Various Situations

Emotion	Situations
Surprise	Leaders face moments that greatly derail their expectations, such as an even-tempered colleague blowing up over a minor issue or when a reasonable request is rejected.
Frustration	Irritable situations, such as someone parking in our space, getting stuck in traffic or an unresponsive boss.
Failure	Facing the consequences of mistakes that should not have been made or the failure of any project implementation.

Reflection Involves Diagnosis and Resolution

Reflection leads to **diagnosis** and **resolution**; once the problems are diagnosed, they can be treated and cured.[8]

We can resolve issues by experimenting with new behaviours to identify the most effective approach. Of course, for this, we must keep at it, trying various strategies until we're satisfied with the results (see Chapter 4 on Self-Discipline for details).

Do note that **reflection is a two-step process**, and **thinking** is just the first step. The next step—**action**—is what leads to change. So do not ruminate, indulge in excessive analysis or dwell solely on mistakes. Brooding on failures will only create anxiety, self-blame and guilt. **Reflect, plan** and **act.**

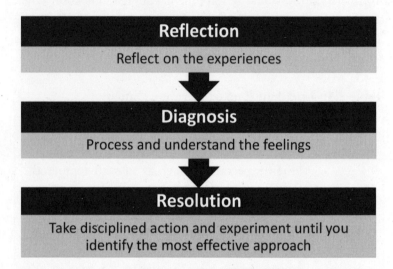

Figure 2.1: Reflection Is about Diagnosis and Resolution

(Adapted from Bennis 2003, 2009)

Why Is Reflection Critical?

Reflection leads to greater awareness of ourselves, others and situations. It facilitates clarity of the options that are available, like the way chess grandmasters can see fifteen to twenty moves ahead. Naturally, with such foresight, one is better equipped to lead.

Reflection is critical for leaders for many reasons, such as:

- It helps in emotional regulation, allowing us to take a step back, challenge some of our assumptions and see things from a new perspective.
- It strengthens our convictions and facilitates personal growth.

- In turn, this brings moderation to our behaviour/ responses and improves our capacity to listen, discern and act.
- It helps develop a better understanding of our strengths and weaknesses, as well as motivation to act.
- It helps us to connect with a deeper life purpose as to why we are doing something. This can bring in innovation and creativity.
- It helps in balancing duality in terms of when to be tough yet empathetic, courageous yet vulnerable and when to be a perfectionist yet tolerant of errors.

Leaders who do not reflect show no accountability for their behaviour and blame others for problems. The implications are serious because they affect the motivation and morale of the people they work with. They fail to build long-term commitment to people and try to impose their authority and power to get results. Obviously, such leaders do not evoke any sense of pride among employees, much less their engagement.

Barriers to Reflection

It is worth reflecting on **why leaders avoid reflecting and resolving**. Managers and leaders often do not examine their feelings and behaviours because it is hard work. Besides, it creates anxiety and fear. Most people do not like to acknowledge their flaws and blunders. Those who mistake it for a spiritual exercise avoid it because of something lacking in their temperament or because it does not align with their beliefs. They fail to realize that reflection is a pure and simple exercise in self-examination. A closed mindset is another reason. Reflection requires an open mindset, calming the thought process and accepting ownership of our actions to resolve dilemmas. However, it can also create irritation, discomfort and guilt. One of the strongest deterrents to reflection is that it can be difficult to see an immediate benefit or substantial returns from this practice, and people often want quick-fix solutions. Reflection calls for remaining calm and thinking slowly, but most people do not find the time or are lethargic about investing in themselves. At times, the absence of external feedback is a deterrent, as we are accustomed to external validation. But the most common reason I've noticed is that people are too distracted, often halting their reflection midway to attend to calls, messages and emails.

How Reflection Has Helped Me

Reflection for me has been a kind of daily exercise in my own gym of leadership. For the past three decades, I have reserved the last fifteen minutes before bedtime for reflection. It has helped me to consciously deal with my fears and consider the consequences of making risky decisions in the interest of pursuing organizational goals. With deep reflection, I have been able to logically get to the heart of issues and adhere to a principled stand. It helped me immensely while streamlining union–management relations in my organization, to stand strong against political pressures or the irrational demands of trade unions.

Through reflecting, I have managed to curb my occasional impulsiveness, own up to my part of the problem as a senior leader and initiate baby steps to improve. With trial and error and relentless practice, I could, to a fair extent, control my impulses.

Reflection has helped me think logically and examine the pros and cons of my decisions, especially in difficult times. I really do not know how I could have managed some of the crises I have been in without reflection. My practice of reflection has helped me speak up on issues that matter the most to me. I own my actions because they come from deep thought. My most critical learnings from reflection have been exercising self-control, listening better and learning to let go of small things.

A Workout for Developing Reflective Muscles

Daily reflection is a discipline that trains us to think logically, act consciously in the greater interest and examine our actions against our values. You need to carefully build this into your routine and allocate time and resources for a daily stocktaking of your performance.

1. **Allocate Time for Reflection**
   In an environment full of distractions, focusing on vital tasks and finding time for reflection can become a challenge. But time is a precondition for deep thinking. To get the full benefits of reflection, you must make it a habit. This will

have a significant impact on your relationships, attitudes and work.

2. **Build Your Reflective Practice**
   Graham Gibbs, a professor at Oxford, developed the process called **Gibbs' Reflective Cycle** to help with reflective practice. It involves the following steps:[9]

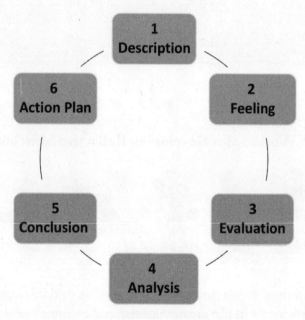

Figure 2.2: Gibbs' Reflective Cycle

a. **Description:** Describe the event and the experience, objectively without any judgement or analysis. Some useful questions are: What happened? Where did it happen? Who was involved? When did this occur? How did it start/end?

b. **Feelings:** Consider your feelings about it without any judgement: How did you feel at that time? What were you thinking? How do you feel about it now?

What are your thoughts now? Note down the positive and negative feelings and thoughts evoked, as they significantly affect our analysis of the event.

c.   **Evaluation:** Evaluate the entire experience. What were the good and bad aspects of the experience? What went well? What went wrong? What were the positive or negative consequences? How did you handle the situation? What did you learn today?

d.   **Analysis:** At this stage, 'why' becomes a driving question to understand the experience: Why did things happen the way they did? Why did it go well/badly? Why did you act the way you did? Why did others act the way they did?

e.   **Conclusion:** We can now consider what and how we could have done differently, and more importantly, what we learnt from the experience.

f.   **Action Plan:** Based on the above, we can devise an action plan for handling similar situations in the future.

3.   Restructure Your Thought Processes

Reflection identifies the source of our problems. This allows you to restructure your beliefs to build new, more robust patterns that balance your actions with your values.

4.   Maintain a Journal

Write the key events, reactions and emotions (both good and unfavourable ones) daily or after each major incident (based on Gibbs' Reflective Cycle) and review them once a week. This will reveal a pattern of thoughts, emotions and reactions. Don't be judgemental and assign blame; just acknowledge the areas that need improvement and devise an action plan to become effective. You may revisit previous journal entries to see if you are able to see things differently. This also helps you track your growth over time.

5. **Seek Help**
   Globally acknowledged and revered faculty and psychotherapist Manfred F.R. Kets de Vries has identified these six reasons driving the 'go it alone' mentality among executives: the fear of being vulnerable, the fear of losing control, the fear of rejection, the need to be independent, over-empathizing with others and a sense of victimhood.[10] I have found that leaders also hide behind the pressure of time to avoid seeking help from a coach, mentor or therapist who can listen unconditionally and act as a 'thought partner'. Such people can help us see the big picture, develop new perspectives, and consider the consequences of different options. They can also help us examine our value systems and vulnerabilities, holding us accountable for the changes we need to make in ourselves.

6. **Plan Reading Time**
   Reading is the key to improving our ability to reflect. Rather than reacting impulsively, it helps build new perspectives and thus take a more balanced and coherent view of the situation. Great leaders set aside time for reading the latest books beyond their subject specializations. Warren Buffett spends 80 per cent of his working day reading and reflecting. He says, 'I just sit in my office and read all day. That is how knowledge builds up like compound interest.'[11]

7. **Meditate**
   Meditation helps connect the body, mind and soul. Regular practice allows the mind to become still and calm enough to look at issues objectively. This helps immensely with self-exploration and self-awareness. Regular meditation is a very potent way to make reflection a regular practice and

is extremely beneficial in controlling emotions in chaotic and stressful environments.

What Not to Do While Reflecting

Although self-reflection is considered one of the main tools to develop self-awareness, it may not always prove to be useful. Tasha Eurich notes, 'The problem with introspection isn't that it is categorically ineffective—it's that most people are doing it incorrectly . . . "why" is a surprisingly ineffective self-awareness question.'[12]

For example, asking, 'Why do I feel angry?' might lead to biased answers that can make us feel more miserable. Instead, 'What situations or people trigger my anger?' can help you identify the cause and become more self-aware, allowing you to find a solution that works for you through trial and error.

This **reflection-awareness-regulation cycle** leads to gradual personal development, building character and clarity of purpose. Despite major setbacks, Mahatma Gandhi and Nelson Mandela accomplished great things because they remained anchored in their larger purpose.

Building a Culture of Reflective Thinking at the Top

Reflecting on what we have achieved so far can help us do a better job next time. Therefore, we must encourage this practice across the board and integrate it into the company culture. Not only does this improve effectiveness all around, but it also holds everyone accountable for their actions. By encouraging this, the organization nurtures its employees and reduces the expectation that the CEO is the only one to demonstrate it.

Collective Reflection and Diagnosis, A Personal Experience

During my stint as CEO of Bank of Baroda (2005–08), I was fortunate enough to implement a major transformational strategy to transition the bank from a staid brand to the most vibrant one in the banking space. We needed to build excitement, develop ownership and foster forward-thinking among the top management, so we instituted daily morning meetings with general managers for collective reflection on organizational issues. In these morning meetings, anyone could raise issues concerning the bank's effective functioning. There was no set agenda. This helped the bank achieve spectacular business outcomes in just three years.

I realized that many business problems had their origins in the internal culture of siloed working, bureaucratized decision-making processes, a lack of ownership and responsiveness, as well as a lack of an innovative and growth-oriented mindset. **We worked together to examine issues of customer complaints, sluggish performances, business and technology innovations, employee engagement and various other critical areas of bank functioning. The idea was to diagnose and find appropriate solutions in an open and reflective mode, and it enabled each executive to consider problems from multiple perspectives, take ownership of their responsibilities, and collaborate in order to learn and succeed together.**

These sessions drastically reduced bureaucratic delays and defensive guarding of turf while enabling executives to assume responsibility for their

own roles. We collectively reflected on our attitudes and response mechanisms towards our customers, as well as ways and means to engage employees in a significant manner. This practice fostered a culture of achieving extraordinary results.

We reclaimed our time and deployed it to implement many complex changes, including in technology. We could achieve this by encouraging reflection and diagnosis, as well as liberating our executives from the corrosive effects of fixed mindsets. **I was truly amazed at the way everyone expanded their visions in their areas of work and effectively used their intellectual and emotional resources to restore the glory of the century-old bank.**

(For details about the morning meeting, refer to Chapter 11 of *Dare to Lead*.)[13]

Questions for Reflection

1. What are your key learnings from this chapter?
2. Create an action plan to develop and improve your practice of reflection using the questions below.
3. Have you used reflection before to improve the quality of your interpersonal relationships?
4. How have you used the insights from reflection:
   a. To effect personal change and overcome your blocks.
   b. To streamline human processes.
5. How do you react to a difficult situation?
   a. I tend to withdraw from the situation.
   b. I tend to blame.
   c. I step back and try to reflect on the reasons for the conflict.

Chapter 3

Self-Management: Building Your Strengths

You should not change yourself, but create yourself, that means build around your strengths and remove bad habits.[1]

—Peter Drucker—

Alok Mohan began his career as an assistant manager of marketing at a leading pharma company. Despite working for over five years, he did not receive a promotion and switched to another pharma company. Two years in, he still hadn't received a promotion, and he started to feel frustrated there as well.

What went wrong for Alok? Why couldn't he adjust to his role and feel a part of the company culture at his workplaces? Alok usually experienced interpersonal problems with his immediate bosses on account of his failure to meet targets and his lack of drive towards achieving the goals set for him. Despite his impressive educational qualifications, Alok demonstrated poor self-management skills and often blamed his bosses, the company culture and others. He felt stuck in a rut, experiencing anxiety over his future. Alok's case is a prime example of the importance of self-management skills.

If you look at job postings—even entry-level ones open to freshers—there is a 100 per cent chance that you will see the word 'self-driven'. It is a skill in great demand. And the higher the role, the higher the expectation of self-management—along with that of managing others. Still, many people in the hierarchy experience a certain degree of helplessness in dealing with pressure. There are, however, many people with excellent self-management skills who can cope with stress and work under pressure. Obviously, they are quite self-aware, reflective, purpose-driven and disciplined, and they make strategic use of their time to manage the myriad demands of the job.

To become truly effective leaders, we need to take charge of our lives, set higher standards and manage ourselves. Because if we fail to manage ourselves, someone else will exploit and manipulate us.

The best way to predict the future is to create it.[2]

—Peter Drucker—

What Is Self-Management?

Self-management is about taking responsibility for planning a purposeful life for oneself. Verse 5 from Chapter 6 of the Bhagavad Gita offers inspiration to remain steadfast on the path of self-management.

उद्धरेदात्मनात्मानं नात्मानमवसादयेत् ।
आत्मैव ह्ययात्मनो बन्धुरात्मैव रिपुरात्मन: ॥5॥

Meaning: Elevate yourself through the power of your mind, and not degrade yourself, for the mind can be the friend and also the enemy of the self.

Thus, it is our responsibility to manage ourselves, without placing too many expectations on our workplace, family members and other affiliations.[3]

Managing ourselves effectively will increase our self-confidence, improve our relationships and increase our productivity. It results in balanced living, even-tempered behaviour and the achievement of both personal and professional goals. **Self-management is the key to our success in all areas of life.** People with poor self-management skills blame others for their failures and live an unfulfilled life with myriad problems, which are often self-created.

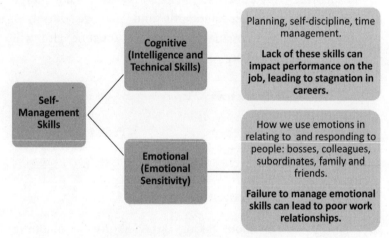

Figure 3.1: Self-Management Skills

(Adapted from the article 'What Makes a Leader' by the leading authority on emotional intelligence, Daniel Goleman, 2004)[4]

Self-management requires a balance of both cognitive and emotional skills. People with fewer technical skills but good emotional intelligence can sometimes be successful leaders. Whereas people with exceptional technical skills and lacking in emotional intelligence can prove to be disastrous leaders. In my long career, I have indeed come across both types of individuals.

Today, leadership development is 30 per cent technical competence and 70 per cent soft skills development. Even in a highly technological environment, no amount of artificial intelligence can replace the use of judgement, mature and wise responses, compassion, etc. Developing soft skills is essentially an investment in the self.

An effective leader must aim to become an **integrated human being** and manage their physical, intellectual, emotional and spiritual health (see Figure 3.2). All areas need sufficient attention, as each is dependent on the other. This is not a one-time process but a quest for continuous improvement.

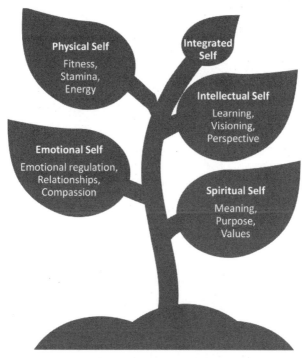

Figure 3.2: Integrated Self

1. **Physical Self:** Physical fitness enhances our ability to maintain stamina and energy for remaining

productive while staying energized and dynamic throughout the day. It also influences our mental and emotional fitness.

2. **Intellectual Self:** To stay ahead and be able to lead from the front requires knowledge and intelligence for quick and efficient problem-solving, innovation and developing a vision for the future.

3. **Emotional Self:** Managing stress, anxiety, disappointments, setbacks and building the best version of ourselves are all critical for creating a balanced personality. Emotional regulation is key to building relationships; it is critical for achieving organizational objectives with the cooperation of people.

4. **Spiritual Self:** Spiritual fitness connects with hope, meaning, values and the purpose of our lives; it helps build resilience against hardships and tragedies. Positivity, optimism, gratitude and forgiveness (for ourselves as well as others) help us connect better with the larger world.

Self-management for creating an **integrated self** calls for acknowledging all the qualities that can be enhanced as well as recognizing all the negatives that require course correction.

One of the biggest obstacles to self-management is resistance to change. Often, people are comfortable with their old ways of being and are reluctant to change due to the considerable effort involved. Besides, it can also be scary. It is not easy to challenge deeply held habits and anxieties, more so when those habits are beyond redemption, unless one takes help from a psychologist. **The human mind in such circumstances is like a pressurized chamber that cannot let go of the old nor can it let in the new.**

Unless a person decides to change, no one else can help him or her.

Table 3.1: Manifestations of Resistance to Change

- Low resilience, pessimism and the inability to manage adversity or transitions.
- Inability to take charge of emotions (EQ), although the IQ may be good.
- Reduced willingness to listen, take feedback and initiate change.
- Lack of initiatives, exploration of alternatives and choice-making.
- Failure to own responsibility.
- Resistance to learning.
- Rigidity and inflexibility.

Those who do not consciously chart out a life strategy and live for the day by satisfying their instincts are the ones who fail to self-manage.

Self-Management Is Critical

Each year, thousands of graduates and postgraduates from different streams of education enter the workstream, but only a few make it to the top and leave a legacy of their leadership and its impact on transforming their organizations.

Often, when I interact with fresh management graduates who are finding their footing in the world of work, I see visible dissatisfaction and demotivation among them over their higher scoring and 'more intelligent' counterparts securing better, higher paying jobs in bigger organizations. I point out that intelligence alone does not guarantee success. Intelligence merely enables a person to enter the job market, but a lack of self-management skills creates many roadblocks to unleash their true potential. I also remind them that self-management skills act as a 'filtering factor' throughout the several stages of growth in their career.

During my career, I experienced new challenging environments in various positions (especially in field jobs), calling for new knowledge, problem-solving skills and moving the system from a comfort zone to a zone of discomfort, to adapt to face competitive realities head-on. Work pressures can sometimes disrupt your set routine, demanding your attention and priorities to face new challenges. **Fixating on a particular style is not beneficial. The traits that serve an executive well in one leadership position often do not work well in another. Thus, self-management means flexibility, coping in new environments and accepting the challenges of transformation with optimism and courage.**

Table 3.2: Leaders Who Practise Self-Management

• Are self-driven, display entrepreneurial drive and take responsibility for themselves.
• Display high integrity, accountability and personal discipline.
• Are masters of their own time and do not waste the time of others.
• Persevere through adversity, courageously facing the situation.
• Are aware of goals and personal strengths.
• Work on their blind spots and seek feedback for improvement.
• Constantly learn, acquire relevant knowledge and build new skills.
• Are creative thinkers and problem-solvers.

A Workout for Managing the Self

It is a given that managing the self is about taking care of all the factors in our personality that affect our capacity for success and overcoming our shortcomings. In short, it means developing our strengths.

1. Prioritize Self-Management Goals

One of the critical things in self-management is to get feedback about oneself and seriously work on it. To reach your full potential, you need to continually improve your self-management skills, take responsibility for your actions and learn from your mistakes. Create a purpose that will keep your priorities straight and motivate you.

In his classic article, 'Managing Oneself', prominent educator, management consultant and author Peter Drucker offers apt advice:

> First and foremost, concentrate on your strengths. Put yourself where your strengths can produce results. Second, work on improving your strengths. Analysis will show you where you need to improve your skills or acquire new ones. It will also show you gaps in your knowledge—and those can usually be filled. Third, discover where your intellectual arrogance is causing disabling ignorance and overcome it.[5]

Make a list of strengths to be enhanced and weaknesses to be reduced, and prioritize them based on their importance. One must relentlessly work on building on one's strengths by developing new skills and acquiring new capabilities. For example, early in my career, I discovered my passion for working on the people side of business, so I chose the human resources function for pursuing my career. I acquired skills, both in the areas of industrial relations which required skills in labour laws and negotiations as also in the area of applied behavioural science, which helped me in developing my capabilities in organizational change process. This gave my career a leg-up and helped me to develop expertise in the entire spectrum of human resource management and organization development.

The more difficult part is working on the weaknesses, which sometimes become habits. For example, being non-listening or unresponsive, having a short temper, a lack of focus, a lack of time discipline, etc. Getting rid of these requires tremendous self-discipline, more rigorous work on oneself and perhaps guidance from a mentor. These weaknesses can create the greatest barriers to one's professional progress. In such cases, managing oneself would entail owning up to the problems and working hard to break the habit patterns.

2. **Managing the Integrated Self (Personality)**
   Work on your emotional, intellectual, physical and spiritual selves for overall health and an improved lifestyle—one that will positively impact your work.

   a. Create a routine of at least four days a week for any form of exercise that is appropriate for building your physique. Exercises such as yoga, walking, running, trekking, swimming, working out in a gym or playing any sport are great ways to not just burn calories but also improve blood circulation, de-stress and rejuvenate the mind and body. Likewise, a healthy, well-balanced diet and paying attention to any illnesses are vital for keeping our bodies fit and in optimal condition for one's leadership journey. The most important thing is managing the physical self.

b. For intellectual growth, learn from the best, follow effective leaders or role models, take cues from the lives of great achievers and transformational leaders, and try to emulate their leadership qualities. Keep up with global trends in technology, management and leadership, the latest developments in your specialization and major issues that can impact the world. Avoid getting sucked into your own specialization and step outside your comfort zone to learn new things. This can provide more options in your career and enable you to better understand the big picture. In other words, it helps to identify both the forest and the trees. You are also better able to adapt to changes and apply your specialist skills as an effective expert in your chosen field. As Nick Lovegrove, an academic and author mentions in his book, *The Mosaic Principle*, 'When we choose this path, we are more likely to become truly *broad-minded*— tolerant, empathetic and understanding of differences in perspectives and points of view.'[6] Pride in intellectual achievements will create ignorance of other subjects; this is self-defeating. Hence, learn to respect everyone who is an expert in their domain.

c. Regulating your emotional self means discovering more about yourself and becoming more understanding, aware and sensitive towards yourself and others. It would mean developing sensitivity to getting along better with more people without hurting anyone and taking responsibility for your own behaviour. Stay kind and dignified in all interactions; be equitable towards everyone. Maintaining a healthy approach to work and life and learning to balance time and effort for both are essential. Finally, practise emotional regulation in all upsetting situations (see Chapter 7 on Emotional Regulation and Anger Management).

d. Take care of your spiritual fitness by practising mindfulness or any form of meditation. Those who find peace in religious practices can dedicate time to it daily; atheists can pursue universal teachings of peace, kindness and other altruistic teachings. Sort out broken relationships, grudges and rough edges in relationships through self-awareness and reflection, followed by dialogue and, wherever possible, forgiveness (see Chapter 1 on Self-Awareness, Chapter 2 on Reflection and Chapter 18 on Dialogue).

In conclusion, self-management may not be easy, but it is the heart and soul of leadership development. It is also a filtering and determining factor that transcends from management to leadership roles. To manage ourselves, the only way is to stay consistent with this 'fitness programme', constantly challenge ourselves and set higher standards. Once we achieve these new standards, we will not want to go back to our old ways of being.

Questions for Reflection

1. What are your key learnings from this chapter?
2. Create an action plan to develop and improve your self-management skills using the questions below.

3. What are your unique strengths that help you manage your 'self' effectively?
4. What aspect(s) of your personality do you need to work on?
   - Physical
   - Intellectual
   - Emotional
   - Spiritual
5. What are the barriers that you experience in managing yourself effectively?

Chapter 4

Self-Discipline: Fuel for Personal Growth

Self-discipline is the fuel for personal growth. This is the discipline we formulate for ourselves and obey ourselves. We're not subjugated to any authority. We're not obeying anyone else. I obey myself; I discipline myself and I do this to grow. The fruit of self-discipline is moderation. Moderation helps you stay balanced. It gives you the equanimity to enjoy the highs and cope with the lows of life.[1]

—Daaji—

Even the best driver can lose control and crash if the vehicle crosses a certain speed. The doctor's timely treatment of a trauma patient within the golden hour increases their chances of recovery. A person who lacks financial discipline will struggle to make ends meet. These examples show the importance—and the impact—of discipline with respect to speed, time and money.

In the environmental context, a lack of discipline shows up as a threat to the climate on account of failure to control emission levels and a lack of disciplined action by various nations, except for the rhetorical pronouncements. Improved education, wealth and a better standard of living, it seems, have not helped the discipline levels in society. It is evident that a lack of discipline puts individuals, societies and nations in danger, leaving them vulnerable to serious problems.

Only personal discipline and self-control can give us the self-confidence and freedom to live life on our terms.

What Is Self-Discipline?

Self-discipline is the ability to maintain focus, resist distractions and complete the task at hand on time. It is a fundamental trait for leaders, as it empowers them to maintain focus, drive results and inspire others. Self-disciplined leaders remain focused and avoid distractions, even when other priorities vie for their attention.

They feel accountable for their actions, decisions and outcomes and are willing to accept consequences. They exercise self-control over their emotions, impulses and reactions, especially in challenging situations, and they remain level-headed during crises. All this translates to a passionate commitment to a high level of work ethic as they push themselves towards excellence.

My friend Rajesh Srivastava shared an example of self-discipline and work ethics that left an indelible impression on me.* He was attending a cricket test match between India and the West Indies. It was India's turn to bat when he noticed three batters walking out in full cricket gear. Two of them walked over to the pitch to open, while the third sat down near the boundary. His curiosity was piqued and Rajesh asked an official who that was.

'Sachin Tendulkar!' the official answered.

'He bats at number four. What's he doing there?' asked Rajesh.

'He is acclimatizing himself!' he replied nonchalantly.

Such discipline! Such a dedicated work ethic! Here's a player whose talent and skills are acknowledged across the world, sitting in the scorching Mumbai sun to acclimatize himself to the conditions! This is when he's at number four, only to come in when India is two batters down, while the batsman due next is in the air-conditioned comfort of the dressing room.

*This incident has been described in his book, *The 10 New Life-Changing Skills: Get Them and Get Ahead!*[2]

Self-discipline is about self-governance. As spiritual guru, Daaji (Kamlesh Patel) says, 'Discipline does not curtail freedom; discipline creates freedom.'[3] For example, if we want financial freedom, we must practise financial discipline. To achieve freedom from disease, we adopt a disciplined lifestyle. Thus, discipline is the way to freedom.

In the pursuit of achieving success in any field or role—as teachers, parents, corporate leaders, sportspersons or actors—personal discipline is the precursor to building stamina and unflinching commitment to achieve one's goals. A person's capacity for self-discipline enhances their ability to influence the environment around them. In some ways, self-discipline helps build what the well-known systems scientist, academic and author Peter Senge calls self-mastery, which is the key aspect of growing as a leader.[4]

It is evident that a lack of discipline can have serious negative impacts in major as well as minute ways. But here is an example of the tremendous benefits of being disciplined: Alex Ferguson is one of the world's most admired football managers, having helped build Manchester United into one of the world's biggest commercial brands. He ascribes his success to his unrelenting focus on placing discipline above all else, even if it cost him several titles. As he explains, 'In the long run, principles are more important than expediency.' He is known to be ruthless with players regardless of their stature and achievements if they lack discipline: 'Once you bid farewell to discipline, you say goodbye to success.'[5]

A common trait among all great achievers is their resolute commitment to discipline in all areas of life. Great sportsmen, great musicians or great achievers in any field follow a strict regimen. Great leaders demonstrate disciplined behaviour both in their thinking and actions.

I find that a leader needs to build personal discipline in the following aspects:

1. **Discipline of Tongue:** Leaders need to be mindful of what they say, how they say it, who they say it to and in what situation. Some leaders have an absolute false sense of their position and show utter contempt for their colleagues and subordinates. They use foul language that causes discomfort and humiliation. While scare tactics and toxic communication may lead to positive business outcomes in the short term, such behaviour can hardly elicit long-term and sustained performance. Imagine such leaders at the top, like an uncontrollable bull, recklessly smashing people's morale. The unfortunate truth is that many such leaders reach high positions (see Chapter 17 on Detoxifying Communication).

   I rate discipline of the tongue as a No. 1 requirement for leaders.

2. **Discipline of Temperament:** People who are in control of their temperament and their emotional responses, even during difficult situations, make the best leaders. They win the support of their colleagues and co-workers with their calm, controlled and compassionate minds. Their toughness at work and occasional demonstrations of anger are far more effective than those who habitually dominate, control and yell to get the work done (see Chapter 7 on Emotional Regulation and Anger Management).

3. **Discipline of Listening:** Leaders who listen with attention with an intent to act always benefit in pursuing growth compared to the know-alls. Non-listeners show contempt for ideas, generate problems on many fronts and end up laying the foundations for a disgruntled culture. Ram Charan, a globally acclaimed management guru and a mentor to hundreds of CEOs of Fortune 500 companies, observes that one out of four senior leaders has a listening deficit.[6] As leaders move up, the capacity to listen shrinks for a variety of reasons, including overconfidence, time pressures and a task-driven culture. The discipline of listening is critical for improving perspective, engaging all stakeholders and promoting a culture of teamwork (see Chapter 16 on Listening).

4. **Discipline of Integrity:** Leaders' character and integrity need to be above reproach within the organization and in their personal dealings, as their personal reputation affects the reputation of the company. It also has a huge impact on the morale of colleagues and co-workers. A single unprincipled act can demolish a painstakingly built reputation (see Chapter 12 on Credibility).

5. **Discipline of Time:** In this fast-moving world, time is a precious resource that needs to be utilized judiciously and effectively. Leaders cannot afford to waste their time and that of others in (un)planned extended discussions on non-issues. Known for his punctuality, film star Amitabh Bachchan famously took a lift from a biker when he found himself stuck in a traffic jam and running late for his shoot. This is a classic example of self-discipline (see Chapter 5 on Time Management). Leaders must also be prompt and respond to people's queries in a timely manner.

6. **Discipline of Thinking, Perspective and Reflection:** Leaders need to consciously and regularly dedicate time to developing new perspectives. This is invaluable in envisioning and acting for the long-term, all-round health of the organization. For example, during my visits to the field, I allocated time to interact with the operating staff and the customers to gain new perspectives about the emerging need for new products and services in order to remain ahead of our competitors.

7. **Discipline in Maintaining a Balanced Life:** Effective leaders need to maintain a fine balance between the personal and the professional. With the ever-increasing demands of the job to extend oneself to the fullest and achieve corporate goals, conscious and disciplined efforts are required from leaders to pursue their hobbies and attend to family responsibilities. Great leaders adroitly maintain this fine balance, periodically restructuring their working style.

8. **Discipline of Passion:** Passions can either be positive or negative. Negatively focused passion is revealed by indulging in immoral activities, hoarding money, incessant criticism of adversaries, jealousy and a

display of unfair, rude and arrogant behaviour. The manifestation of such uncontrolled passion can have dangerous consequences for leaders. On the positive side, a passion for problem-solving, leadership actions, compassion and work accomplishments can contribute to a leader's success.

9. **Discipline of Practice:** Finally, no habit is changed by mere good intentions; it requires disciplined practice. Virat Kohli became a legendary cricketer through discipline. He followed a daily regimen of three to four hours of physical exercise in the gym.[7] Cricketing sensation Hardik Pandya takes his cook along on all his domestic and international trips to follow a balanced diet.[8] Even world-renowned musicians spend four to five hours daily on *riyaz* (practice).

10. **Discipline of Manners:** Leaders need to treat everyone with dignity and respect, regardless of their gender, age, status or position and without letting their own emotions or prejudices come in the way of politeness.

11. **Discipline of a Healthy Lifestyle:** Leaders should follow a regular exercise routine as per their age and physical condition and eat healthy food.

Why Is Self-Discipline Critical?

According to a 2013 study by Wilhelm Hofmann (University of Chicago), self-disciplined people are happier because they do not allow their impulses to dictate their choices.[9] As a result, they are more capable of:

- Resolving goal-based conflicts
- Making positive decisions more easily
- Making informed, rational decisions without stress

Self-discipline can be contagious, as it inspires others. In leadership roles, it enhances the credibility of the leaders and their moral strength to change the status quo and facilitate transformative changes. I learnt a lot about self-discipline from my father as I watched him make ends meet through a strict routine. He made time for his family while managing two jobs. Following in his footsteps, I live a strictly disciplined life in order to efficiently manage my personal and professional obligations. Over the years, such discipline and work ethic have helped me create a better balance between myself, my work and my duties to my organization while achieving results.

Thus, self-discipline helps us lead a balanced life, meet our work (and personal) priorities, and focus on our personal growth. As the Dalai Lama has said, 'A disciplined mind leads to happiness, and an undisciplined mind leads to suffering.'[10]

Table 4.1: Traits of Self-Disciplined People

- Passionate, self-driven and content.
- Confident, agile, dependable and responsive.
- Punctual and respectful of commitments.
- Fastidious, organized and seeking excellence.
- In control of their emotions.
- Lead a balanced life.

A Workout for Building Self-Discipline

How do we improve our discipline? How do we challenge ourselves? Any number of lectures or sermons on improving discipline cannot help unless we make a personal resolve. Like many skills, self-discipline is best improved with willpower, prodigious efforts and regular practice. The encouraging thing is that it is a learnt behaviour, not an inherent ability, and we can train ourselves to engage in it more often.

1. Practise Self-control

Self-control is about building endurance or stamina; it is the willingness to undergo some pain for the things that matter in the long run. Start small, but persevere, and your efforts will reap results. Stacked up over time, they will translate into self-discipline. For this, you need to exert great determination and willpower.

The Buddha says in Verse 159 of *The Dhammapada*: 'One should do what one teaches others to do; if one would train others, one should be well controlled oneself. Difficult, indeed, is self-control.'[11] This verse emphasizes that true self-discipline may be a challenging endeavour but it is also a realistic one. It is generally observed that those who are self-disciplined show self-control of a higher order, and vice versa. Perseverance, grit, delayed gratification and willpower are keys to self-control, but how do we develop them? If a bad habit is formed, often some dramatic events or a change of context can help us give up such habits, although in certain cases, the chance of a revival of the old habits is high.

While it may be difficult to have 100 per cent self-control, it can be exercised with a daily restructuring of our time.

2. Exchange Bad Habits for Good Ones

When an unwholesome practice becomes a habit or addiction, it may be useful to initiate new interests or revive an old hobby. Author and speaker James Clear observes that bad habits are autocatalytic: 'the process feeds upon itself'.[12] He suggests that a reliable approach to breaking bad habits is to reduce our exposure to the cues that cause them.

To avoid biased TV debates, I do not watch any evening programmes except some musical shows on weekends. A retired friend of mine realized that his daily indulgence of a peg or two of alcohol was aggravating his diabetes. He was quite concerned, so he decided to revive an old hobby. He reached out to his music teacher requesting that he conduct music lessons in the evenings. Slowly, his dependence on an evening drink decreased. Thus, changing one's environment can play a key role in maintaining self-control. The same applies to distractions.

3. Remove Distractions

As a leader, you must choose between multiple priorities and urgent tasks. When working, silence emails, turn off cell phones and block tempting websites. Whenever you have an off-topic thought, note it down and deal with it later. This will help you build discipline, prioritize goals and tasks and manage your time. A week of such notes will reveal the patterns of distractions in your routine, and you can plan on tackling them. Changing your work style will take time, so be patient in eliminating distractions from your workday.

4. Seek Discomfort

Self-discipline is about doing what is good for us. What we like (carb-rich foods) may not always be good for us, and what we dislike (healthy foods) may be good for us. Self-discipline is all about choosing something good, irrespective of how it feels. By seeking discomfort voluntarily, one can cultivate self-discipline.

According to Stoic philosopher Epictetus, 'voluntary discomfort' is the practice of deliberately putting yourself through uncomfortable situations so that discomfort no longer holds you back.[13]

Be tough with yourself. Get up at 4 a.m. and go for a run, and try fasting. Abandon softness and be determined to complete all your work. Do whatever feels hard for you. Author and podcaster Ryan Holiday explains the logic:

> All self-discipline begins with the body, but it does not happen magically . . . It is like you temper a sword, exposing it, for brief instances, to heat and cold, to environments that attack the steel and harden it. And so, the best of us become the best by undergoing the same challenge, by forcing our bodies to change and adapt.[14]

5. Build New Habits

Developing self-discipline requires us to let go of some unwholesome habits and cultivate favourable and empowering ones. American novelist Trina Paulus once said, 'How does one become a butterfly? You must want to fly so much that you are willing to give up being a caterpillar.'[15]

In doing so, the first step is to identify your life goals and reflect on why they are important. Next, break down your goals into monthly, weekly and daily units, and identify the new habits that need to be cultivated to achieve these smaller units of your goal.

For example, to develop the habit of reading, you may decide to read one book a month and then look at the number of pages to be read every day. Next, reflect on the adjustments you need to make to your schedule to accommodate the reading. Stay consistent with this reading habit until it becomes a part of your routine.

6. **Get an Accountability Partner**
   Sometimes, even when we chart out a plan, it is difficult to follow. You may be daunted, reluctant or even find it boring. In such instances, having someone remind you of your goals and intentions and hold you responsible will be helpful. You could ask a family member or friend, or even seek expert help for this.

   The quest for self-discipline does not mean punishing or denying ourselves legitimate time for rejuvenation, but to exercise self-control and not indulge in excess. The goal is to move towards a more balanced and organized life, one that aligns with our aspirations.

Questions for Reflection

1. What are your key learnings from this chapter?
2. Create an action plan to develop and improve your self-discipline using the questions below.
3. What self-discipline traits do you value? Which of these do you already practise?
4. In which areas of life do you find it difficult to practise self-discipline? What prevents you from practising self-discipline in these areas?

Chapter 5

Time Management: How to Work Smarter with Your Time

---

*If time were money, most of us would be in debt
and some of us would be bankrupt!*

—Anonymous—

I was catching up with my friend Anupam when he shared with me how his daughter, who works in an executive role, was always running breathlessly from one meeting to another, chasing deadlines and getting exhausted. She had neither the time nor energy for quality time with the family, even on weekends. Although she was only in her early thirties, she had chronic health issues indicating growing anxiety, stress and burnout.

Does this sound familiar? Everyone seems to be struggling with time management, rushing to complete all daily tasks and attempting to maintain order.

When we fail to be disciplined about time, it has far-reaching effects. Obviously, it affects all involved parties and their other commitments for the day. But there is an often-overlooked set of victims as well. Poor time discipline has a cascading effect on those lower down the pecking order, thus victimizing a whole host of people in its wake. For example, a poor time manager may arrive late at a meeting, keep changing the time of meetings, give the same time for a personal meeting to several people or stay back late and expect subordinates to do the same. Of course, it has a huge impact on one's morale and personal life.

To avoid this, we need to smartly manage our time and not let it manage us. Or else we will all be like the White Rabbit from *Alice in Wonderland*, perpetually playing catch-up with time.

Advantages of Mastering Time

Before we go into greater detail, let's ask ourselves: Why is time management important? Time management is crucial because time is a limited resource. And while we need to be respectful of all resources, we must also exercise extra care when a resource is scarce. If we treated time like we do money, we would be much more mindful of it and treat it with the respect it deserves.

Effective time management improves results in **three critical areas: effectiveness, efficiency** and **productivity**. It is one of the pillars of good leadership.

Time is, hands down, our most coveted, most unrenewable resource.[1]

—Brené Brown—

With time working for you, you will be able to:

- Strategize and design the future of the organization;
- Focus on strategic issues and matters of importance;
- Pursue change and transformation;
- Improve responsiveness and problem-solving processes;
- Increase productivity and business outcomes.

- Achieve organizational goals.
- Have a real work–life balance.
- Improve connections and motivate people.

To be masters of our time, we must be aware of our working styles and plan our work accordingly. This will allow us to focus on strategic priorities and achieve multiple goals.

Why Some Leaders Succeed and Others Fail at Time Management

Effective time managers always contextualize their roles to the problem at hand, asking themselves, 'What is my primary job? What are the expectations for my role? What are the problems that I need to solve?' They're also willing to accept that someone else can solve the problems better because they respect their own time as well as that of others. Those who grumble about lack of time need to work on planning, prioritization and delegation.

Table 5.1: Effective Managers versus Ineffective Managers

Effective Time Managers	Ineffective Time Managers
Reflect on their time-spending patterns and work out a plan to shun dysfunctional and time-wasting habits.	Surrender to their habits and settle for lazy living. They lack the initiative to reflect on or implement any improvement plans.
Constantly restructure and refine their time deployment in various activities, focusing on things that matter.	Despite good intentions, they fail to accept responsibility for self-management, especially effective time management.

Effective Time Managers	Ineffective Time Managers
Don't procrastinate on decision-making by effectively planning their time. They believe in being on time, being prepared and being responsive. Their reliability index is high.	Keep postponing important things and continue inefficiently managing their work and personal lives. Hence, they are not reliable.
Do everything with a purpose and do not squander their time. They are organized and self-disciplined.	They do not show any sense of purpose and settle for a status-quo approach to work and personal life.
Plan their calendar days, weeks and even months in advance.	Don't plan their days and undertake the bare minimum to exist.
Make time to respond to the concerns of colleagues and subordinates. They are hands-on, non-bureaucratic and do not waste others' time by nitpicking. They also place a high level of trust in subordinates and delegate tasks efficiently.	Spend a considerable amount of time on insignificant issues and lack trust in others. They micromanage and/or delegate inefficiently.
Make time for self-renewal and personal growth through reading, writing and pursuing their hobbies.	Any personal time for self-renewal is a luxury for such managers. They indulge in unproductive socialization.
Finally, they are dependable and committed to accomplishing the tasks.	Accomplishing tasks is a burden, and they do not show any aspiration for growth. They settle for mediocrity.

Effective time managers are masters of their routines, whereas bad time managers are slaves to their workdays. Figure 5.1 illustrates some common outcomes of ineffective time management.

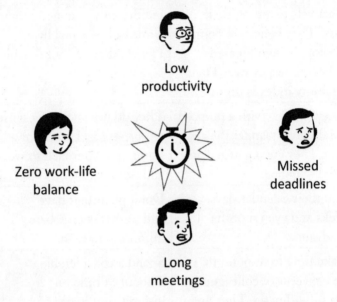

Figure 5.1. Common Symptoms of Ineffective Time Managers

Common Fallacies in Time Management

We all perform under various constraints. There are system-imposed and boss-imposed constraints, such as meetings, priorities set by the boss, workflow, etc. However, leaders often spend a disproportionate amount of time addressing the problems of subordinates. Experts on management and leadership, William Oncken et al., describe this phenomenon in the article 'Who's Got the Monkey'.[2]

They employ the 'monkey on the back' metaphor to examine how subordinates consume leaders' time and explore potential solutions. Some bosses unknowingly invite problems—monkeys—from subordinates and use up their time trying to tame them. In the process, they lose much of their discretionary time (time available to managers after budgeting for all official engagements, which they can utilize for themselves). Leaders must nurture a workplace culture that encourages and empowers subordinates to find solutions on their own, rather than relying on their boss for answers at every turn. While problem-solving brings its own high, it also has other benefits. It makes the team feel more involved, allowing them to course-correct similar situations in the future without the boss's intervention. It boosts overall morale and instils trust in the leader of the team, and vice versa. It inculcates accountability and responsibility in the team, motivating it to aim higher. At the same time, it allows the leader to be a mentor and supervisor instead of micromanaging and breathing down the team's neck, thereby increasing their discretionary time.

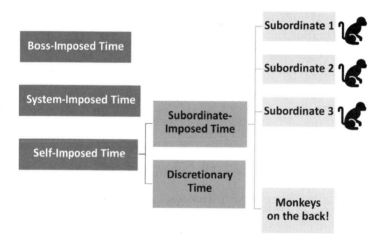

Figure 5.2: Components of Time at Work

The other fallacy is one's own need to micromanage and control because of a lack of faith in the skills and capabilities of others. Such leaders end up busy with mundane and routine work at the cost of more important and strategic issues. Thus, leaders may sabotage their time either through personal or organizational limitations.

One of my senior colleagues, a CEO, would meticulously go through every official note or memo and raise several queries, some of which were avoidable. Once these were clarified, he would raise further questions (queries upon queries). Everyone in senior and top management positions found this frustrating, often leading to a pile of papers awaiting decision-making. During the annual finalization of the balance sheet, this gentleman would spend innumerable hours discussing every single problematic account with auditors before they were classified as non-performing assets.

When leaders spend so much time on something that can—and should—be delegated to functional executives, they are, in fact, reducing time for their core work.

While this banker was hard-working and had remarkable stamina, the organization failed to undertake many strategic and time-bound initiatives (for instance, technology-driven transformation), and its market position declined. A leader's (mis)management of time has a ripple effect on everyone's time down the hierarchy as well as the organization's performance. In this case, the end result was that the bank's performance rating fell dramatically, marking a strategic shift in the bank's overall performance.

A Workout for Time Management

Time is the one resource available in equal measure to the highest, the mightiest and the lowest on the organizational ladder. Everyone has twenty-four hours in a day; no one gets extra. Legendary investor and author, Ray Dalio sums it up well in his popular book, *Principles*:

> Some people spend a lot of time and effort accomplishing very little while others do a lot in the same amount of time. What differentiates people who can do a lot from those who can't is creativity, character and wisdom. What makes an executive effective is how he or she uses the time.[3]

Effective time management requires three crucial phases: **planning, prioritizing** and **delegating**. You need to chalk out your activities well in advance, order and address what is most important, and delegate all that is not tied to your core work function. Let's see how we can achieve these three goals.

1. **Reflect on Your Time Management Style**
   The starting point for developing muscles for effective time management is to diagnose your daily habits (sleep–wake times, time spent on phone calls, texting, social media, etc.) and reflect on the impact of these habits on the availability of time for 'must-do' activities to pursue your career goals and personal effectiveness. Unless you can identify the excessive use of time in any habit and work seriously to disengage, it would be difficult to create any additional time to pursue your career goals and have a balanced life.

2. **Plan Your Time**
   Any resource that is scarce must be prioritized and planned for better productive use. The purpose should be to strike a healthy balance between personal and professional lives. The essence of planning is writing down your monthly,

weekly and daily activities. At higher levels, the most critical thing is to create a balance between long-term and short-term priorities and accordingly allocate time. To do this, you could rope in a very competent, organized and efficient secretary who can help plan meetings and appointments, keep track of your long- and short-term commitments on a daily basis and restructure your time in case of exigencies.

Regularly audit your calendar and to-do lists to clear out everything except for mission-critical and high-value tasks. This will help you balance your time budget.

3. Use the Time Management Matrix

Stephen Covey's Time Management Matrix (TMM) is an excellent tool to prioritize tasks and plan schedules.[4] First, you identify your tasks. Next, you categorize the tasks according to the TMM. This helps gain clarity on what deserves your time and what will bring better rewards.

Figure 5.3: Time Management Matrix

For Q2—not urgent, but important tasks—make the schedule nearly non-negotiable as these will be core tasks that have a high value. Mastery over Q2 will help reduce your Q1 pile; it will prepare you well for all crises, if not prevent most of them, thereby reducing the need for firefighting.

Unnecessarily deviating from a meticulously planned schedule can result in a **'time bankruptcy'**, so be sure to avoid it. For example, if you resolve to spend forty-five minutes at the most on a presentation, set up a time-tracking app to alert you when the time is up.

I know of a CEO who would keep track of the end time of every meeting that he attended and make sure to leave at that time. The message was loud and clear: he meant business and his time was precious. This sent the right signals, and meetings in his organization were conducted with discipline regarding time.

I also know a senior executive who would give at least half a dozen people one window to meet him. This earned him a notorious reputation while squandering time—his own and others'.

4. Delegate and Creatively Outsource

One of the key reasons for ineffective time management is the tendency among many leaders to centralize decision-making and continue to be control freaks. To avoid the trap of centralization, the twin strategy of delegation and creatively outsourcing some tasks can create a lot of free time. Otherwise, you end up focusing on operational busywork instead of the critical issues demanding your attention.

For creating additional time resources for oneself, it is also critical to delegate activities in such a manner that subordinates undertake the responsibility and gain confidence. For example, in 1994, I was a new deputy general manager, personnel to the corporate job (after thirteen long years in training function at the staff college), and my boss asked me to independently lead a union–management meeting, normally chaired by him. I was initially nervous, but I could lead the meeting with great success, which enhanced my confidence. This saved my boss a full day of participating in this meeting and, in the process, I gained huge confidence.

Eminent researchers Julian Birkinshaw and Jordan Cohen point out in their 2013 article, 'Make Time for the Work That Matters', that by delegating unimportant tasks and replacing them with value-added ones, one can free up nearly a fifth of one's time and improve productivity.[5] One can then focus on more worthwhile tasks with the hours saved.

5. Use Time Blocking

Time blocking, a powerful time management tool, divides your workday into scheduled work blocks according to the type of work. It allows space for deep focus and allows you to immerse yourself in the task at hand for a few hours, thus maintaining context and eliminating interruptions. Many trackers and calendar-based apps are available that help with time blocking quickly and easily. Always create a time budget in the same way you create a financial budget or plan. This will help you keep track of your tasks and, thus, better allocate time to them. When you exceed your budgeted time, it has a domino effect on the rest of your calculations. And once you are in the red, it is hard to return to solvency.

6. Cut Out the Clutter in Your Inbox

Technology can either be a great asset in time management or turn you into a prodigal time waster. Use social media apps such as LinkedIn, Facebook, WhatsApp and Instagram with discipline and prudence. Do you really need to be a member of an unmanageable number of groups? Is it necessary to respond to every post and participate in every discussion? For working executives, it can be the biggest distraction and also kill productivity. You can save a lot of time by very selectively using these apps.

Digital experts, Nandan Nilekani and Tanuj Bhojwani, in their book, *The Art of Bitfulness*, have proposed the interesting concept of Inbox Zero, where you go through your inboxes regularly to achieve a 'zero items pending' result through the algorithm determined below.[6] The central idea is for you to decide how to process each item in your inbox.

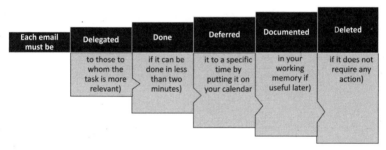

Each email must be	Delegated	Done	Deferred	Documented	Deleted
	to those to whom the task is more relevant)	if it can be done in less than two minutes)	it to a specific time by putting it on your calendar	in your working memory if useful later)	if it does not require any action)

Figure 5.4: Creating Inbox Zero

7. Keep Meetings Short

Meetings consume 70–80 per cent of the time of any senior executive. While meetings are necessary for collective decisions and discussions on key issues, most meetings can be shortened, restructured or merged. Insist on crisp presentations and businesslike discussions at meetings. If you are in a leadership role, avoid the temptation of taking charge and speaking, allowing others to do so instead. Make sure to decide the exit time for every meeting and stick to it.

8. Learn to Say 'No'

To effectively manage time, learn how to say 'no' politely to distractions such as meetings, discussions and public events, especially if they are not important to you or the organization. It may be difficult to say 'no' to attending meetings convened by very senior and top bosses, even if one does not find immediate relevance for her work. However, you can, with some tact and diplomacy, avoid attending a meeting convened by an immediate or horizontal boss by informing them that you are engaged in an urgent task that has also been assigned by the boss. Sometimes, you are successful, and the rest of the time, it is your luck.

9. Create a 'Magical Twenty-Fifth Hour' for Learning

One of the greatest advantages of better time management, especially for busy executives, is the ability to focus on self-renewal. By improving your time management muscles through the various steps listed above, you can create a magical twenty-fifth hour for your own learning and personal growth.

I have used many of these tips during my time as CEO when I headed a large government-owned bank. My responsibilities, among other things, included visits to the reporting ministry, meetings called by regulators, the board and other parties, travel (both domestic and international), visits to zonal and regional offices, town halls with employees, customer meets, etc. About twenty general managers heading various functions reported to me.

As a first step, I reorganized and strengthened my secretariat in the context of my strategic priorities to undertake technology-driven business transformation. To accomplish this, I also put employee-centricity and customer-centricity on equal footing and piloted programmes under my direct charge by creating two separate helplines for employees and customers, respectively. I delegated most operational issues to two executive directors and functional general managers, which helped me focus on my strategic priorities to undertake a major transformation of the bank and allocate a major part of my time to this endeavour.

Apart from restructuring my time in the office, I also reorganized my time beyond the office setting, as the workload was overwhelming and needed a huge amount of my engagement.

As I was keen to allocate time for my personal well-being, I did not sacrifice my hour-long morning walk. Instead, I utilized that time to discuss functional issues with a senior general manager and a fellow morning walker, and the two of us discussed important and critical issues relating to his functions, which was one of the most critical profit-generating functions of the bank. It greatly helped me process papers and make decisions later in the day.

During about forty-five minutes of commute time to the office, any one of the general managers would join me with a prior appointment to discuss issues relating to their function. During all my local travels and from the office to the airport, my executive secretary would often join to brief me on various matters. I wanted to get the most out of every minute I had at my disposal. There was so much to do, and twenty-four hours appeared insufficient. I wanted the best return on investment (ROI) on my time.

In general, I divided my day into the following tasks:

- Strategic discussions on key issues with all general managers through morning meetings, from 9.30 a.m. to 10.30 a.m. This helped in building coordination between various functions and de-bureaucratizing decision-making.
- Decision-making time for business issues: 11 a.m. to 2 p.m.
- Meetings with customers and other visitors: 2.30 p.m. to 4 p.m.
- Strategic discussions on the transformation project: 4 p.m. to 6 p.m. (technology team, consultants and HR group)
- External linkages and board matters: 6 p.m. to 7.30 p.m.

With rigorous planning, prioritization, delegation and daily reflection about the way I spent my time, it was not very difficult to get the best possible return on my time, thereby improving the overall productivity of my top team and helping us achieve all our business goals.

Such productive time management allowed me to handle various functions in a very systematic and strategic way.

Being busy does not necessarily mean being productive. On the contrary, an excessively busy person is a victim of mismanaged time and can stay busy for years without getting anywhere. In our endeavour towards leadership, we will benefit from developing a healthier perspective on our relationship with time. Only by doing this can we make time our best ally.

Questions for Reflection

1. What are your key learnings from this chapter?
2. Create an action plan to develop and improve your time management skills using the questions below.
3. How do you generally manage your time?
   a. I have enough time for all activities.
   b. I manage somehow.
   c. I struggle with time management.
4. What constraints do you face in managing your time? What steps have you taken to improve your time management?

Chapter 6

Resilience: Bouncing Back from Setbacks

Do not judge me by my successes, judge me by how
many times I fell down and got back up again.[1]

—Nelson Mandela—

Seema lost her father to Covid-19, which was a big blow to her, but she made it a point to complete the rigorous apprenticeship for a certification that she had already applied for. Michelle lost her leg in an accident at the age of nine. Today, she is a successful professional who has travelled the world and conducts group therapy and counselling for an amputee support group. Arun lost his job during the recession. When he could not find another job despite his best efforts, he put together his savings to start his own business, which is now very successful.

These individuals underwent great loss and adversity, only to emerge stronger. They didn't give up in the face of hurdles, finding new avenues to lead meaningful lives. The spirit to persevere and prevail over obstacles is what resilience is about.

Employees across the globe experience daily challenges that can have a destructive cumulative effect. Frustration, anxiety, regret, worry and depression have now become common maladies in this non-stop competitive and disruptive world. Work, for many, is a source of discontent for a variety of reasons. Inequities, a lack of an open and transparent environment, toxic bosses, a lack of empathy from customers and rigidly enforced deadlines all cumulatively disrupt mental peace.

What Is Resilience?

Resilience is the human capacity to meet adversity, setbacks, humiliation and loss of respect without crumbling. It is the process of overcoming upsetting emotions during failures or adversities and finding the strength and willpower to bounce back, adapt, cope and recover from trauma. In the words of Harvard Business School professor Ranjay Gulati, 'True resilience involves more than recovering from or resisting the effects of adversity. It is the ability to emerge even stronger.'[2]

Low resilience leaves one vulnerable to emotional pain, deep isolation, fear, anger and stress. It can make us withdraw into ourselves, unable to view people and situations from the right perspective. If this pattern continues, it can make us emotionally arthritic.

Ginni Rometty, former chairman and CEO of IBM, describes in her book, *Good Power*, how her father abandoned his wife and four children with no money, and how the family had to fend for themselves. Considering the hardships they faced, it is nothing short of a miracle that all the siblings were wildly successful. Rometty's younger sisters were head of strategy at Accenture and chief procurement officer at Coca-Cola, her brother was head of the largest commodity trading firm in the US. In her memoir, Rometty observes: '. . . it wasn't luck that propelled each of us to transcend a tragedy in our childhoods and forge ambitious paths. The singular characteristic that describes us is resilience.'[3]

Resilience is about not giving up, giving in or letting fate or misfortune break us. Resilient people show equanimity under pressure and cope well with disruptive changes. They are proactive, possess self-worth and have good reflective abilities. They are humble, yet their confidence is high, and they are not defeated by their failures. Such people have the physical, emotional and mental stamina to sustain and absorb pressure and stress.

One of the greatest examples of resilience in action is the performance of the Indian cricket team in the Brisbane Test against Australia in January 2021. This was after they experienced a humiliating loss (36 all out) only a few weeks earlier, in the first test match, despite bruises and injuries suffered by half of the team. The Brisbane match was a power play of India's collective resilience and saw them achieve the famous 2-1 series victory. This is a classic example of sustained confidence and recovery from the trauma of failure.

Different Types of Resilience

Broadly, we can say that there are three kinds of resilience, and all of us have at least one of these in some measure.[4]

Natural Resilience	Adaptive Resilience	Restored Resilience (Learned Resilience)
This is an instinct or ability that we are born with. It makes us enthusiastic and helps us see life as an adventure. As children, most of us learned to ride a bicycle, even if we scraped our knees, because the result was rewarding. But if, as a child under the age of seven, we faced trauma, it would have diminished our natural resilience.	This is developed when we face adversities through coping, adapting and transforming. The more challenges we face, the more opportunities we must learn from and evolve, thus increasing our adaptive resilience. The key is determination, optimism and self-belief in achieving what seems insurmountable.	This can be developed by learning and honing certain techniques that can **restore our natural resilience** and help us deal with trauma in a healthier way.

Figure 6.1: Types of Resilience

It is entirely up to us to captain our lives to take decisive action and to deal with adversity head-on. It requires us to have our heads firmly on our shoulders and a pragmatic perspective on reality. Trudging along stubbornly, nursing false hopes for an unattainable goal, is not resilience but denial. A truly resilient person is a realist and humble enough to know when it is time to give up and to live to fight another day.[5]

Why Is Resilience Important?

Resilience is critical for leaders, especially in today's fast-paced and often unpredictable world. Leaders must often steer through unforeseen challenges, setbacks and changes, so their ability to bounce back and adapt is crucial for their own well-being as well as the well-being of their teams and organizations. Resilient leaders can inspire others, maintain focus during tough times and effectively navigate through adversity. It also allows them to lead by example and create a positive and supportive work environment.

Perhaps this is why many Eastern cultures focus on developing resilience in their practices. For instance, Buddhism dwells on the four noble truths and the eightfold path.[6] The ancient Greek philosophy known as stoicism emphasizes equanimity in the face of both joy and sorrow.[7]

On a professional level, anxiety, pressures and stress are now recognized as major issues that need serious attention. Even the World Health Organization has recognized the impact of stress on employees in the workplace.[8] It is therefore the responsibility of leaders and organizations to help their employees cope with stress and to create nurturing environments rather than stressful ones.

Morgan Stanley became the epitome of resilience during and immediately after the 9/11 terror attacks in the US. This is how they exhibited resilience at every step:

- The first step was the implementation of the evacuation plan (established earlier, after the 1993 World Trade Center bombing) immediately after the bombing of the first tower. In doing so, they saved the lives of over 2500 employees.
- The second step was to move operations to their backup site. This allowed them to continue functioning while other companies took weeks or months to resume operations. Some companies never recovered.
- The third step was to convert their credit card call centres into toll-free emergency hotlines to find their missing employees. Later, they also set up grief counselling to help employees cope with trauma and anxieties.[9]

Morgan Stanley's crisis handling shows how their leaders learnt from previous threats and prepared their employees for emergencies. It was this preparedness and quick action that saved their employees when the second plane hit the exact spot where their offices were! Their resilience helped Morgan Stanley bounce back from a situation that caused many others to shut down their businesses.

Characteristics of Resilient Leaders

Diane Coutu, author and senior editor at *Harvard Business Review*, mentions that most research on resilience points to three characteristics commonly seen in resilient people:

- A strong acceptance of reality.
- A deep belief, often buttressed by strongly held values, that life is meaningful.
- An uncanny ability to improvise.

She further observes, 'Resilient people face reality with staunchness, make meaning of hardship instead of crying in despair and improve solutions in thin air.'[10]

Presented in Table 6.1 is a comparison of leaders with high and low resilience.

Table 6.1 Leaders with High Resilience versus Leaders with Low Resilience

Leaders with High Resilience	Leaders with Low Resilience
Positive view of life, optimistic and courageous	Negative view of life, pessimistic and weak
Emotionally robust, can recover faster from crises, become stronger	Over emotional, do not recover well from crises, develop anxieties
Flexible and learning attitude, growth mindset	Reject new ideas and advice, fixed mindset
Prepared for eventualities, risk-taking	Unprepared for challenges, risk-averse
Passionate and driven, high levels of commitment	Passive and directionless, not very committed

A Workout for Developing Resilience

We all face difficult moments in life. How we respond to them is what matters. Do we recover and move on, break down or stagnate? Giving up is not an option. Resilience can be developed, improved and enhanced (and involves working on restored or learnt resilience). It also requires us to strengthen ourselves on physical, mental and emotional levels to support and enhance our adaptive resilience.

In his article, 'Resilience for the Rest of Us', Daniel Goleman mentions two ways to be more resilient, based on two types of challenges. The first type of challenge is a major failure or setback, a big life-altering adverse incident, for which resilience can be built by talking to ourselves and giving ourselves a 'cognitive intervention and counter-defeatist thinking with an optimistic attitude'. The second type of challenge includes:

> frequent annoying screwups, minor setbacks and irritating upsets that are routine . . . Resilience is, again, the answer— but with a different flavour. You need to retrain your brain. The brain has a very different mechanism for bouncing back from the 'cumulative toll of daily hassles'. And with a little effort, you can upgrade its ability to snap back from life's downers.[11]

Building resilience is a valuable skill that can help you navigate challenges and bounce back from adversity. There is no uniform method for building resilience. It will depend on the context and the process of socialization of individuals. Building resilience is like restoring oneself from a deep negative world view to a pragmatic understanding of the reality around oneself, reclaiming oneself from a mental logjam and restoring confidence to restart and thrive.

Here are some effective ways to build individual resilience:

1. **Accept the Reality and Adapt**

    Life is unpredictable, and we need to be open to change and disruption. Being adaptable is crucial, as it can help us stay resilient in the face of unexpected challenges. Cultivate flexibility in thinking, embrace change and be open to new ideas and perspectives.

    It is important to understand the ground reality in terms of the competitive environment, task-obsessive culture, impatient customers, the digital landscape and an increasing shrinkage of job opportunities. These factors can create stress and cause mental weakness unless we develop new skills and abilities to cope with the new reality. We need to accept the fact that our current skills will not be enough to ensure growth in the future. In addition, when faced with bigger adversities, we need to be realistic and look at all options, yet be compassionate enough to ensure coping without causing additional stress. Reflect on these questions and take remedial action where necessary:

    •   What am I doing to cope with this new environment/adversity?
    •   Am I building new skills/abilities?
    •   What is my contingency plan?
    •   What are my constraints in terms of job mobility?

- For daily challenges, what strengths can help me cope, and what weaknesses can hold me back?
- Am I prepared to deal with the tough environment ahead?
- Am I making thoughtful decisions and not focusing on inaction?

While reflecting on these questions, be ready to face the truth and accept reality. Treat oneself with kindness and understanding; accept that setbacks and failures are a part of life and learn from them rather than dwelling on self-criticism.

2. Take Charge of Yourself

The most common reasons for low resilience are a lack of personal discipline, which leads to incomplete or delayed tasks; a disinclination to listen; a fixed mindset; toxic thinking and behaviour; a lack of accountability; refusal to improve and a lack of emotional control. Such people react negatively to unfavourable feedback, do not improve their performance or display a learning attitude.

Building resilience essentially means taking charge of ourselves and creating a vision for our lives based on our core values and aligned with a purpose. This can provide a sense of direction and motivation during challenging times. Also, we can practise self-care, tending to our physical, mental and emotional well-being to help gain discipline over ourselves.

We must believe in our abilities and create concrete goals and a purpose for life. With the right approach, adversity can teach a lot, and with the wrong approach, it can destroy lives.

We are the captain of our life's ship, and we must steer it safely in times of turbulence.

(How to know oneself better has been discussed in Chapters 1 and 2; how to take charge of the self is discussed in Chapter 3, and how to build the discipline needed to strengthen the self is discussed in Chapter 4.)

3. Build Emotional Restraint

This essentially means taking control of our emotions and shifting from being reactive to being responsive and responsible. For example, when deeply hurt by someone's remarks, you may stop communicating and isolate yourself from work or other activities. However, a controlled and functional approach is to bounce back from the feelings of hurt and frustration and build confidence to discuss the issue with the concerned person. This helps build emotional resilience and the potential resolution of the problem through mutual understanding. The key to resilience is staying focused on the important things rather than fixating on negative emotions.

Gandhi and Mandela provide excellent examples of strong emotional restraint and resilience in the face of provocation. Gandhi faced many humiliations at the hands of colonial powers, but he bounced back each time with renewed vigour and energy without deviating from his non-violent ways of confronting issues. Similarly, Nelson Mandela, after having spent most of his youthful years (twenty-seven years) in jail, came out and advocated peace and reconciliation. Mandela exercised a choice between retribution and reconciliation.

4. Challenge Yourself in Increments

A good way to build resilience is taking on something that you find challenging or intimidating. For example, if you feel certain languages are hard to master, try learning a different but somewhat familiar language. If you are a Hindi-speaking person, it may be easier for you to pick up the Gujarati language. This will bolster your confidence, and eventually, once you gain proficiency, you can explore a more difficult language. This helps you gradually overcome inhibitions and realize that you can achieve just about anything if you are determined. Similarly, in my physical training, I started with an achievable goal of walking 3 kilometres at a stretch, and then I gradually increased it to 7 kilometres. It is important to set realistic and achievable goals that align with your aspirations and subsequently progress along the way to achieve the ultimate target. This will help you develop resilience to sustain it as a habit.

5. **Shift Your Perspective**

   Reframe challenges as learning experiences and opportunities for growth. Develop a positive outlook on life, focus on the aspects you can control, and emphasize your strengths and past successes to bolster your confidence. Become aware of your patterns of response, move beyond your comfort zone when required and, rather than being near-sighted, approach the situation through the larger context to gain new perspective and insight about the business and stakeholders. I experienced a major change of perspective in my work when I was asked to take up a senior business role late in my career. It helped me gain new perspectives on human problems at the operational level.

6. **Take the Time to Rest and Recover**

   Often, people push themselves harder in an attempt to build resilience, but research has proven that this approach has the opposite effect and wears us out. A balanced life can help us recharge and handle stress better. Allowing ourselves sufficient time for rest and recovery is essential, especially when facing adversity. Maintaining a healthy work–life balance, with proper rest, good sleep and the right diet, repairs and regenerates the body. Any gentle form of exercise will improve blood circulation, and even a simple stretch can release some stress. Spending time with loved ones, indulging in hobbies and solving puzzles all allow the brain to rewire our synapses to learn from adversities.

The key to resilience is trying really hard, then stopping, recovering, and then trying again.[12]

—Shawn Achor and Michelle Gielan—

---

7. **Get Help**
   If you feel stuck in negativity or are overwhelmed by stress and emotional difficulties, seek help from a friend, a therapist, a counsellor or a mentor. This will provide you with a non-threatening environment for self-reflection, receiving feedback, processing your thoughts and feelings and initiating personal change. Whatever the source of your stress—the daily grind or a traumatic event—counselling or psychotherapy are likely to help.

8. **Develop Problem-Solving and Crisis-Management Skills**
   Breaking down problems into smaller, manageable tasks enhances our ability to tackle them. Seek creative solutions, explore different perspectives and learn from mistakes. Crisis and conflict management training can prepare us to deal with emergent crises and conflict situations. This can help leaders in aspects such as mobilizing resources and efforts during crises, building morale, bringing people together, etc.

9. **Practise Yoga and Meditation**

To deal with tension and stress, especially in times of adversity, it is important to calm down the mind and its turbulence. Engage in activities that promote resilience, such as journaling, meditation, mindfulness or gratitude exercises. These practices can enhance your self-awareness, reduce stress and promote your emotional well-being. Yoga and meditation are time-tested methods that help achieve calmness and inner peace, as well as support recovery from trauma, which is much needed to build and sustain resilience. In a study conducted by IIT Bombay, 450 students who practised yoga and meditation regularly were observed over two years.[13] The findings revealed an increase in positive energy, the ability to relate to others, connectedness, compassion and better grades.

10. **Build a Support Network**

Surround yourself with supportive and trustworthy individuals, whether family, friends or mentors. Share experiences, seek advice and lean on their support during challenging times. They can provide new perspectives on the situation, help you reflect on the factors that may have caused or exacerbated the problem, and provide you with options to course-correct. A mentor can help you come out of a negative mindset and overreactions and steer you towards new pathways based on optimism, positive initiatives and larger goals.

It is within our control to defeat the negativity and hopelessness that come with adversity. These steps can greatly help restore your momentum. By incorporating these strategies, you can enhance your ability to navigate difficulties and emerge stronger.

Going Beyond Resilience: Building Antifragility

Nassim Nicholas Taleb, a global expert on risk analysis and a statistician, in his seminal work, *Black Swan*, explains the concept of **antifragility**: 'Antifragility is beyond resilience or robustness. The resilient resists shocks and stays the same; the anti-fragile gets better.'[14] In other words, systems improve when they experience disorder or harm, and instead of going back to the status quo ante, they strengthen and evolve. For example, when you train with more weights than you are used to, there is an additional strain on your muscles (what you consider disorder or harm). This triggers an antifragile response of muscle-building, thus creating greater resistance, endurance and strength in the body.

Authors Héctor García and Francesc Miralles suggest the following steps to be more antifragile:[15]

- **Create more options:** To take care of adversity in any aspect of life—finances, relationships, occupations and skill sets—avoid putting all your energy and resources into just one thing.
- **Bet conservatively in certain areas and take many small risks in others:** The conservative approach protects us against large setbacks, while small risks in multiple areas may bring greater rewards.
- **Get rid of things that make you fragile:** Set 'good riddance goals' in addition to new life resolutions. Certain people, things and habits that make us vulnerable are a case in point.

If we fear adversity, consider it a misfortune and avoid confronting it, we lose the opportunity to learn from it and grow. Choosing the attitude of antifragility helps us to see the misfortunes as challenges or as experiences from which we can learn, alter our goals and become stronger.

An Example of Antifragility

Srikant Bolla, who was born blind, wanted to pursue science after his matriculation.[16] But the state law did not allow him to study math or science, as studying graphs and diagrams was considered a challenge for blind students. Srikant went to court and won the case, securing 98 per cent in the HSC board exams. He faced his next hurdle when he wanted to study engineering at IIT but was denied admission by coaching institutes, who told him that preparing for the entrance exams would be like 'pouring rain on a small sapling'. So, he applied to MIT, USA, and completed his engineering. At each stage, Srikant triumphed through sheer resilience. Now a successful entrepreneur and the founder of Bollant Industries, he is a living example of the phrase 'when the going gets tough, the tough get going'. Srikant is a classic example of antifragility, using every setback as an opportunity to elevate his life goals. Pursuing an antifragile attitude makes us stronger and helps us stay focused.

Create a Culture of Resilience

The need to build resilience is not limited to individuals alone, as challenges can hit organizations as well. **Transformation and resilience go hand in hand. Companies that strive for sustainability and innovation, particularly in disruptive environments, are inherently resilient.** In times of calamity, resilient organizations have managed to stay ahead, as seen in the case of Morgan Stanley. Leaders need to continuously prepare the organization so that it responds effectively to disruptive changes in a calibrated manner while meeting the changing needs of customers.

Having said that, leaders must be mindful of the demands they place on their teams. Sometimes, organizations fail to provide sustaining structures and processes, creating excessive stress and pressure for their operating managers and employees. When leaders fail to listen to their problems and provide no tangible solutions, even the most hard-working and committed employees succumb to stress.

In this context, the observations of authors and experts in communication, learning and development, Liz Fosslien and Mollie West Duffy, are very apt:

> Resilience, or the ability to withstand hardship and bounce back from difficult events, is useful when it comes to working. But, too often, it's presented in a way that overlooks structural issues and instead encourages employees to grin and bear whatever tough stuff comes their way—and to do so on their own, without disturbing their colleagues . . . it's much, much easier to be resilient in an environment that 'makes' it easy.[17]

Here are some ways to build a culture of resilience at the grassroots level for individuals and teams.

1. **Create growth-oriented challenges:** Assign tasks to individuals and teams with increasing levels of difficulty each time they succeed; such challenges will help them build resilience. And if they fail, they will learn valuable lessons that will prepare them for the future.
2. **Create a support system for resilience:** Appreciate and mentor employees to create a safety net in case of failure. This humaneness in your approach will make your people trust you and embolden them to take

calculated risks, which can further build their capacity for resilience.

3. **Encourage the practice of reflection:** Encourage your team to regularly reflect as individuals and as teams on their successes and failures. Help them understand their weaknesses, their strengths and the lessons from both that can help build their resilience as individuals and as a team (see Chapter 2 on Reflection).

4. **Help employees manage stress:** Provide coaching or counselling and conduct stress-busting team exercises to help employees decompress. Communicate openly about challenges and setbacks. This creates a culture of transparency and trust, which can help mitigate stress and build resilience. American psychologist George S. Everly Jr. calls this developing a 'psychological body armour'.[18] Some individuals may want to deal with crises in their own ways and that is perfectly fine, but the leader can let the employee know that other options are available.

5. **Encourage passion for work:** It can be a powerful tool to help individuals navigate adversity with determination, positivity and a sense of purpose. Create an environment in which team members are encouraged to pursue their passions and leverage them as sources of strength and motivation. Help them align their passions with the organization's goals and objectives. Encourage them to find connections between their personal interests and the work they do to contribute to the team's and organization's success.

In my experience, passion ranks higher than competence, and our own passion as leaders motivates employees to join in realizing the purpose of the organization.

Resilience can be promoted at the organizational level through larger initiatives. A 2020 survey by Microsoft-IDC showed that, with the right approach, crises can indeed become opportunities.[19] The findings brought out four key factors that contributed to organizational resilience: technology, people, data and processes. Thus, to build organizational resilience, leaders need to:

- Fortify the organization's resilience by investing in the right digital **technology** for accelerated innovation and transformation.
- Invest in **people's** capabilities and skills to unlock their potential to accelerate transformation; ensure rewards and incentives.
- Leverage **data** to develop new revenue streams and capitalize its value to drive innovation and increase competitiveness.
- Redesign and deploy **processes** that empower people to continuously drive sustained innovation.

Here are some ways to build organizational resilience:

1. **New capacity building:** Enhance the abilities, resources, structures and processes within communities and organizations, and create systems to effectively anticipate, withstand, respond to and recover from adverse situations or crises.
2. **Encouraging collaborative resilience:** Build unity and team spirit. When the Bank of Baroda slid from its No. 1 position to No. 4 among peer banks, we took several steps to bring cohesion to the top team and build passion at the grassroots level by listening to employees' concerns and initiating several programmes

to build optimism and positive aspirations. We initiated smart communication mechanisms to reach out to employees and customers with a foolproof system of responding to every single concern in a defined time. We also initiated several employee-centric and customer-centric initiatives with the full participation of the team. Collectively, these steps instilled renewed vigour to fight the decay and slide, and in a short period of three years, the bank regained its prime position in the industry.

3. **Sustainable innovation:** Innovative and creative problem-solving for daily challenges helps prepare everyone for real crises. Instead of following the crowd in times of crisis, organizations can take calculated risks that will help them stay ahead.

4. **Reaching out to loyal customers in crises:** In times of economic crises, you need to retain your customer base and make it known that you are still in business, lest they assume otherwise and jump ship.

While introducing any of the above, in improving the organization's resilience, leaders need to be mindful of three things: **cohesion at the top** (unified decisions and efforts can drive transformations smoothly), **passion in the middle** (a team that believes in the organization's vision stays invested and motivated for the transformation) and **new capability building at the grassroots level** (to unleash the higher potential of the people for sustainable innovation).

Indian organizations have displayed resilience in various ways, especially in the face of challenges such as economic downturns, natural disasters and global pandemics. Here are some examples of how they did it.

1. Rapid **adaptation to digital trends**, transitioning to remote work set-ups by leveraging digital tools for collaboration and communication.

2. Resilience through **innovation**, particularly in sectors such as healthcare, agriculture and renewable energy.

3. Technology-driven **resilient supply chains**, diversified sourcing strategies and explored local manufacturing options to mitigate risks even in disruptive times.

4. **Agile business models** to keep up with the changing market dynamics; traditional brick-and-mortar businesses created an online presence, and the retail and hospitality sectors pivoted to offer home delivery and takeout services.

5. Active engagement in **corporate social responsibility** (CSR) initiatives, contributing to relief efforts, providing medical supplies, supporting frontline workers and offering financial assistance to affected communities.

6. **Financial prudence** through healthy cash reserves, reducing debt burdens and diversifying revenue streams to weather economic uncertainties and emerge stronger from downturns.

7. **Collaborations and partnerships**, both domestic and international, with government agencies, industry associations, research institutions and others to facilitate knowledge sharing, resource pooling and collective problem-solving.

Thus, Indian organizations have exhibited resilience through a combination of adaptation, innovation, collaboration and prudent management practices, enabling them to overcome challenges and sustain growth in dynamic and unpredictable environments.

In summary, no one is immune to challenges, whether big or small, personal or professional, from human error or natural calamities. We can never know when we might be hit by adversity, but we can certainly control our preparedness to face such situations—on an individual level, as a leader and as an organization. By doing so, we move from a crisis mindset to an opportunity mindset. Then every challenge, calamity and crisis can become the springboard or stepping stone for growth, transformation and greater resilience. A serenity prayer, attributed to Reinhold Niebuhr, a Lutheran theologian (1892–1971), sums up the idea well: 'God, grant me the serenity to accept the things I cannot change, the courage to change the things I can, and the wisdom to know the difference.'[20]

Questions for Reflection

1. What are your key learnings from this chapter?
2. Create an action plan to develop and improve your resilience using the questions below.
3. What are the typical everyday situations that stress you?
4. How do you deal with your stress? Are your coping mechanisms helpful?
5. Have you ever faced a crisis? How did it affect you and how did you cope?
6. What steps are you taking to stay mentally strong?

Section 2

Emotional Regulation

Chapter 7

Emotional Regulation and Anger Management: Taming Your Temper

Anyone can be angry—that is easy, but to be angry with the right person and to the right degree and at the right time and for the right purpose and in the right way is not in everybody's power and is not easy.[1]

—Aristotle—

In the prevailing highly competitive and pressurized environment, one of the most common problems faced in the workplace is mood polarity. Whether this is triggered by personal problems or work pressures, the fact is that workplaces are becoming increasingly toxic, and the behaviour of leaders is becoming a matter of concern as never before.

In early 2024, I attended an annual top management meeting (in my capacity as an external expert) to review the training function in a large organization. I was quite concerned when at least two members proposed that training systems conduct workshops on emotional regulation and anger management, as these issues are reaching epidemic proportions in the organization. This confirmed what I'd lately been hearing about toxicity in the workplace via executive sources and media reports.

A close friend's daughter, who works for a media and advertising company, revealed during a dinner that she felt confused by her boss's mood swings, which expressed themselves as irritability and even downright yelling. The boss failed to provide any clarity or action plan for organizing the work for her team, which resulted in late nights as a rule and a sense of incompletion for the team. As a result of the prevailing work environment, my friend's daughter no longer feels normal, and her own emotions are becoming dysfunctional. She feels that her anger is bottled up, and one day it may just explode. Is this not becoming the new normal?

Emotions influence everyone in the workplace, from the lowest-rung employee to the CEO. We often don't realize that our emotions are manifested through unprovoked and angry responses. Emotional regulation is a critical skill that contributes to the success of managers and leaders, and its absence can make the workplace a psychologically unsafe place.

Emotional regulation is critical because it is the foundation of self-management. As researchers in social psychology, Wegner et al. have noted, '. . . a well-regulated person, will have a better balance and judgement of their feelings and actions. Emotional regulation allows us to carefully judge which affective outcomes to embrace and which ones to avoid.'[2] On the other hand, people with poor emotional regulation may fall prey to polarities in their emotions, resulting in unpredictable behaviour.

Emotional regulation helps a leader stay calm in volatile situations and think clearly during difficult circumstances. Leaders must have the capacity to manage their own emotions as well as those of others if they are going to help create successful teams. Effective emotional regulation by leaders helps in resolving misunderstandings or conflicts, facilitates an anxiety-free environment, and improves engagement and team culture. Those in leadership roles need to be sensitive to its positive impact and demoralizing consequences if it is not managed properly.

In the mid-1990s, when I worked as a senior-level functionary in the personnel department at my bank's corporate office for about two years, my immediate boss and I often had to deal with a CEO who, though a perfect banker, was severely lacking in managing his emotions. He often insulted executives, responded with sarcasm, belittled others and gave the impression of a know-it-all. If anyone offered a suggestion during official discussions, his quick retort was, 'Are you teaching me?' No one dared open their mouth when he spoke, and he talked non-stop. People refrained from expressing their ideas, fearing the risk of speaking out. The whole atmosphere was toxic, with him being cryptic, inconsistent and moody, and executives avoided facing him.

It was a typical case of emotional derailment, and its consequences were obvious. Despite a high level of technical skills, his lack of emotional skills posed the biggest problem to his leadership, and the entire top management in the corporate office experienced helplessness. I have been a close witness to this egregious display of emotional deviance at the top, as well as its consequences on the morale of people. Fear gripped the executive corridors. Sometimes, one could be the recipient of exaggerated appreciation, as I was when I visited him in his office when I was on a visit to the corporate office (I was posted in Kolkata at the time). I was surprised by such mood swings. His executive secretary later confided, 'On another day, you would have been the victim of his wrath.'

This is a classic example of the criticality of emotional regulation and stability in one's behaviour. Those who fail to maintain emotional regulation in a leadership role, more so at the top, hold the power to emotionally paralyse their colleagues and employees with disastrous consequences. Unfortunately, selection at the top levels largely depends on one's technical knowledge!

Daniel Goleman famously asserted that 90 per cent of the difference between outstanding and average leaders can be attributed to emotional factors, not intellectual acumen.[3] In the present disruptive environment and task-driven culture, it's much more critical for leaders to manage their emotions and their expression in a manner that does not demoralize employees or strain relationships. Most young managers in my training programmes point out the negative impact of their superiors' uncontrolled anger on their work, as well as the contagious effect it has on their own behaviour.

As a part of my leadership programmes, I would give participants an exercise to identify things they were most concerned about and wished to work on. Interestingly, most of them pointed out their failure to cope with their own emotions, which manifested as anger. Many participants openly admitted that anger overpowered them often, paralysing their concentration and severely damaging their interpersonal relations. Regulating emotions and anger management were at the top of their to-do lists.

Anger and its expression seem to be the new norm. 'The angry young man' has become a much-adored image. Social media is full of trolling, with anger expressed in its most ugly manner. Even politicians often make unguarded statements laced with anger, sometimes bordering on hatred. What is it all leading to? Is there an **anger epidemic** waiting to happen?

There are several reasons why anger may be such a troubling issue. We all suffer from problems; there's work pressure, competitions, one-upmanship, intense pressure for results, the boss's behaviour, family problems and so on. However, the results are mostly damaging.

A volatile temper is one of the worst traits a leader can have; it affects us far more than the person we are upset with. It is a very simple fact that anger first affects the person who experiences it, and uncontrolled anger can cause severe damage to one's health and relationships.

We must deal with anger at the individual level before it becomes part of our DNA.

Let us analyse the emotion of anger a little more dispassionately.

What Is Anger?

Anger is an intense emotion that is just as natural as happiness. It is normal and, at times, healthy, but also the most stigmatized emotion. It is a strong feeling of displeasure and antagonism. Right from childhood, we are told that anger is bad and must always be avoided.

Everyone gets angry, some more often than others, and it can be healthy if expressed with the right intent. **Feeling or expressing anger does not make us abnormal.** In the real world, we face anger almost daily, whether our own or that of others.

Generally speaking, if a human being never shows anger, then I think something's wrong.[4]

—Dalai Lama—

The fact is that anger can be **functional** or **dysfunctional**. As a functional emotion, it can facilitate transformation, but as a dysfunctional emotion, in the form of uncontrolled anger, it can become a major problem.

Anger normally arises because a desired event does not occur or because an event we do not approve of occurs. It involves feelings of defiance, antagonism and resentment towards the person(s) or situations that provoke us or that we perceive as threats.

In an interaction with about ninety participants of two leadership training programmes, the main reasons people listed for getting into a temperamental rage were **personal reasons**, including delays, arrogance, non-cooperation, lack of appreciation, etc. There were also **organizational reasons** relating to excessive stress and fatigue due to routine long hours, workplace discrimination, bias in performance appraisals, an inconsiderate boss, sexual harassment, etc. Other triggers for anger included biological reasons such as a lack of sleep, depression, hormone disruption, etc.

In the daily transactions of life, we encounter many disagreements, differences of opinion or dissent, which we sometimes express politely and at other times not so politely, depending on the context, such as repeated violations of rules or instructions. Therefore, we cannot classify every act of dissent or difference of opinion as a manifestation of anger, and not every expression of anger is bad. As mentioned earlier, anger can be functional or dysfunctional.

Anger Is Not Always Bad—It Can Be a Positive Trigger for Change

Can anger ever be good? Yes. Anger, if used and expressed properly, can trigger positive changes in people and organizations.

It is normal, or even desirable, to be concerned or even angry about a situation that may be detrimental to our personal or professional lives.

Anger by itself is not problematic, but the way a person reacts during the wave of anger—through a lack of civility, insulting words, comments or threats—is problematic.

Here are some ways in which anger can have functional roles:

1. **Self-Preservation:** In the face of perceived threats or injustice, anger can serve as a mechanism of self-protection. We can set safe boundaries, defend ourselves or take action to signal to others that certain behaviours and actions are unacceptable. When anger is expressed assertively and respectfully, it helps others see that their behaviours or actions are unacceptable. This helps diffuse the situation and create healthier relationships.

2. **Motivation for Change:** Anger can serve as a trigger for personal and social change. **Anger for Social Change** can mobilize people to fight for causes dear to them, for instance, awareness of climate change, equal rights for women, laws against rape, anti-racism and prevention of animal cruelty, discrimination against the marginalized, etc. **Anger for Organizational Overhauling** can target redundant and rigid ways that do not serve the organization, its people or its customers. **Anger for Self-Transformation** can help us overcome our limiting habits by strengthening our willpower and improving our lifestyle and relationships.

3. **Mobilizing Support:** In certain contexts, expressing anger can rally support and solidarity from others who share similar concerns or experiences. It can draw attention to important causes, such as trade union action, and drive collective action for positive change.

While anger can have functional roles, it is important to exercise control over its expression and ensure that it does not lead to destructive outcomes.

Archbishop Desmond Tutu mentions that he was not afraid of anger and righteous indignation in pursuit of peace, justice and equality: '**Righteous anger is usually not about oneself. It is about those whom one sees being harmed and whom one wants to help. In short, righteous anger is a tool of justice, a scythe of compassion, more than a reactive emotion.**'[5]

Dysfunctional Anger

Dysfunctional anger has its roots in an egocentric nature and can be triggered by frivolous reasons, such as someone cutting into our lane when driving. It can be based on prejudices, biases and personal angularities. Such anger is deaf to logic and reason; it can erase relationships in seconds and also destroy our health. We may experience a mental lapse; as anger takes charge, it consumes and intoxicates, making us unstable and distracted. In such dysfunctional anger, we may even yell or become hysterical. Thus, dysfunctional anger is the biggest punishment we inflict upon ourselves.

Leading organizational behaviour expert Udai Pareek has made a clear distinction between functional and dysfunctional anger through the concept of **Confrontation/Assertion versus Aggression** based on the theory of **Transactional Analysis (TA)**.[6] According to him, in the process of dysfunctional expression of anger, the target becomes the 'Person', whereas in functional expression of anger, the focus is on 'Confronting the Problem' rather than blaming the person. The distinction is best exemplified by Gandhi's dictum: 'Hate the sin; not the sinner.'[7]

Targeting an individual and holding him singularly responsible for a problem is an expression of dysfunctional anger (except when the problem occurs solely on account of that person). The right approach would be to channel the anger into diagnosing the deeper causes of the problem and articulating and addressing them; in such situations, the focus would shift from individuals or a group of people to systemic issues. Therefore, this kind of expression of anger can actually lead to an overall ownership of responsibility for problem-solving and improvement.

Anger can take many forms, such as yelling, irritability, rage, uncontrolled expressions and the use of harsh words. Often, the whole body shakes and quivers when we are in a fit of rage. Research has revealed that dysfunctional anger can literally change our physiology and cause long-term health problems like insomnia, high BP, headaches, stomach problems, depression, deep anxiety and even stroke.[8]

Angry-looking people are deemed untrustworthy; their furrowed brows, wrinkled faces, clenched teeth and flailing arms create a sense of discomfort that pushes people away. We are definitely not comfortable when such people handle our business or finances.

The expression of anger is not entirely bad, but legitimizing it by using our positional power certainly is. Authority or power can put us in an **ego trap**, where we demonstrate authority by expressing our dysfunctional anger.

In such cases, **anger is used as a lever of power** to:

- Enforce instructions (right or wrong) by using threats and imposing our authority.
- Perpetuate and expand the power base of our authority.
- Clear competition or threats to power through insults and humiliation.

Despite their impact on people's motivation and morale, such egotistical tactics can improve outcomes, at least in the short term. But what happens with long-term exposure to ego-driven anger?

The Anger Trap—How It Can Destroy Our Personality

The ill-effects of anger are best narrated in the Bhagavad Gita (Chapter 2, Verses 62 and 63) mentioned below:

ध्यायतो विषयान्पुंसः सङ्गस्तेषूपजायते ।
सङ्गात्सञ्जायते कामः कामात्क्रोधोऽभिजायते ॥62॥

क्रोधाद्भवति सम्मोहः सम्मोहात्स्मृतिविभ्रमः ।
स्मृतिभ्रंशाद् बुद्धिनाशो बुद्धिनाशात्प्रणश्यति ॥63॥

In his commentary on the Bhagavad Gita, Swami Parthasarathy provides a vivid interpretation of Verses 62 and 63, graphically represented below.[9]

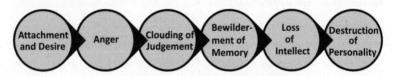

Figure 7.1: The Anger Trap

Parthasarathy explains that when we excessively muse on objects, we develop attachment and desire, and anger arises from those desires. When the anger keeps mounting up, we lose control of our minds and plunge into delusion.

The effect of anger is such that the damage does not stop there. Delusion leads to loss of memory; we forget what is right and wrong, what is good and bad. This impairs our ability to make judgements. We forget our position, obligations and relationship with the world. A loss of memory leads further to a loss of intellect. With this comes the biggest blow—we perish, and our personality is destroyed. Therefore, the indiscriminate entertainment of angry thoughts can lead to an individual's degradation and destruction.

The accumulation of dysfunctional and unresolved anger intensifies its impact. Unreleased pent-up anger can be fatal when released; it is like an unguided missile—where it lands, which target it hits and how much destruction it causes is unfathomable. No amount of apologizing can undo the damage, and frequent expression of anger in this manner may lead to social ostracism due to our unpredictable behaviour.

If we are not aware of the dysfunctionality of our anger, we are in danger of becoming 'rageaholics' and the consequences can be dangerous. The issue of managing anger is a high-stakes proposition, as it can cost us our careers, personal relationships and health. Unfortunately, many try to rationalize it as part of their nature, irrespective of its consequences.

Most people believe that anger is uncontrollable, but we can actually take concrete steps to manage it. Short-tempered people who are especially vulnerable to uncontrolled anger need to work much harder. It requires a great deal of effort, and one way to deal with it is a deep dive into self-awareness to discover the underlying emotions and broaden our perspective. The following section provides a few insights into managing anger.

A Workout for Developing
Emotional Regulation and Anger Management

Controlling anger requires practice and the development of healthy coping mechanisms. Essentially, it involves emotional regulation. Uncontrolled emotions and their expression have the potential to multiply all our progress by zero, undoing all the work that we've put into it so far.

1. Emotional Regulation

Emotional regulation is the ability to recognize, understand and respond to emotions in a healthy way. It encompasses 'both positive and negative feelings, how we can strengthen them, use them and control them . . . Essentially emotional regulation is about modulating responses triggered by emotions.'[10]

Here are some ways to regulate our emotions.

a. **Practise Awareness:** Become aware of your emotions, thoughts and triggers—internal and external factors, such as other people, the context, etc. (see Chapter 1 on Self-Awareness). Our starting point is to understand our natural reactions. For example, what makes me upset and why? How do I react to negative feedback? How do I deal with uncertainty and confusion? Why do I not assert myself in certain situations? How do I cope with adversity?

b. **Be Adaptable:** Being rigid and fixed in our ways can make us blind to appropriate coping mechanisms and can worsen our emotional dysregulation. Be open to new ways of coping and learn to adapt to the situation.

c. **Be Objective:** Getting drawn into emotional drama can drain our energy, leaving us feeling overwhelmed and confused. If someone is yelling at you, do not respond immediately; let the person cool down and then you can speak to them. Looking at the situation and people objectively helps us arrive at practical problem-solving. You can try thinking of what practical suggestions you would have given a loved one if they were in a similar situation.

d. **Seek Emotional Support from Yourself:** Psychologists believe each of us has immense capacity to develop healthy emotional and mental qualities. These qualities can act as our guide and anchor in times of emotional turmoil. We can practise mindful self-awareness and look for answers, which we often already have access to. And if we are unable to find the answers, we can always reach out to a therapist.

With emotional regulation, we can filter important information and act with confidence. It helps create a strong emotional foundation, based on which one can practise the following steps to manage anger:

2. Mind Your Behaviour

It is our responsibility to control our behaviour that may cause anger in others. For example, it is for us to control our emotions (especially dysfunctional anger) by using the right choice of words or actions, expressing emotions in an acceptable way, controlling anxiety in responding to other people, remaining respectful, not being defensive in arguments and interactions, and taking a view based on facts and data instead of being judgemental and responding abruptly.

In unpleasant situations, pay attention to the early physical and emotional signs that indicate anger. These may include an increased heart rate, tense muscles, irritability, shorter breath or negative thoughts. By becoming aware of these initial signs, we can intervene and manage our anger before it escalates.

To manage your anger, pause and take a few deep breaths. If possible, step away from the situation or the person causing your anger. This can help you disengage emotionally and create space for clearer thinking.

Emotional self-control does not come automatically. We must work towards it. I have personally worked on controlling my anger by consciously becoming aware of such signals and using these mechanisms. Over time, it has helped me control and express my anger in a more moderate manner.

3. Practise Equanimity

This helps us remain level-headed and empathetic even in challenging or distressing situations, allowing us to respond—rather than react—to life's twists and turns. The first step in achieving this is being able to control our dysfunctional emotions. Unless we calm down, we cannot achieve good outcomes. There are several ways to build mental quietness and calmness, such as meditation, mindfulness (e.g. Vipassana), yoga or other similar exercises. Such practices help us to stay present in the moment and prevent emotions from escalating.[11] The challenge is to distance ourselves from negative thoughts and deep biases and realize that they are not absolute truths.

At times, there is a need to delve deeper into mindfulness or meditation through training in the right techniques and regular practice. Such training helps us quiet the mind, observe our thoughts and understand what makes us angry. We can reflect and decide what to focus on and what to ignore. Regular practice of quieting the mind will improve calmness, concentration, awareness and the power of reflective thinking.

Deep breathing exercises can help us calm down and regain control. Slowly inhale through the nose, hold the breath for a few seconds and then slowly exhale through the mouth. Repeating this several times while focusing on the breath helps us relax. As performance psychologist Dana Sinclair notes, 'Breathing is a natural sedative and is undervalued as a tool for managing the tension that pressure creates. It sounds goofy to some, but the most efficient way to get calm is to pay attention to your breathing . . . Proper breathing can help you cope with stress, sleep better, be less angry or moody, and refresh your energy. It can slow your heart rate and reduce your blood pressure.'[12]

4. **Practise Reflection**

Reflect on the sources of your anger to identify what types of people or situations create it and why. This will reveal your prejudices, biases and hurts, as well as your style of response, behaviour and feedback. Anger often arises from negative thought patterns and cognitive distortions. Question the validity of such thoughts: 'Are there alternative explanations for the situation? Am I jumping to a conclusion? Are there deeper underlying emotional causes that trigger the anger? Could I have reacted in a different way?'

Thus, your emotional landscape can be mapped by deeply reflecting on anger, both at the intellectual level (difference of opinions and level of understanding) and the emotional level (bias, prejudice and angularity), and then planning the course correction (see Chapter 2 on Reflection). Recognizing our triggers makes us better equipped to regulate our emotions.

You can deepen this reflective process by incorporating the following steps:

a. **Journaling:** Write down your feelings and thoughts when you're angry. This helps you gain insight into your emotions and identify patterns.

b. **Reframing Negative Thoughts:** Challenge irrational or extreme thoughts that fuel anger. Replace them with more balanced perspectives.

c. **Monitoring Your Progress:** Keep track of your anger triggers, reactions and coping strategies. Reflect on what is working well and where there is room for improvement.

5. **Use 'I' Statements and Own Your Anger**

When expressing concerns or frustrations, use 'I' statements instead of accusatory language. For example, say, 'I feel upset when . . .' rather than 'You always make me angry when . . .' This approach allows one to express emotions without placing blame, reducing defensiveness in others.[13]

It is critical that we own our anger. As the Dalai Lama once indicated, 'If we can discover our role in creating the situations that upset us, we are able to reduce our feelings of frustration and anger.'[14] Besides, when we recognize that the other person also has their own fears, hurts and fragile human perspective, we have a chance of escaping from the normal reflex of anger.

Owning up to even 50 per cent of the responsibility helps us substantially reduce the problem. Which gives way to several options to resolve our anger, such as initiating a conversation, problem-solving, negotiating a new working methodology or resorting to machinery under the law.

6. **Learn to Let Go**

Many cultures around the world advocate the practice of forgiveness and letting go in order to be free of anger and facilitate resolution and healing. Forgiveness does not mean that others are allowed to continue hurting us; it means letting go of the bitterness so that we are free of its toxicity. This practice can help convert dysfunctional anger into functional anger. But forgiveness may sometimes encourage the wrongdoer and set a bad precedent. We must assertively and respectfully communicate our needs and boundaries without being aggressive.

Another aspect is that we don't always need to react to every situation and plan rebuttals. Getting worked up and excited can only cause us pain and frustration, and reacting emotionally will only worsen the situation. Sometimes, it is better to let go. We cannot control everything that people say or do; we can only control our own actions. So, avoid reacting to provocations, choose your battles carefully and do not waste time on frivolous matters. If needed, take a break from the person or situation that caused anger and learn to relax.

And if the issue has caused deep hurt or challenged your integrity, you must express those feelings, but it is critical to do it in a civilized and acceptable manner without humiliating or insulting the recipient. It is a tough task, but that is where the challenge lies.

However, you must not ignore graver issues involving a violation of ethical standards. You must take a principled stand and rectify the wrong by seeking justice through legal means.

7. Practise Empathetic Anger

There are two ways to do this. The first is to channel the anger productively and the second is to handle the anger with empathy.

Anger research by Brodsky et al., as mentioned by Adam Grant in his book *Originals: How Non-Conformists Change the World*, suggests that anger can be productively channelled by focusing on the victims who have suffered from it instead of venting about the harm caused by the perpetrators. He indicates that focusing on the victim activates what psychologists call empathetic anger— the desire to right the wrongs done to another.[15] He mentions the research which demonstrates that when we are **angry at others**, we aim for retaliation or revenge. But when we are **angry for others**, we seek out justice and a better system.[16]

Empathy can help us handle anger as we try to see things from the perspective of others involved in the situation. Understanding their feelings and motivations can not only help us respond with empathy but also reduce anger. It is prudent to see both sides before forming opinions. As the Dalai Lama observed:

> Often we direct our anger at another person, someone who we think has hurt us or offended us in some way. If your anger is not very forceful, you can try to look at a different aspect of the person. Every person, no matter how negative she seems to be, also has positive attributes. If you try to look at that side of her, the anger will immediately be reduced.[17]

8. Practise Self-Care

Taking care of our physical and emotional well-being can reduce overall stress and irritability, thereby making it easier to regulate emotions and anger. We can engage in activities that help relax and recharge, such as exercise, meditation, hobbies or spending time with loved ones. One of the best ways to release aggression and anger is through a physical outlet, such as swimming or going for a walk.

We may also engage in creative pursuits, such as drawing or solving crossword puzzles, listening to music, etc. A friend of mine, who is very fond of poetry, often recites some verses whenever he is upset about something. He says that reciting poetry calms him down and helps him divert his mind gently and sensitively.

Reminding ourselves of our good qualities, practising self-acceptance, being flexible and being grateful for the blessings we already have can transform how we relate to and react to emotions.

9. Seek Support

Sometimes, sharing helps alleviate anger. Talking about our anger can also provide perspective, encouragement and guidance as we work on improving our anger management skills. If we find it too challenging to control our dysfunctional emotions, we may consider seeking support from a trusted friend, family member or mental health professional who can guide us in exploring the underlying causes of our anger and teach us additional coping strategies.

In summary, an effective leader's first code is to treat others with grace and dignity and provide succour to others in their time of personal and professional crises. However, regulating emotions is a multi-step process requiring prodigious commitment and work on the self. Unlike medical sciences, which can resort to a surgical procedure to remove a tumour, no single method works in dealing with a serious issue like dysfunctional anger. While managing one's anger can be challenging, it is achievable with focused effort.

Questions for Reflection

1. What are your key learnings from this chapter?
2. Create an action plan to develop and improve your emotional regulation using the questions below.
3. What kind of situations and people make you angry? Are you able to regulate your emotions in dealing with them?
4. Have you ever channelled your anger to improve situations?
5. In what situations does your anger overpower you?

Chapter 8

Compassion: Empathy in Action

What is that one thing which when you possess you have all other virtues? It is compassion.[1]

—Buddha—

In the mid-1960s, my elder brother used to commute by bicycle to attend graduate classes at Agra College. While returning home, he would sometimes drop in at the Arms and Ammunition Shop, where my father worked as an accountant. On one such day, the owner of the business, Mr Paliwal observed that my brother was not adequately dressed for Agra's harsh winter. He handed my brother a slip of paper addressed to a well-known woollen store and asked him to visit them. My brother was quite perplexed, but did as he was told. When he visited the store, the owner told him to choose the best woollen cloth for his jacket. This compassionate gesture by Mr Paliwal sparked in me a desire to help others in need. As I grew in my career, in my own small way, I dealt with problems of employees with a sense of compassion. In my role as a CEO, I institutionalized some policy measures, keeping in mind the special hardships that employees undergo in difficult times.

In 2020, during the Covid-19 crisis and nationwide lockdown, Bollywood actor Sonu Sood was in the limelight for helping stranded migrant labourers. He was right there on the ground, arranging food and transport for their journeys back to their villages. His actions went beyond pity, sympathy and even empathy. It was an act of compassion when he stepped out of the comfort of his home to reach out to those in deep distress.[2]

In such moments of despair, when everything feels bleak and hopeless, a little understanding, help and support restores our hope and gives us strength. **Empathy** and **compassion** are the two primary qualities that have helped many of us cope despite the severity of challenges. **Compassion is especially recognized as one of the foundational qualities of a leader.**

Be kind, for everyone you meet is fighting a harder battle.[3]

—Plato—

What Is Compassion?

Compassion is the sense of concern we feel when confronted with the suffering of others, and it motivates us to act in a manner that relieves the suffering. People commonly understand it as the expression of empathy through action. It is a three-stage process with three components: understanding, feeling and acting (see Figure 8.1).

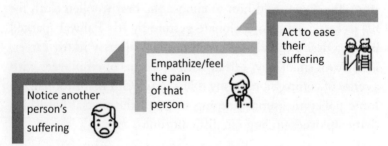

Figure 8.1: Compassion Is a Three-Stage Process

Thupten Jinpa, a former monk and academic specializing in philosophy and religious studies, explains in *The Fearless Heart*, that every expression of compassion has three aspects:[4]

- The cognitive aspect—'I understand your problems.'
- The affective component—'I feel what you feel.'
- The drive or motivational component to act—'I want to help you out of this.'

Jinpa adds, 'Compassion offers the possibility of responding to suffering with understanding, patience and kindness.' Thus, compassion, the feeling of empathy and then acting with kindness and generosity evoke the feeling that **we are all together** in this.

In the organizational context, employees at all levels need to show compassion for the problems of customers, vendors and other stakeholders. Many of the problems concerning delays and hassles can be solved by compassionate managers and leaders.

Empathy versus Compassion

Often, people use 'empathy' and 'compassion' synonymously. They are, however, different in meaning, although one is an extension of the other.

Empathy is the ability to connect with the pain and despair of those who are suffering. Empathy is when we feel for others, but there is no action to alleviate the suffering; it is not the same as compassion. Empathy has only one component—feeling— but compassion has three components—understanding, feeling and action.

Empathy helps us make an emotional connection in the sense that we feel others' suffering, but there is no desire to alleviate it or help in any way. Whereas **compassion** is an interpersonal process involving noticing, understanding, feeling and the desire to act to alleviate the suffering of the other person.[5] Research by neuroscientists Tania Singer and Olga Klimecki demonstrates that empathy can be exhausting; it can sap our energy and create a pessimistic outlook, while compassion can inject us with energy to help others.[6]

Benefits of Compassion for Individuals

Acts of compassion are certainly beneficial to the receiver, but givers also derive many benefits. Experts on compassion, such as Dr James Doty and others, have shown how the practice of compassion has a direct positive effect on the mind–body mechanism.[7] Studies at Emory University have also demonstrated 'that a regular practice of compassion meditation reduces negative neuroendocrine, inflammatory and behavioural responses to psychosocial stress'.[8] Here are a few more:

- Brings purpose to life.
- Gives a sense of fulfilment and joy.
- Shifts perspective from narrow self-agenda to broader world view.
- Helps to regulate painful or negative emotions since we are able to see other's perspectives.
- Promotes psychological well-being.
- Makes us feel energized since we become free of the emotional baggage.
- Contributes to better relationships.

All these benefits contribute to personal growth, and compassion's biggest benefit is that it makes our problems appear small compared to what others are facing.

Benefits of Compassion for Organizations

Organizations' obligations to their employees go much beyond a mere contractual relationship of pay and getting the work done. Rather, the organization and its stakeholders, at all levels, are in a symbiotic relationship that is enhanced by compassion. Compassionate leaders are not calculating; they are moved by the plight of others to help—without taking into consideration the benefits that they will undoubtedly derive for themselves as well as the company. When the top management acts with compassion, the employees feel motivated to give back more to the organization.

Compassionate leaders often make the well-being of their employees a priority. They try to:

- Create a good balance between employees' performance and well-being.
- Help employees recover from problematic and traumatic situations and restore their morale.
- Build sensitivity across the organization to employees' problems and offer effective resolution with speed and alacrity.
- Allay the fears and anxiety of employees and give them confidence.
- Engage people through constant interactions.
- Rise to the occasion to do their absolute best and are not driven solely by cost to the organization.

Research studies in 2018 by leadership experts Hougaard et al. have found that compassionate leaders bring a number of benefits to their organizations:[9]

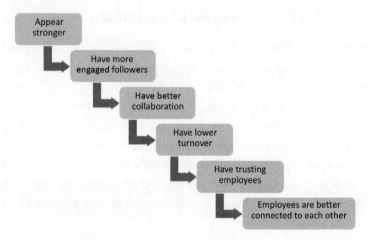

Figure 8.2: Benefits of Compassion for Organizations

(Adapted from global leadership experts, Hougaard et al., 2018)

Compassion Does Not Mean Compromising on Performance

Organizations are mostly conceptualized as economic enterprises, and they mainly pursue business growth through the efficient deployment of resources. In this scheme of things, there is no explicit place for softer human considerations or humanistic values; hence, the expression of compassion happens as an exception rather than as a norm. Sometimes, even with the best intentions, companies neglect to pursue these considerations as part of their responsible corporate philosophy.

In most places, employees' personal and emotional problems are often under-prioritized in a non-stop, performance-driven workplace. The incessant emphasis on increasing productivity and efficiency can be overwhelming. On top of that, narcissistic and aggressive leadership styles can create deep emotional problems for employees.

During the peak of the pandemic, we have seen examples of companies that, in their bid to stay afloat, took on bigger projects on shorter deadlines without hiring extra staff to bear the excess workload and while experiencing a shortage of existing staff on account of sickness and the loss of loved ones. Emotional and mental burnouts, higher workloads, pay cuts, lay-offs, losing loved ones and homes—the cascade of challenges was just too much to handle. Many people who were otherwise mentally and emotionally healthy slipped into anxiety and depression. The overwhelming pressure pushed many individuals to re-evaluate their personal and professional priorities, and what soon followed was the **Great Resignation.**[10]

On the other hand, while facing the same pandemic, some organizations acted with empathy and compassion. They relaxed the rules and introduced initiatives to help their employees cope and feel supported in tough times. Such a compassionate leadership culture helped employees connect with the organization and experience a degree of sanity in the workplace.

Relying purely on a performance-driven approach is like running a sprint; the speed and the thrill of achieving targets are fantastic, but the success is short-lived! Long-term, sustainable success and growth (both for employees and the organization) call for a balance.

This can only happen when equitable steps are taken to provide support to employees in their most difficult times and by creating opportunities for their growth within the organization. Its impact on their engagement can be enormous.

A Workout for Developing Compassion

Research at Cambridge University suggests that some people are **genetically predisposed** to being more **prosocial** (altruistic, empathetic or compassionate).[11] Certain genes carry this trait, and women are more predisposed to this trait compared to men.

This does not mean that those who do not have this gene cannot develop compassion. Individuals who have been exposed to an environment of compassion at home, in school or at college and have witnessed at least one family member, teacher or mentor acting out of compassion consistently will imbibe it from them. Thus, compassion is not defined by nature or nurture alone, but by a combination of both.

Hougaard et al. mention in their 2018 study on compassion involving over 1000 leaders that '91% of them said compassion is very important for their leadership and 80% said they would like to enhance their compassion but do not know how.' They validated that compassion is a much-sought quality. Yet, seldom do management or executive training programmes prioritize training on cultivating compassion (perhaps due to the absence of any reliable methodology), and it is often left to individuals to develop it by themselves. The good news is that compassion can be cultivated and learnt by everyone, and with practice we can become more compassionate.

1. **Embrace Your Humaneness**

   Stand by people when they need support at critical times in their lives. The main role of leaders is to serve their people, not control or boss them around. Emotions, not intellectual prowess, touch people's hearts. Thus, emotions can be used to show concern and love, empathize genuinely and show compassion with a sense of service.

   > My friend Subhash Kalia, former executive director of Union Bank of India, often shares his experience of observing the highest level of humaneness in his boss: 'I was on probation as an officer at the Aligarh branch of my bank in 1973. One day, I received information about my mother's untimely death in Delhi. Due to a transport's strike, buses or other vehicles were not available. The branch manager, Mr Mehrotra, felt my pain and drove me on his scooter from Aligarh to Delhi, a distance of 150 km, in the fierce summer heat of June, enabling me to perform the last rites for my mother that very day. I can never forget this act of humaneness!'

2. **Compassion Cultivation Training**

   Whether compassion is innate or cultivated is a topic of debate. The **Compassion Cultivation Training** programme at Stanford University is a revolutionary course that teaches individuals how to cultivate the mindset and practice of compassion. It was co-developed by Thupten Jinpa.[12]

   This training programme helps transform our perspective on life and change the way we relate to ourselves and others as fellow human beings. Thus, while it helps cultivate compassion, the programme is also a powerful method for promoting psychological well-being.

Based on this programme, Jinpa's book *A Fearless Heart* shows that compassion can be a path through suffering, a key to robust health and even an effective way to reach one's goals.

3. Practise Self-Compassion

In *A Fearless Heart*, Jinpa also mentions self-compassion as the 'replenishing of the well-spring of kindness and compassion that lies within us'. He also highlights the importance of self-compassion—if we cannot be compassionate towards ourselves during our sufferings, then 'we don't develop adequate resources within ourselves to be able to give more to others'. This means that by continuing to drive ourselves harder and harder, we may experience breakdown or burnout.

Jinpa also talks about how self-compassion is a fundamental and instinctive ability to care for and be kind to oneself. Such self-care can be practised by attending to the basic need to be healthy in body and mind through good nutrition, sleep, exercise, meditation, relaxation, etc.

4. Use Your Compassion Muscle

Compassion does not always mean monetary aid. We can help in many ways—with our time, material resources, knowledge and skills or by doing pro bono work for others—and it can even be a joyful experience. For this, we must identify what we can and are willing to do and start doing it.

Start with something small, such as teaching children from marginalized communities, sending food to a sick neighbour, helping someone with their accounting and taxes, creating social media posts for a friend's new business venture or raising funds for a charitable cause—your options are aplenty.

5. **Volunteer with Charitable Organizations**
Often, we are unsure about where to begin practising compassion. In such cases, volunteering for charitable causes is a great way to start. Most of these organizations have a structured framework for volunteering, with various avenues of service that provide a great learning experience. Regular volunteering will also help develop wisdom and compassion. Some well-known organizations such as Teach for India, Akshay Patra and others are doing amazing work in their fields of service. You can join them as volunteers to help the poor, educate the underprivileged and work in hospices, soup kitchens, etc.

Despite being an important part of leadership, compassion is not always demonstrated in organizations, and it seems to have taken a back seat to competition and profit margins.

Building a Culture of Compassion

The leadership's commitment to employees is tested during times of crises in employees' lives or as a result of external factors such as the pandemic. It is during such times that compassionate leaders come forward and demonstrate their leadership, both at the personal and the organizational levels.

Organizational culture is built over time by the founders and leaders. Altruistic qualities such as compassion are institutionalized when they originate at the very top and flow down every level of the organization. Ratan Tata is a great example of a compassionate leader, and the Tata Group is also well known for its compassionate policies for employees.

After the terror attack in Mumbai on 26 November 2008, Tata Group provided monetary compensation that included the settlement of a full last salary for life for the family and dependants and also supported the education of dependants. Within two weeks of the 26/11 incident, Ratan Tata, Tata Sons and R.K. Krishna Kumar, then vice chairman of Indian Hotels Company Ltd (IHCL), formed the Taj Public Service Welfare Trust to not only provide relief to those affected by the terrorist attacks but also to set up a system to help and rehabilitate those recovering from such tragic events.[13]

Such compassionate gestures towards the bereaved families of deceased employees go much beyond monetary aid, making them feel deeply cared for. Institutionalizing compassionate policies that care for people under stress and go out of their way to help such employees cope gives them succour and fosters their trust in the organization. Corporate social responsibility (CSR) is another way of institutionalizing compassion that unites the whole organization for a cause. Often, organizations donate skills or take up pro bono projects that create a larger impact for the beneficiaries. However, CSR should not be merely viewed as a statutory responsibility.

Another good example of a leader's compassion being reflected in the organizational culture is that of Patu Keswani, an IIT- and IIM-qualified professional who started the Lemon

Tree Hotels chain in 2002 after an illustrious professional career at Taj Hotels. While the hotel industry recruits the most polished and sophisticated staff, Keswani decided to hire 10 per cent of the staff (mostly in the maintenance and kitchen areas) from among those who had disabilities and/or were illiterate. As of March 2022, 231 of the 2761 employees at Lemon Tree Hotels belong to the disabled category, including those with speech and hearing impairments, orthopaedic impairments, visual impairments, and Down's syndrome and autism. Keswani's policy has won the organization several awards from both governmental and non-governmental agencies. It has also considerably reduced attrition to 15 per cent, compared to the industry-wide churn rate of 40 per cent. Today, Lemon Tree operates a hotel in Gurugram entirely staffed with people with disabilities, probably making it the only employer in the world to hire people with zero formal educational skills.[14]

There is no statutory requirement for a private hotel group to recruit people with disabilities, so Patu Keswani's extraordinary vision purely emanates from his compassion. On the face of it, it was a very risky choice for a service industry like a hotel, but Keswani's innate compassion gave hope and meaning to the lives of many who are now living as active members of society.

My Experience with Institutionalizing Compassion

When I undertook a large-scale transformation of the Bank of Baroda as its CEO, the task was quite complex.

We had planned to introduce new technology in the banking operation without disturbing or disrupting the existing system or level of customer service. This meant hard work and late hours to ensure the implementation of the new technology. Naturally, the employees were overworked and even fatigued, but the job had to be done. I was well aware that our managers and frontline staff faced the dual challenge of burnout at work and issues arising at home due to their longer work hours. This was a pressing concern during the transformation programme.

This was when I organized dozens of town halls across the country, meeting several thousand of our frontline employees. I listened to their concerns and activated many changes in our HR policies. New initiatives aimed at building compassion into the very fabric of our policies were introduced. A trained personnel specialist was posted in my office to pilot these programmes under my direct supervision.

1. **Sampark:** A twenty-four-hour hotline was made available to 40,000 employees to connect directly with the CEO for problems that required immediate attention and resolution. Hundreds of employees received immediate help for work-related and personal issues through this initiative.
2. **Paramarsh:** A host of professional counsellors were introduced in metro cities to provide counselling to employees and their families who experienced serious personal crises.

3. **Khoj:** A talent identification scheme was designed to provide proper grooming and development to the right candidates instead of hiring from outside. These candidates served as the 'change champions' in the bank's transformation journey.

In many ways, the pandemic proved to be a litmus test for the values and priorities of individuals and organizations. It shook us and forced companies to take a long, hard look at what truly matters in this grand scheme of life. In other words, it underscored the importance of compassion at every step. Although the pandemic is over, the after-effects still linger. With man-made and natural calamities happening all over the world, compassion is the only way humanity can mend what's broken and reach the equilibrium that's necessary to coexist peacefully.

Not just in times of calamity, but even in everyday life, there is a need to embrace compassion through policies for better education, better standards of living, the dignity of labour, fair wages, and policies to broker a truce along borders and rekindle friendships. Therefore, compassion must become part of the tapestry of humanity. This quote by Thupten Jinpa is apt: 'A compassionate mindset is necessarily less self-preoccupied, more at ease, and less inhabitant. It is no exaggeration to say that with others, we become free.'

Questions for Reflection

1. What are your key learnings from this chapter?
2. Create an action plan to develop and improve your compassion using the questions below.

3. Has any compassionate act impressed you enough to change your outlook? How have you incorporated it into your life and actions?

4. What situations motivate you to show your compassion?

5. Do you extend compassion to everyone—friends, colleagues, family and even strangers? How and from whom do you expect to receive it?

6. Have you been able to practise compassion even in a situation where you had to step out of your comfort zone? What skills do you need to build to do so?

Chapter 9

Courage: Conquering Your Fears

You cannot be truthful if you are not courageous.
You cannot be loving if you are not courageous.
You cannot be trusting if you are not courageous.
You cannot inquire into reality if you are not courageous.
Hence courage comes first,
And everything else follows.[1]

—Osho—

This is the story of the CEO of a cement manufacturing company, which had a stellar reputation for being an employee-centric organization committed to strong values and paying their employees really well (as per industry standards).

A new person, who had joined as the union leader, was trying to build his own image as a leader among the workers. At the time when negotiations for wage settlement were in progress, this young, ambitious leader climbed on the high perimeter wall of the factory compound and threatened to jump if all the demands were not accepted. The CEO, who was in the head office at that time, received frantic calls from his deputies and officers at the factory. He took stock of the entire situation and made a well-calculated decision (he knew most of the blue-collar staff personally, as he spent time with them on the factory floor and knew this young man well).

The CEO gave the factory's senior-most officer instructions to inform the young leader over a public address system that he had declared the company would not be held to ransom. He also asked him to climb down so that discussions could be concluded. The young, upstart union leader quietly climbed down from the wall and joined his colleagues at the negotiation table.

In the above case, if the CEO had succumbed to the union leader's blackmail, it would have sent the wrong signals and set a bad precedent. This would have likely encouraged the unions to use further intimidatory tactics to get things done. Therefore, the CEO's decision to stand firm in the greater interest of building a culture of problem-solving through discussions and dialogues was indeed courageous.

The world is changing faster now than at any other time in history. To keep pace with these disruptions, meet the demands of the competition and/or market, and increase growth, businesses need leaders with the foresight and courage to take bold initiatives across many fronts. When a business fails to do this, it inevitably crashes. Therefore, businesses need leaders who can act with courage, take risks, face the consequences, learn their lessons and move on.

Essentially, courage requires conviction and the desire to take on challenges and move beyond our comfort zone. This could mean starting a journey as an entrepreneur by leaving a cosy corporate job, leaving a well-paying job to work in the social sector or moving the company in a new direction to weather storms better.

Life shrinks or expands in proportion to one's courage.[2]

—Anaïs Nin—

What Is Courage?

Merriam–Webster defines courage as 'mental or moral strength to venture, persevere and withstand fear or difficulty'. In other words, overcoming obstacles through conscious risk-taking.

Courageous people have the strength and clarity to be who they are, rather than turning into what other people expect or desire them to be. They believe in themselves and stand up for what they believe in, even when others do not feel the same way.

Courage is a core quality of leaders who take bold initiatives to change the organizational culture (the existing ways of doing things or status-quoist attitudes) in order to align the business to the needs of the time. It may even call for major paradigm shifts, such as designing a new compelling vision and revisiting organizational processes, management styles, attitudes and policies.

Universally, courage is considered the most desirable quality in leaders, yet most leaders suffer from a **courage-deficit syndrome**. It is like a nutrient deficiency with its accompanying negative consequences.

Courageous acts don't always have positive outcomes. In fact, most acts of courage often occur in uncertain situations, potentially leading to unexpected negative outcomes or adverse side effects. No wonder, then, that an individual experiences fear and anxiety when required to act with courage. Nelson Mandela, the great revolutionary and reformer, once said, 'I learnt that courage was not the absence of fear but the triumph over it. The brave man is not who does not feel afraid, but he who conquers that fear.'[3]

Various Types of Courage

Different people have different notions about courage; hence, it may be a good idea to understand the types and nature of courage. Psychologists Cooper Woodard and Cynthia Pury mention three major types of courage in their research article 'The Construct of Courage: Categorization and Measurement', as illustrated in Figure 9.1.[4]

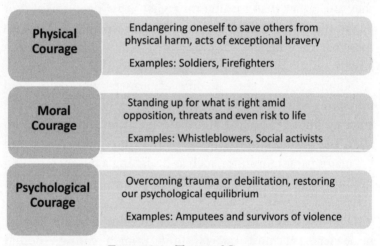

Figure 9.1: Types of Courage

In the professional setting, courage, typically moral and psychological, can take many forms; Table 9.1 provides a few examples.

Table 9.1: Manifestations of Courage

Manifestations of Courage	Means of Expression
Courage of conviction	Speaking up for what is right and taking a principled stand
Courage to guard self-respect	Capacity to sacrifice position and power for self-respect
Courage to be disliked	Capacity to suffer isolation
Courage to transform	Disturbing comfort zone, sharing vision and engaging people
Courage to pursue personal growth	Challenging assumptions about oneself, reflecting on them and pursuing a plan for self-improvement
Courage to be creative and original	Experimenting with new ideas and fostering an environment for such ideas
Courage to be a curious learner	Openness to new things and learning from juniors, too

Being Brash and Stubborn Is not Being Courageous

Being courageous is a positive quality, whereas being brash and stubborn is a negative trait. Those who use brashness or stubbornness as a demonstration of courage often suffer from power syndrome or plain showmanship. Such people do not deserve to be leaders, as their actions cannot be justified and may, in fact, result in conflicts. Even in provocative situations, leaders must act firmly and with level-headedness.

Leadership experts Kaipa and Radjou suggest that leaders should not hold on to any decision doggedly, and given the contextual factors, they should know when to hold and when to fold to achieve greater benefits. They observe that,

> . . . wise leaders take a middle path and exhibit **flexible fortitude**, which means using one's discernment to gauge when it is appropriate to hold on to things and when it is appropriate to let them go . . . wise leaders demonstrate their flexible fortitude in different ways like they stick to decisions when appropriate, they inspire others to support their decisions and see them through, they revise or reverse decisions willingly when the context shifts and they draw on the collective will-power to push through transformational decisions.[5]

Why Is Courage Crucial for Leaders?

Leaders often face complex and challenging situations and are required to make tough choices, especially when those decisions are unpopular or carry significant risks. As noted earlier, they largely need to exercise psychological and moral courage.

To make the business future-ready, leaders need foresight and courage to navigate uncharted territories, step outside their comfort zones, embrace innovations and take risks while encountering criticism, setbacks and failures. Courage helps them weather all challenges while relentlessly pursuing their vision, and they bounce back from failures with renewed determination and optimism. The same goes for individuals who are stuck in their careers; they can achieve success when they break free from limiting roles, shift to a growth mindset, and are willing to take on new challenges, experiment and learn.

The other dimension of exercising courage is defending your values and living your life with integrity. As individuals rise in rank, they are expected to manage change and transformation in their organizations, which often requires courageous initiatives.

In business, courage is no longer just a discretionary skill but an essential quality; handing over an organization to a risk-averse leader can be dangerous. Those organizations that have shown a commitment to high values and ethics, even at the cost of impacting profits in the short run, can create sustainable change and win the confidence of their stakeholders. **Courage is thus a defining characteristic that separates winners from losers.**

Leaders driven by sturdy principles and motivated to create a future for their teams take courageous steps. They often risk their careers to achieve the larger objective. Examples can include initiatives such as:

- Designing a new future for the organization and preparing all stakeholders to understand the logic and rationale behind the transformation.
- Rocking the boat as necessary with resolute will and conviction to pursue the organization's vision.
- Enforcing an accountability system, particularly for those in senior management positions.
- Confronting those who indulge in unethical practices.
- Taking on bullies, internal and external, to protect their team and organization.
- Shouldering responsibility for mistakes, learning from them and standing by their team in times of adversity.
- Taking a righteous position in matters of principles and values.
- Heeding their inner voice and owning their fears.

Exercising Courage Must Be a Calculated Decision

Why a large number of managers and executives fail to exercise courage in their work lives can only be explained by the human tendency to 'not get into any problem', anxiety and fear of failure, fear of consequences on one's career and fear of disturbance of mental peace. Like any other leadership skill, exercising courage can be developed with resolute determination, willpower and daily practice in one's working schedule. It needs a thorough understanding of one's motivation, anxiety level, purpose and contextual factors. Kathleen Reardon, professor of management and organization at USC Marshall School of Business, has put such factors in a logical sequence and called it the courage calculator.

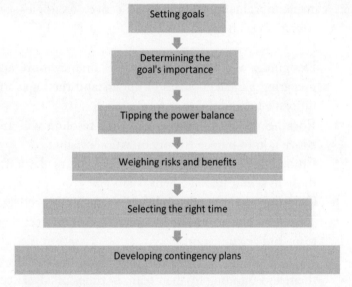

Figure 9.2: Courage Calculation
(Based on Kathleen Reardon's Courage Calculator, 2007)[6]

Reardon states that taking courageous action is akin to an intelligent gamble, requiring an understanding of what she calls 'courage calculation' . . . a method of making success more likely while avoiding rash, unproductive or irrational behaviour. She charts out six steps in the process.

- **Setting goals:** Ask yourself: Does my primary goal stem solely from my professional ambitions? Is the goal within reasonable reach? Is it to prevent a senior manager from acting on faulty information? What is the possibility of success?
- **Determining your goal's importance:** How important is it that you achieve your goal? Does the situation call for immediate or nuanced and less risky action? Weigh your belief in the cause against the risks involved.
- **Tipping the power balance:** Establish relationships with those around you to influence them and gain sway over people who otherwise hold sway over you. This will give you a broader base from which to make bold moves.
- **Weighing risks and benefits:** This component of the courage calculation focuses on trade-offs. Who stands to win? Who stands to lose? What are the chances of your reputation being tarnished beyond repair if you go forward? Will you lose respect for the job or cause others to lose theirs?
- **Selecting the right time:** In *The Book of Joy*, Archbishop Desmond Tutu described good leaders as having an uncanny sense of timing: 'The real leader knows when to make concessions, when to compromise, when to employ the art of losing the battle to win the war.'[7] Courage does not mean recklessness or brash actions. Restraint is key when circumstances are unfavourable.
- **Developing contingency plans:** If you do not meet your objective, what then? Will you lose credibility? How will you salvage your reputation? Contingency planning is really about resourcefulness. People who take bold risks and succeed are versatile thinkers; they

prepare themselves with alternative routes. Courageous managers prepare themselves for many eventualities, including worst-case scenarios.

How Timid and Faint-Hearted Leaders Can Cause Damage

Without courage, a leader may resist transformation and stick to the status quo, preventing the organization from adapting to challenges and innovations. Such leaders, gripped with fear, are risk-averse and unwilling to move beyond their comfort zone; they eventually lead their organizations to slide and finally to collapse. They are the biggest risks to their organizations and cause a loss of morale among employees. They are not able to create trust, manage resistance to change or make decisions on crucial issues. They cause paralysis in their organizations and create grounds for their collapse. Thus, it is important to ensure that the potential leaders are courageous and committed.

A Workout for Developing Courage

Courage, like any other leadership skill, can be developed and it improves with practice. Courage is also contagious, motivating and inspiring people around us.

Manfred F.R. Kets de Vries observes that apart from some genetic factors that may lead to our capacity for greater risk-taking (though not always), non-biological factors such as psychological make-up, values and beliefs, along with conditioning by early role models, can help us take risks and show courage.[8] He also observes that our skills, self-esteem, self-efficacy and capacity to deal with fear also enhance our ability to be courageous.

Most managers or leaders are not born with courage. When you prevail over problems with some basic conviction, you gain the confidence to be courageous.

As a personnel officer at my bank in Uttar Pradesh, I had to deal with union–management conflict issues early in my career. I attended meetings that tested my courage, requiring both intellectual and emotional preparation. I was prepared with facts (hard data) and an understanding of the logic behind the adversary's actions. I understood my fears, owned my anxieties and weighed the risks involved. Most of the time, this approach validated my stand. In the meetings with trade unions, my homework, openness and friendliness, even with those holding opposite viewpoints, helped me raise issues without fear.

My basic nature to persistently confront and resolve difficult issues also enhanced my confidence to experiment with courage. One such issue of grave significance was the reorganizing of union–management relations at the corporate level.

My Experience of Confronting Issues with Courage

Between 2000 and 2003, as executive director of the bank (in the position of deputy chief executive), I took it upon myself to streamline the prevailing messy pattern of industrial relations in the bank. The most glaring difficulties I faced included huge criticism and vilification campaigns from trade unions for disturbing their comfort zone by defining the domains of issues they could negotiate on. Worse still, my immediate boss, the CEO and executive chairman of the bank, demonstrated a wishy-washy approach to dealing with trade unions, who interfered on a daily basis in running the bank's operations smoothly. It was a difficult situation, as I felt isolated in resolving the union–management conflict.

Left with no alternative, I took up the issue in one of the board meetings (as executive director, I was also a board member) and sought the board's intervention, with the board eventually advising the CEO to take immediate action to stop the vilification campaign of the trade unions against me. It was personally a very tough decision for me to invoke the board's authority in advising the CEO to take decisive action, but circumstances demanded such an extraordinary action on my part. In the entire tenure of this episode, I reflected on the consequences daily, worked on my fears and eventually gathered the courage to deal with the problem.

In hindsight, I realize that if I had hesitated at that time, our subsequent course of transformation of the bank would have been stalled by the prevalent militant trade unionism.[9]

I don't think I was courageous in my childhood; rather, I was quite timid. However, right from my first job, I've walked on a road that requires courage. I have enjoyed flashes of success because of my adherence to certain basic principles and convictions. For me, exercising courage has never been a rash act. What always sustained me in such circumstances was the logic of action, clarity in articulating my point of view, and not being overly concerned about its implications for my career.

Based on my professional experiences, during which I faced many difficult situations and eventually emerged successful, I propose the following steps for building one's courage muscles:

1. Confront the Issues

Some people may be uncomfortable using the word 'confront' as it has a negative connotation, but to me, it means confronting issues such as shaking the status quo, internal bureaucracy, apathy towards customers, a lack of agility, delays and challenging a culture that may not be conducive to achieving one's purpose. It also meant speaking the truth to superiors and taking a stand when the situation warranted it. This establishes your credibility.

The Enron scandal could be exposed in 2001 because of the courageous action of then vice president of Enron, Sherron S. Watkins, who wrote a letter to the founder, Mr Lay, about wrong accounting practices being undertaken in his company. It took courage to do so.[10] The will to sacrifice power and position is the ultimate test of exercising courage.

There are several examples to inspire courage, but it will depend upon the risk-taking capacity and the circumstances surrounding an individual. From an organizational perspective, while it may not be pragmatic to question every violation or behaviour where the legality of issues and values is involved, silence can jeopardize the interests of the institution. If confronting any issue or person feels too intimidating, you can seek support from friends, colleagues or mentors to encourage and guide you as you work on building your courage.

2. Conquer Your Fears

Almost everyone has the potential to be courageous. What sets certain individuals apart is the measure of their courage through their ability to overcome their fears, inhibitions and limitations.

What we fear the most is usually what we need to do the most. Identify the things that scare you or make you uncomfortable. Acknowledge your fears and set achievable goals to conquer them. Start by confronting minor fears and gradually work your way up to the bigger ones. Each time you face a fear, you build confidence and resilience. Eventually, you will feel courageous enough to take risks. I have read many stories of courageous actions by ordinary people, and I am particularly impressed by the life of America's most well-known media superstar, Oprah Winfrey. Her story of facing life's setbacks with courage is very inspiring. Oprah, too, confirms that it is fear that inhibits our initiatives. She observes, 'Your fears can rob you of your life. Each time you give in to it, you lose your strength, while your fear gains it.'[11]

The more we conquer our fears, the more motivated and confident we are to take courageous steps.

Decades ago, after I had spent twenty-four years in HR, my CEO asked me to move to a business role at a senior level. Gripped by the fear of failure, I was nervous about taking on the role without any preparation. I even considered resigning, but through constant reflection and processing of my feelings, especially a fear of failure, I developed the confidence to take up the new role. My HR and organizational development background gave me the edge to reach out to field staff, seek their engagement, learn from them and work out an ambitious plan for business outcomes. I succeeded in my maiden business role, which eventually laid the foundation for my becoming a CEO. Had I surrendered to fear and not worked on it, I am not sure where it would have led me.

3. **Speak Up**

   One of the biggest roadblocks to courage is the failure to speak up, usually on account of self-doubts and mental blocks. A lack of confidence or conviction creates doubts such as: Will I be able to effectively communicate my views? Will I be able to control my emotions while presenting my views? Will I be seen as a disruptor? Will I be making a fool of myself? Other reasons could be a lack of understanding of the full picture or even a lack of confidence in their presentation or linguistic skills.

   Reflect on these and consider

   - If your fear is about self-image or self-doubt, it can be overcome through self-management (see Chapter 3 on Self-Management).
   - If your fear stems from linguistic limitations, it can be overcome by reading and conversing daily (see Chapter 15 on Communication).

   Initially, you may require some practice sessions before you can actually exercise courage.

   In the organizational context, there are various levels, such as the board, regulators and the government, where you face some extraordinary situations and you need to speak up rather firmly about your point of view.

My Experience with Exercising Courage

While working as the CEO of Bank of Baroda (2005–08), I faced an unusual situation. In order to refurbish the bank's image (based on a national study), we decided to rebrand the bank through various measures that involved a logo change and the appointment of a brand ambassador. Our rebranding exercise created a buzz and was enthusiastically received by customers as well as employees.

However, some vested interests complained to the government of the day that the colour chosen for the logo resembled the emblem of the political party in opposition and raised tendentious allegations about my support for that political party. One day, the concerned minister called me and instructed me to withdraw the logo. My team and I were stunned. After careful consideration, I decided to meet the powers that be in the government and inform them that withdrawing the logo would severely dent the image of the bank. I argued that the colour of the logo was one of the colours in our national flag and the allegations were based on frivolous logic.

To preserve my self-respect, I was even prepared to quit my position as CEO if the decision was forced upon me. Perhaps the government saw the merit in my argument and did not pursue the issue. This experience heightened my motivation to defend the right decision and vindicated my belief that leaders need to build convincing logic and exercise courage to put across their point of view.

4. Express Functional Anger

Anger towards status-quo attitudes and injustice can serve as fuel for a courageous leader. This **functional anger**, coupled with passion, personal integrity and the nobility of the cause, can be a great motivator to lead with courage (see Chapter 7 on Emotional Regulation and Anger Management).

On that fateful night, when Gandhi was pushed out of the first-class compartment on to the Pietermaritzburg railway station platform in South Africa, the dominant emotions would have been anger and humiliation. But Gandhi channelled and converted that emotion of anger to fuel his lifelong mission of India's freedom struggle.

5. **Visualize and Reflect on Your Progress**
Spend some time visualizing yourself successfully facing your fears. Imagine yourself feeling confident and empowered as you overcome obstacles. You may also practise mindfulness to help you stay present and grounded, especially when facing challenging situations. Also, take time to reflect on your progress and celebrate your successes, no matter how small they seem.

In summary, developing courage is essential for personal growth. We need to step outside our comfort zone and take on new challenges and calculated risks, try new experiences and pursue goals that may seem daunting. Embrace uncertainties and view failures as opportunities for growth. For a leader, the courage to challenge long-established legacy issues and confront dysfunctionality of any kind in business is critical. Courage exercised in pursuit of organizational interests and society at large seldom goes to waste; despite temporary setbacks, it prevails and inspires people. As the stoic philosopher Seneca said, 'It is not because things are difficult that we do not dare, it is because we do not dare that things are difficult.'[12]

Questions for Reflection

1. What are your key learnings from this chapter?
2. Create an action plan to develop and improve your courage using the questions below.

3. What inhibits you from standing up for what you believe in?
4. Think of a situation where you would have liked to be more courageous. What could you have done differently? What would have been the result?
5. Think of an instance where you saw courage in action in the workplace. What were the outcomes, whether positive or negative?

Section 3

Managing Relationships

Chapter 10

Relationships: Making Meaningful Connections

You can go at life as a series of transactions, or you can go at life building relationships. Transactions can give you success, but only relationships can make for a great life.[1]

—Bill Lazier—

Ameer Haq (name changed), an IIT graduate in computer science with fifteen years of experience in the industry, joined a large corporate firm as the chief technology officer (CTO). He was a bright, young executive with new ideas. The CEO, who had inducted him laterally and at a high annual compensation, was especially fond of Haq and supported him in all his endeavours. Haq carried out some critical initiatives to reorganize the technology function, but his colleagues and seniors found him brash, overconfident and insensitive. He had scant regard for rules and regulations, rubbed his juniors the wrong way in internal meetings and used the CEO's name to push his agenda. He casually used foul language, and in one instance, his behaviour with a colleague led to a collective outcry. However, the CEO's support emboldened him for continuing his brash behaviour. After about six months, the CEO left for greener pastures abroad and Haq faced the wrath of his colleagues. Despite his obvious intellectual prowess and acknowledgement of his expertise, Haq ended up scoring a self-goal due to a lack of interpersonal deftness and failure to build relationships, and had to eventually leave.

People like Haq can be found in any industry and at any level. The higher they move, the worse their behaviour. People like him get away with such behaviour because the leadership fails to take timely action, often for considerations of technical competence, ignoring the behavioural and relationship competence, allowing relationships to flounder. Effective leaders focus on promoting collaboration and addressing any deviance that may sabotage it. This admittedly delicate task is a critical undertaking for a leader.

Where there are people, there are bound to be disagreements. They are inevitable but also important; they force us to consider a point of view that we may have overlooked or brushed aside. These disagreements can escalate into conflicts at home and the workplace, but we must not allow them to damage our relationships. Relationships based on authenticity and trust can resolve such differences through dialogue. However, if we are egocentric and have scant regard or respect for the other party, there will obviously be no scope for dialogue and thus no problem-solving, just festering resentment and ill will, which will sooner or later corrode the work environment and harm the organization.

What Is Relationship Management?

The criticality of relationships for leaders cannot be overstated because they establish trust, facilitate communication, enable collaboration and shape the culture; in other words, they lead to results and growth. Leaders who prioritize building and nurturing relationships are better equipped to inspire and empower their teams to achieve success.

The business of business is relationships; the business of life is human connection.[2]

—Robin Sharma—

In its very basic form, a relationship can be purely transactional, such as a professional one, but that too can be uplifting and transformational.

The late Edgar H. Schein, a Swiss-born American business theorist, social psychologist from MIT and global expert in organizational culture and leadership, noted four levels of relationships that occur in the professional setting:[3]

Level Minus 1: Total impersonal domination and coercion.
Level 1: Transactional role and rule-based supervision, service and most forms of professional relationships.
Level 2: Personal, cooperative, trusting relationships, such as friendships and effective teams.
Level 3: Emotionally intimate and totally mutual commitments.

In work relationships, Schein introduced the concept of 'personization', which he defined as the process of building a mutually working relationship with a fellow employee, teammate, boss, subordinate or colleague. This is the beginning of a genuine and healthy dynamic between the team and the boss. In this dynamic, we try to see that person as a whole and not just the role they occupy. This assumes that you are open and honest with one another and feel safe sharing when things are not going well. Personizing should not be confused with being nice or extending generous benefits; it is concerned with everything related to building relationships that get the job done while avoiding manipulation of any kind.

Table 10.1: Components of a Healthy Relationship

• A stress-free ecosystem of understanding and trust
• Mutual dependence, timely and end-to-end responses for better productivity
• People-centric approach for enhanced team morale and internal collaboration
• Positive attitude
• Creative problem-solving
• Support during crises
• Going beyond the call of duty, not merely role-taking but role-making

When the above components are visible, there is better cooperation and partnership among all stakeholders, and when any of the above components are missing, the relationship can go awry.

One of the defining tasks of leaders is to establish and nurture genuine trust, respect and cooperation among stakeholders so that they have at the very least, smooth and healthy working relationships. The following strategies are extremely helpful in this regard:

1. Expressing Gratitude

A simple act of gratitude can enhance the quality of relationships and even help rebuild ones that have gone sour. If we look back on the occasions that someone expressed their gratitude to us, we'll realize that it made our day and lit up our face with a smile.

Gratitude is usually expressed in three ways—acknowledgement, appreciation and authenticity—which are the keystones for building relationships in all walks of life.

Table 10.2: The Three A's of Gratitude

Acknowledgement	This means recognizing the individuals/teams for their effort. For example: A boss goes to the desk of a subordinate to acknowledge their contribution to a project.
Appreciation	This involves expressing your feelings about a job well done and specifying the achievement. For example: When a restaurant owner appreciates the ingenuity of the chef in creating a special dish and uses it to promote the restaurant or puts up a poster or banner of the chef posing with the dish.
Authenticity	This means being genuine in your appreciation without any other motive, such as to gain goodwill or cooperation. For example: Publicly honouring those who have made significant contributions in their field, highlighting their work and giving appropriate incentives to facilitate their work.

Leaders can use genuine appreciation and acknowledgement in an authentic manner to build relationships, not just for the sake of it, but to express that they truly care. This helps them run the company for the greater good of all stakeholders, not just for the bottom line.

2. Build Connections

Get to know your people. This goes a long way towards building relationships and making people feel seen and valued. Demonstrate your interest in them.

As CEO, I operated from an exclusive floor. And though there were about 400 people in my office, there was rarely a chance to interact with them; at the most, I met people in the atrium or in the corridors and waved at them. This was a sore point for me, and I pondered over how I could connect with my people. Then it occurred to me to celebrate their birthdays on my floor. Thus, the tradition of birthday celebrations started. On the first of every month, I invited all the staff with birthdays in that month. There were flowers and cake, and I would shake hands and chat with them. The whole affair lasted about twenty minutes. This gave me a great opportunity to shake hands with practically every member of the staff throughout the year and to acknowledge how much they mattered. It gave me immense pleasure and I could see as much happiness on their faces.

With this simple gesture, I was able to authentically express my gratitude by acknowledging and appreciating every single employee. This went a long way towards building relationships with the employees at the corporate office.

3. Cultivate Influencers

Influencers can play a great role in creating a facilitative environment by removing roadblocks or bureaucratic hurdles. Thus, building relationships with influencers is extremely important.

During the early 1980s, I was pursuing a PhD in the sensitive area of industrial relations on strategies in union management. As an observer, I initially experienced some indifference from union functionaries, especially while attending their meetings with management. At this stage, I reached out to M. Rajagopal, general secretary of the recognized workmen's union, who was intellectually inclined and broad-minded. When I shared the purpose of my research and asked for his cooperation, he came fully on board and became an influencer of critical importance in collecting field data for my research. With his support, I could attend meetings between trade unions and management at the corporate and regional levels. Rajagopal also helped me interview some former CEOs.

In my later work as CEO, I also nurtured relationships with key influencers, for instance, board members and government bureaucrats, during the transformation project of the bank. Cultivating relationships to seek a purpose-driven and performance-focused goal (not a narrow personal agenda) is critical to a leader's success.

Why Is Relationship Management Critical?

The fate of an organization depends on the collective effort of its people. When employees are happy and engaged, they can work smoothly to facilitate growth. It is thus critical that leaders develop relationships internally with those who keep the wheels of the organization turning.

Bill George, former CEO of Medtronic and now a professor at Harvard Business School, explains the strategic importance of building relationships:

> The capacity to develop close and enduring relationships is one mark of a leader. Unfortunately, many leaders of major companies believe their job is to create the strategy, organisation structure and organisational process. Then they just delegate the work to be done, remaining aloof from the people doing the work. The detached style of leadership will not be successful in the twenty-first century. Today's employees demand more personal relationships with their leaders before they will give themselves fully to their jobs.[4]

A leader, especially in the modern scenario, must build authentic, meaningful relationships to help everyone evolve.

Among the several bosses I worked with, I particularly carry memories of S.P. Talwar (CEO, Bank of Baroda, 1993–95) who came from Union Bank of India at a time when there was general despondency in the operating units on account of a strong hierarchical and bureaucratic culture that led to delays in decision-making and frustration among employees and customers. In about two months' time, Talwar was able to bust the internal bureaucracy, accelerate the process of decision-making and connect with employees and customers. All these initiatives built an excellent architecture of relationships both within the bank and with customers, government officers and regulators. Talwar was **informal, hands-on** and **accessible.** He broke the barriers of formalities and hierarchies by directly phoning executives, sometimes over four levels below him, to get a sense of the business environment, get feedback on business problems and encourage field functionaries to take decisions without fear. Above all, he was humane and compassionate, breaking the shackles of rules to help people during crises.

As a CEO, he brought down the barricades in communication within the corporate office by holding meetings with general managers almost every alternate day and resolving complex issues stuck in interdepartmental conflicts. We experienced new energy in the organization and an atmosphere of problem-solving and productive discussions. Relationships among the top management and between the corporate office and regional units dramatically improved. Overall, Talwar was able to create an ecosystem of ease and collaboration through his understanding of human processes and quick problem-solving that helped to improve relationships at every level, and its impact was visible in the bank's growth.

Why Do Relationships Fail?

When the components of a healthy connection are missing, the relationship cannot grow. In some cases, the give and take is so strongly skewed in one party's favour that it reeks of manipulation or exploitation.

Many times, power dynamics come into play in relationships that operate in rigid hierarchical situations. This can leave the subordinate feeling unheard, their hopes and aspirations ignored or, worse still, dismissed. One needs to consider the changes in attitude that have taken place across generations. The false sense of superiority that was once accepted and deferred to is now a thing of the past, and all employees must expect—and are entitled to—respectful behaviour regardless of their position in the system. We must also be wary of people-pleasers; complimenting people to keep them happy without any real appreciation for them is inauthentic, transactional and serves only to fulfil some purpose. These relationships are purely cosmetic and superficial, and once they achieve their goal, they often vanish.

The success of relationship management depends on the effectiveness of one's people management skills. How one can excite and energize people for the overall objectives of the department or company, how one can create passion in people by showing sensitivity to their problems, both work-related and personal, how one can demonstrate empathy and compassion in times of crisis, how one can show humility in day-to-day interactions, and how one can use every possible opportunity to appreciate and recognize the work of their people. Leaders who fail to follow this and act with arrogance, indifference and a lack of sensitivity cannot develop any worthwhile relationships, and this will certainly be a great deterrent to achieving corporate objectives through the willing cooperation of people.

Logging Out of Dysfunctional Relationships

Reciprocity is what sustains relationships. Excessive investment in building relationships by one party can backfire for the simple reason that the other side may take it as an entitlement or develop cold feet towards reciprocating. It may be worthwhile to have a complete exit from a relationship where one party is toxic, demanding or even exploitative. However, if the relationship is within the family and close friends, it will be desirable to invest both intellectually and emotionally in repairing and restoring such relationships through discussions, some personal gestures and patience.

The same is true of relationships between companies or partnerships where greed to covet or possess, harmful intentions to plot coups and hostile takeovers, or acts to malign the credibility of business partners become serious issues. In such cases, it may be the right thing to sever the relationship before it is too late.

It will, however, require deep reflection and prudence to take such a call, as haste, abruptness, anger and impulsiveness can create incalculable harm.

A Workout for Developing Relationship Muscles

In their book, *Beyond Entrepreneurship 2.0*, researchers and academics at Stanford, Jim Collins and Bill Lazier say, 'Leaders who build great companies are "hands-on" always putting their personal touch on the business. There is simply no excuse for being detached, removed, distant, or uninvolved.'[5]

Thus, it is important to train oneself in understanding relationships and building them, since the very root of success, progress and even joy in professional lives depends on the strength of relationships.

Here are some **steps to build relationship muscles**:

1. **Work on the Self:**
   - Understand yourself and **develop self-knowledge** through reflection and introspection. The better you understand yourself, the better you can understand others and nurture relationships. Steer clear of ego traps. **Be flexible, develop patience** and take initiative to resolve or break impasses in relationships (see Chapter 1 on Self-Awareness and Chapter 2 on Reflection).
   - **Work on** all your weaknesses. Be responsible, respect other people's time and be dependable; it shows a caring attitude (see Chapter 3 on Self-Management, Chapter 4 on Self-Discipline and Chapter 5 on Time Management).

2. **Build Trust:**
   - Establish a **common goal or vision** that can foster a sense of belonging and shared purpose, as well as bring together individuals and teams within the ecosystem.
   - Build positive relationships by creating a **collaborative process** to spot new opportunities and stay in touch with the issues and concerns of others. For instance, I held daily meetings as CEO with twenty-five top executives to discuss strategic issues and set in motion a hassle-free collaborative process for policy-making and its implementation.
   - Be a **problem solver**; be **consultative**; avoid unilateral decision-making and respect the viewpoints of others.
   - Be a **role model** and set a good example in behaviour, etiquette and courtesies.
   - Be **authentic**, avoid making promises that cannot be delivered and express views firmly but politely (see Chapter 11 on Authenticity).
   - Create trust by being **credible and ethical in all dealings**. Always demonstrate by your conduct that you

care for and respect relationships and are always there in need (see Chapter 12 on Credibility).

- Be **accessible**, visible and hands-on; provide the necessary resources and support their day-to-day work-related problems, which can include training and mentoring.
- **Operate with humility** and avoid pride in all circumstances (see Chapter 13 on Humility).

3. **Build Positive Relationships:**
   - Stand by others during difficult times, extend timely support and show compassion as an organization and as a leader. Practise empathetic understanding of the problem.
   - Celebrate successes to recognize the achievements of individuals and teams, create a culture of collaboration and improve relationships.
   - Create an environment where people feel comfortable sharing their ideas.
   - **Create inclusive work environments.** Ensure that diverse groups with different backgrounds, experiences and viewpoints are represented in various discussions to improve the depth and breadth of ideas, which can improve overall perspective (see Chapter 14 on Fairness).
   - To **inspire** team members, act with emotional intelligence and be an effective coach or mentor.
   - Communicate effectively; **be responsive**—how you communicate with a person says a lot about your relationship with them. Lack of responsiveness often negatively affects relationships (see Chapter 15 on Communication).
   - **Control emotions** while giving feedback and encourage everyone to improve further by focusing on people's

strengths and potential (see Chapter 7 on Emotional Regulation and Anger Management).

- **Listen with an intent to act**; listening acts as a balm to heal injured relationships (see Chapter 16 on Listening).
- Communicate with dignity and respect; avoid taunts, indecent language and overreacting, as **toxicity injures relationships** (see Chapter 17 on Detoxifying Communication).
- Use dialogue to have **meaningful conversations**, prevent negative vibes from causing more damage, reflect on what may have soured the relationship and remedy it (see Chapter 18 on Dialogue).

Training for Building Relationship Management

There are numerous ways to impart relationship training. Basically, in relationship training, the focus is on the self—self-awareness, emotional regulation, authenticity and credibility. Training based on the self is normally undertaken by using several psychometric tools, such as the TA-based managerial style questionnaire,[6] FIRO-B (Fundamental Interpersonal Relations Orientation) (for details on FIRO-B, see Chapter 1 on Self-Awareness),[7] which help individuals understand their behaviour and that of others, and the MBTI (Myers–Briggs Type Indicator), a self-help assessment test that helps people gain insights about how they work and learn.[8] Using the T-Group methodology is another way to understand the self (see Chapter 1 on Self-Awareness).[9]

Relationship management is not an optional skill but an essential one, as it is the very backbone of leadership. It is, in fact, an amalgamation of all other skills, making it critical for your success. Any effective leader will know that positive relationships are a fundamental part of any organization and are major enablers of engagement, creativity and productivity that shape the organization's credibility and reputation.

Questions for Reflection

1. What are your key learnings from this chapter?
2. Create an action plan to develop and improve your relationship management skills using the questions below.
3. Reflect on the comfortable relationships in your life and list the factors responsible for them.
4. In relationships that have gone sour, what could you have done to repair them?

Chapter 11

Authenticity: Being Your Real Self

The privilege of a lifetime is to become who you truly are.[1]

—Carl Gustav Jung—

In our daily lives, we often choose things that are the real deal. We want authentic south Indian food, an authentic Ayurvedic massage, authentic pashmina shawls, authentic silk and authentic this and that. What does this tell us? It tells us that we care for the genuine rather than the fake or duplicate. Likewise, we expect the people we deal with to be real, open, transparent and without any pretensions or promises that they cannot fulfil. Those who deal with us also expect us to be real in our behaviour, actions and communication. Is this an exaggerated expectation? Is this difficult to practise? Given that we expect those in leadership roles to be authentic in their behaviour, we need to explore and understand the concept of authenticity in greater detail.

What Is Authenticity?

Simply put, **authenticity is the congruence between the real self and the visible self.** In today's world, where the focus is on style, authentic leaders remain rooted in their values (guiding principles that dictate behaviour and action). They are unpretentious, honest and open with others. They are aware of their limitations, accept when they are wrong and have the humility to admit their mistakes.

Authenticity is the competence to express one's ideas without any extraneous considerations. An authentic person is the same, whether in public or in the privacy of their home.

---

*Authentic leaders use their **natural abilities**, but they also recognize their shortcomings and work hard to overcome them. They lead with purpose, meaning and values.*[2]

—Bill George—

These **natural abilities**, as mentioned in the quote by executive fellow at Harvard Business School and author Bill George, may even include 'negative' emotions such as anger to effect positive change.[3] They show conviction and commitment to principles. They often rock the boat and risk their personal interests to protect their principles. They are autonomous.

Authenticity thus demands a high degree of self-knowledge, integrity, trustworthiness, emotional depth, sensitivity to others, the confidence to bear the consequences of our actions and healthy self-esteem. It is not about being self-righteous or insensitive to contextual considerations.

Figure 11.1: Characteristics of Authentic Leaders

Figure 11.1 demonstrates the interconnectedness of various traits of leadership that make an authentic leader. For example, an authentic leader is expected to be a person with integrity and trustworthiness with a high orientation towards self-awareness and emotional regulation.

What Authenticity Is Not

Some people have wrong notions about authenticity and might act dangerously. Authenticity is not about being brash or stupidly naive. It is always contextual and should be expressed with mature judgement, or else it can lead to avoidable controversies and undesirable consequences.

1. Aggression Is Not Authenticity

Being authentic does not mean being rude, bossy, uncompromising or self-righteous. Authentic leaders show a deep understanding of issues and flexibility in tough situations and are compassionate and empathetic. They are aware of their feelings and, more importantly, know how to express them. They do not recklessly display raw emotions but process and express them with measured judgement in different situations. Leaders have a public image to maintain and must exercise restraint in articulating their feelings, especially if how they feel is inconsistent with their role in public office.

As David Gergen, professor and director of the Center for Public Leadership at Harvard Kennedy School, rightly observes, 'Authenticity does not mean that every thought of a leader must be expressed. Nor does it mean that every emotion should be worn on your sleeve. Rather, authentic leadership demands that as you navigate, you stay true to your values and principles . . . as contexts change, you adjust your tactics.'[4]

2. Rigidity Is Not Authenticity

Authenticity is often misunderstood as inflexibility. In simple terms, authenticity requires us to be present and true in each moment while still adapting to the situation. An authentic leader is not rigid but observes, learns, evolves and transforms as per the needs of the hour.

Herminia Ibarra, an expert and leading researcher in organizational behaviour, emphasizes that the greater good must guide us in expressing our feelings.[5] She talks about **adaptive authenticity**. She emphatically observes that it would be wrong to become caged into a rigid concept of the self. Instead, we must try to **build a new self** that is **open to new possibilities**. She suggests that we expand our horizons, learn in new situations and experiment with new behaviours by undertaking many diverse roles and developing our leadership skills in different contexts. For example, in a difficult situation, we may need to mask our feelings for the sake of the greater good and put on a brave face and a confident tone. While we must express ourselves with tact, it does not make us any less authentic.

Why Is Authenticity Important?

One of the key roles of leaders is to constantly learn and remain curious about developments (especially in ever-changing digital scenarios) and have new perspectives that could help their organizations adapt to emerging contexts. They must also create a learning environment across the organization and promote an ecosystem of authentic communication at every level for people to articulate their points of view, which is critical for the growth of any organization. A lack of authenticity can deprive articulation of the best ideas, thereby stunting the progress of institutions.

At another level, leadership, among other things, should mobilize employees to achieve a common vision through enthusiasm and engagement. A leader's role is to inspire employees through exemplary behaviour. Can an inauthentic, insensitive and opaque leader achieve this? The answer is a resounding 'NO'. Authenticity is, therefore, an essential trait. Here are a few of its other benefits:

1. **Establishes Trust and Credibility:** Authentic leaders foster trust due to their perceived genuineness and honesty. When leaders are true to themselves and others, their followers feel secure and have confidence in their intentions and decisions. This builds credibility and enhances the leader's ability to influence others.

2. **Fosters Connection:** Authentic leaders are reliable and accessible. They create a sense of connection with their

followers by remaining true to themselves. People are more likely to engage and communicate honestly with leaders they perceive as authentic and who are able to create an environment of collaboration and open dialogue.

3. **Makes Space for Learning:** Authentic leaders embrace their strengths and weaknesses, acknowledging that they are human and capable of mistakes. This humility allows them to be open to feedback, learn from their experiences and continuously improve. Their authenticity encourages a culture of learning and growth within the organization.

4. **Increases Employee Engagement and Motivation:** Authentic leaders create an environment where employees feel valued, respected and appreciated. By being genuine, leaders can connect with their team members on a deeper level and understand their needs, aspirations and motivations. This helps leaders tailor their approach to inspire and motivate based on each person's unique strengths and interests.

5. **Creates a Culture of Authenticity:** Authentic leaders set the tone for the organization's culture. When leaders lead with authenticity, they encourage their team members to be themselves, fostering a culture of authenticity and acceptance. This can lead to increased employee satisfaction, engagement and overall well-being.

6. **Drives Alignment of Purpose:** Authentic leaders are clear about their values and purpose. They align their actions with these core principles, which helps them make decisions that are consistent with their beliefs. This consistency builds a strong organizational culture and fosters a sense of purpose among team members.

In summary, authenticity is important for leaders because it creates a learning environment of trust, connection and credibility where individuals and teams can thrive.

Table 11.1: Critical Behavioural Patterns of Authentic and Inauthentic Leaders

Authentic Leaders	Inauthentic Leaders
Are open, do not have hidden agendas, work with clarity and transparency and walk the talk.	Are secretive, evasive, manipulative, have hidden agendas and often go back on their words.
Have a learning mindset and never hesitate to receive feedback and improve themselves.	Are often learning-averse know-it-alls who dislike feedback and are not inclined to improve.
Maintain integrity at all times and do not sacrifice their values for personal gains or power.	Lack integrity and may push others under the bus for personal benefit or power.
Display courage to change the status quo and make an impact on the organization.	Lack the courage to change the status quo and, as a result, allow organizations to stagnate.
Accept their failures and do not apportion blame on others.	Are unable to tolerate failure and blame others for their shortcomings.
Are intensely committed to 'people processes'* and sensitive to the problems of others.	Display peripheral commitments and a lack of faith in 'people processes' and are indifferent to the plight of others.
Are open to other viewpoints and can live with contrarian opinions.	Are not open to other viewpoints and do not accept contrarian opinions.

* 'People processes': Aspects of policy, practices and behaviour to promote fairness, justice, cooperation, collaboration and team spirit.

Today, the world is looking for authentic leaders in all spheres of life, from politics to boardrooms. Many organizations fall from grace not because of the external environment alone but because of people at the top, especially the board members who lack the candour and authenticity to raise the right question at the right time. It is because of this broad institutional culture that many corporations are consigned to the dustbin long before reaching their potential.

A Workout for Developing Authenticity

Authenticity is not exclusive to the top rung of the organization. Anyone can practise authenticity in their actions and behaviour, and the sooner the better.

Can Authenticity Be Developed?

Yes, it can. Leaders can also build their authenticity muscles in the same way athletes develop their muscles through continuous practice and sweat. Athletes display their commitment and stamina while pursuing their goal of being the best, and leaders can also make a similar effort in building authenticity. Practice is the keyword.

Being authentic and leading a meaningful life requires patience and a continuous endeavour to understand ourselves, develop a strong moral compass, have the courage to confront ourselves in times of dilemma and constantly reflect on and clarify our values. A sense of purpose, a solid value system and a burning desire to make an impact in our organizations or society in general—these are what make an authentic person or leader.

Here are the steps to build your authenticity muscles:

1. **Start an Experiential Learning Cycle**

    Practise being authentic in all situations. Identify your obstacles to authenticity, overcome them through trial and error, and reflect on the outcomes, persisting with unrelenting focus. See Figure 11.2 for detailed steps in the process. Often, this new experience is not as risky as we might anticipate. Our authenticity, even in a pliable culture, sets us apart.

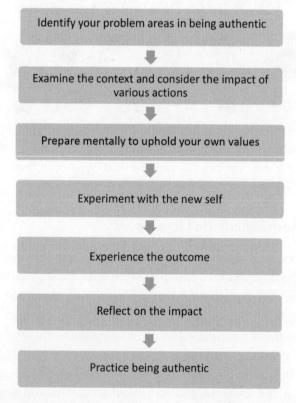

Figure 11.2: Experiential Learning for Developing Authenticity*

(*Adapted and expanded from Kolb's Experiential Learning Cycle, developed by American psychologist David Kolb in 1984)[6]

2. **Own Your Vulnerabilities**
   We can develop authenticity by being aware of our vulnerabilities and not being secretive about them. Brené Brown, a renowned researcher and author, has championed vulnerability as a strength.[7] She has shared her personal struggles, failures and insecurities, which have resonated with millions of people worldwide. She strongly promotes the power of vulnerability in building meaningful connections and fostering trust. Sharing personal challenges, admitting mistakes and being open to emotional harm (vulnerability) means being true to oneself and acting in alignment with one's core values (authenticity). Expressing vulnerability strengthens a leader's authenticity score.

   As a result of my late exposure as a business manager, I shared my limitations of experience in business with my operating managers, which helped me win their confidence and develop collaborative relationships.

3. **Build Trustworthiness**
   Authentic behaviour creates trust, as there is little scope for misunderstanding or manipulation. Establish trust by being respectful of everyone, irrespective of their status, caste, religion, gender or hierarchical level. Only through honest and transparent behaviour can we remain authentic in our dealings. During my first major posting as deputy general manager in Uttar Pradesh in 1995, I did not figure in the list of promotions to general manager. However, my disappointment disappeared after I received a call from the CEO explaining that I was wait-listed for a promotion, which would be announced in the next few months. This candour in communication helped me develop greater trust in the top management.

4. **Build Personal Integrity**

   Have the courage to stand up for what you strongly believe in and stay true to your values, even though it may not be in the best interest of your immediate career ambitions. This will strengthen your ability to face tough challenges in your leadership journey. Manipulative behaviour, pliability and double-talk may sometimes temporarily help, but they will not build your reputation as a leader. If you look at the lives of some great leaders in various fields, their journeys haven't always been smooth, but they've been able to realize their goals despite temporary setbacks.

5. **Be Straightforward and Transparent**

   Corporate politics can be challenging to navigate when you value authenticity. While one needs to understand the politics, it is important not to get involved in them. It is best to avoid taking sides or actively organizing people unless established principles are at stake. Mature responses and remaining anchored in one's value system are the best ways to deal with such situations. In short, do not indulge in politics, speculation or backbiting. Be sincere and forthright, while also being sensitive.

My Experience with Practising Authenticity

I joined the board of a subsidiary of a well-known company in the financial sector (in investment banking with businesses such as capital markets, asset reconstruction, merchant banking, mutual funds, etc). The board, headed by a non-executive chairman (NEC), included some eminent bankers and finance professionals. In one of the board meetings, a certain proposal authorizing the NEC with executive powers in significant areas such as appointments, credit sanction, etc. was brought up. I pointed out that it may not be proper to delegate executive powers to the NEC as his role was 'non-executive', but most of the directors overlooked my observation. I, for one, believed that the decision was not in consonance with the sound principles of governance. Later, other independent directors joined me as some other governance issues came up. The issues were raised with the promoter, but no action was taken. I waited for a reasonable time for the right decision and finally submitted my resignation to the board. I also mentioned the reasons for my resignation from the board, which was rather unconventional.

I knew my resignation would result in a monetary loss on account of the board fee plus commission on profit, and it could also restrict any further invitation to join any board. It, however, opened up other opportunities by way of invitations to address conferences on corporate governance and many speaking invitations from academic institutions and other professional institutions. There are always consequences, both positive and negative, for one's principled and authentic actions. It is for individuals to take a call. I too had a choice: be a pragmatic opportunist or remain my true self.

6. Build Self-Esteem

It is easier to be authentic when we are confident about ourselves. We can develop a high degree of self-esteem and self-confidence through mindfulness and self-compassion; it will allow us to understand the feelings of others and operate transparently (see Chapter 8 on Compassion).

7. Tackle Inauthentic People

While authenticity is necessary for being a better leader, we must also know how to deal with inauthentic people to avoid being manipulated.

- Accept the fact that they are inauthentic and don't justify or rationalize their behaviour.
- Be honest and call them out when they wrong others.
- Don't blindly trust; validate everything they say—check and double-check.
- Recognize their manipulative behaviour and avoid being dragged into their schemes.
- Hold them accountable for their mistakes.
- Maintain distance and establish healthy boundaries.
- Be compassionate towards yourself, and do not take their behaviour personally.

I have a personal code to never take credit for the achievements of others, pretend to know what I do not, bully people into doing something unethical, be opaque and secretive or suppress my feelings when I need to express them.

Like most leaders, I've also faced 'authenticity dilemmas' and the tensions associated with them. There were several times when I felt the need to speak out, but the consequences could have been terrible for my career. On these occasions, I examined the situation to check if it aligned with my professional responsibilities and core values. This thorough scrutiny helped me confront my self-doubt and gave me the confidence to conquer my fears. Being in tune with my authentic self was very liberating. It gave me clarity and helped me articulate my views clearly, even if they challenged others' opinions or beliefs. By being authentic and standing up for my values, I led a major transformation for my bank.

These are the lessons I learnt:

- Question your intent when you're not doing what you want to do.
- Rock the boat, when necessary, in the greater interest of the organization even at the cost of your own self-interest.
- Engage in authentic dialogue with employees and all other stakeholders; practise and make it a habit.
- Show your vulnerability; continuously practise 'unmasking' during conversations and dialogues.
- Use your power for quick problem-solving and be a hard taskmaster but an authentic, compassionate leader.

Expressing our views without being disrespectful or judgemental is a great virtue. Leaders can be great influencers through their behaviour and actions. Frankly, you may not find many supporters of your authentic and logical voice, but your actions count.

My authenticity has brought me accolades as well as criticism and, in some cases, enmity, but I persisted and held on to my values. Even the best leaders in the world are criticized, so why bother?

Promote Authenticity in Your Team

Leaders must also foster leadership qualities among their team members. You can cultivate authentic behaviour in your teams by:

- Creating a culture of open communication.
- Encouraging people to articulate their grievances and respond in a positive manner by dealing with emotional issues without bias.

- Having one-on-one dialogues with members who are too assertive/aggressive, too quiet/docile/withdrawn, those who tend to derail agendas or fail to contribute.
- Ensuring that your team members understand and are committed to the organization's overall vision and purpose.

The success of all this will depend very much on a leader's sensitivity and ability to cope with their own anxieties and emotions.

Authenticity in behaviour, communication and action is key to leadership. Of course, it does not come easily, and it requires disciplined practice and determination. Life will test and challenge your authenticity, values and principles, and you will be tempted by the inauthentic and easy way out.

Let me conclude this chapter with a quote by Bill George, executive fellow at Harvard Business School:

> If you want to be an authentic leader and have a meaningful life, you need to do the difficult inner work to develop yourself, have a strong moral compass based on your beliefs and values, and work on problems that matter to you. When you look back on your life, it may not be perfect, but it will be authentically yours.[8]

Questions for Reflection

1. What are your key learnings from this chapter?
2. Create an action plan to develop and improve your authenticity using the questions below.
3. Do you always expect your bosses and colleagues to be open and transparent?
   a. Yes, always
   b. Depends on the context

4. Do you always try to practise being open and transparent in dealing with your bosses, colleagues and subordinates? In what ways have you benefited from being open?
5. What are the occasions where you are not able to be transparent? What is holding you back?

Chapter 12

Credibility: Building Trust and Reputation

Credibility is a leader's currency. With it, leaders are solvent.
Without it, they're bankrupt.[1]

—John C. Maxwell—

One of my core childhood memories is listening to my mother recite Tulsidas' *Ramcharitmanas* early in the morning. The rhythm and cadence made it easy to remember, and I learnt the words well before I understood their meaning. When I did, I took them to heart, particularly the line from Verse 28 (2) of *Ayodhya Kand* that many people may be familiar with, courtesy of Bollywood:

रघुकुल रीत सदा चल आई, प्राण जाई
पर वचन न जाई ॥28(2)॥

Meaning: The tradition of the Raghu (Ram) lineage is to honour your word even at the cost of death.

Honouring your word—doing as you say, saying as you do—is the foundational stone of building credibility, and I have striven all my life to live up to this credo. It is this that made me dependable, an asset that could be relied upon, and built trust and reputation and helped me rise through the ranks.

In my personal life, I have had many role models who taught me the value of being dependable. At the very beginning of my career, I had the opportunity to learn the importance of credibility in the professional sphere. I was also lucky to work with some highly credible bosses whose personal integrity and alignment of their words and actions, along with a higher sense of accountability, made an indelible impression on my young mind.

I encountered the finest example of credibility in my very first job. This was in 1971 when I was a probationary officer at a bank. I had taken up the job, excited at the prospect of the training and other experiences the role claimed to offer. The reality, however, was far from this rosy picture. Highly frustrated and disillusioned, I dashed off a letter to the then head of personnel, L.B. Bhide, regarding my disappointment. This was a risky and unusual step, considering that it was a hierarchy-driven conservative organization, and I didn't really expect such a high-ranking officer to notice, let alone respond to my letter.

To my utter surprise, Bhide not only replied to my letter but also initiated steps to resolve the issues that I had raised. He wrote to the bank's apex college at Ahmedabad, asking them to admit me to the next induction programme, and to the regional manager, Rajasthan zone, about my job rotation on various operational jobs, and soon, my problems were sorted out.

Bhide's intervention taught me enduring lessons on leadership, specifically how a **responsive** and **problem-solving approach** can help build **credibility**. Since then, I have followed these three principles in practising leadership to achieve some extraordinary results.

The issue of responsiveness is of particular importance. Unless we respond to people's problems, there is no way we can engage them or persuade them to participate in the growth of the organization. As we consistently address problems, we gain credibility and inspire people.

This quest to remain committed to being responsive and ensuring that there is no gap between the promises made and delivered has guided many of my leadership initiatives in various roles, including at the junior level.

As I progressed in my career and occupied senior positions, I pursued it for the purpose of being in leadership roles. Sometimes, with small successes and greater disappointments, and other times, with greater success and minor disappointments. In my role as CEO, with greater executive power, I strove to create a culture of credible management by building accountability, responsiveness and fairness in dealing with employees and customers. For example, I made sure that we took the concerns of our frontline employees and customers seriously and considered them for implementation as soon as possible. At a personal level, it became a kind of mission for me to weave credibility into our culture.

I have also been greatly inspired by the life of Mahatma Gandhi, whose global impact, even now, is largely due to his personal credibility. For example, if he talked about the welfare of Dalits, he lived in Dalit colonies; his belief in communal amity was followed up with his frequent fasts to bring the communities closer. A famous quote paraphrased from Gandhi's book, *The Story of My Experiments with Truth*, 'Be the change you want to see,' encapsulates his credibility.[2] A lack of credibility demolishes leaders' reputations, dilutes their authority and diminishes their chances of achieving results.

It's not surprising, then, that in a 2011 global research study by academics and authors James M. Kouzes and Barry Z. Posner about the qualities people admire and seek in a leader, 'honest', 'forward-looking', 'inspiring' and 'competent', which they grouped under 'credibility', got the most votes.[3] In a 2023 joint survey by *US News* and The Harris Poll, Americans said they wanted leaders who were trustworthy above all else.[4] It is a seemingly universal result across a range of demographic breakdowns, including gender, race, generation, household income, political party, urbanity and geography. It is therefore evident that credibility (trustworthiness of leaders) remains the No. 1 leadership trait.

What Is Credibility?

Credibility is the quality of being **trusted, believed** or **accepted as true, real** and **honest**. It is one of the foundational characteristics of good leadership, as it influences work attitudes and business outcomes. We evaluate our leaders and supervisors based on their trustworthiness—whether they do as they say. **Credible leaders are the ones who will put principles ahead of their own interests.** Our actions, manner of speech, decision-making style, communication patterns, behaviour and all other attributes influence and affect those who work with us. In some sense, credibility demands a commitment to the expectations created. It is the perception others have of our integrity, expertise, reliability and competence. Credibility is earned through a combination of factors such as honesty, consistency, expertise and reliability.

People prefer working for credible and principled leaders who reward merit over relationships. Opportunistic leaders who fail to deliver on their promises and leave employees feeling used, exploited and disillusioned are seldom respected. Essentially, **credibility is demonstrating an alignment between our words and actions**. However, credibility is not a stand-alone quality but an outcome of several other aspects of our personality, such as authenticity, trustworthiness, honesty and dependability.

Integrity is a foundational aspect of credibility. In the professional sense, it would mean not to dilute principles or ideas to please people, particularly those in authority, but to articulate our views honestly and with conviction, without fear or expectation of any personal gain.

It is challenging to build and maintain credibility without integrity because people won't trust someone they perceive as lacking honesty and moral principles. Conversely, someone with integrity is more likely to be seen as credible because they consistently demonstrate honesty, reliability and ethical behaviour. Despite being distinct concepts, integrity and credibility undoubtedly interconnect. Together, they define the character of a leader.

Integrity and credibility are essential ingredients of leadership. No integrity = no leadership; no credibility = no leadership. A lack of credibility and integrity is not merely about scandals or swindling but about having a strong moral compass. It is about the instinct to use discretion and power to benefit others, not oneself. It is also about how we face a crisis situation; how we say 'no' to a powerful person or authority figure; how we endanger our own job to defend our principles; how we confront a tricky situation with courage; and how we take personal responsibility for the failure of our juniors. Leaders need to possess a strong foundation of values that shape their integrity and character.

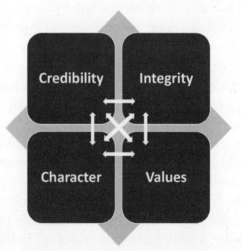

Figure 12.1: Interconnectedness of Credibility, Integrity, Character and Values

Example of Credibility in Leadership

Seetha, the CEO of a large IT services company still in its early days, wanted to build a culture of meritocracy that would lead to high levels of trust in the organization. She acknowledged the fact that, as a leader, she needs to demonstrate the right behaviours that promote trust. She started posting her annual goal sheet on the company's intranet. During the half-yearly review of the business, the CEO's accomplishments were visible to all employees. They could also see that their CEO was perhaps struggling with a few of the goals and had not been able to accomplish all of them. However, by making her goal sheet public and making herself vulnerable, Seetha was able to successfully demonstrate the management's commitment and credibility. Thus, she was able to build and enhance trust levels in the management–employee relationship.

Why Credibility Matters

Practically all the scriptures of various religions talk about the importance of credibility and reputation for leaders. For example, in Chapter 3, Verse 21 of the Bhagavad Gita, Lord Krishna speaks about the expectations placed on a leader:

यद्यदाचरतिश्रेष्ठस्तत्तदेवेतरो जनः |
स यत्प्रमाणं कुरुते लोकस्तदनुवर्तते || 21||

Meaning: 'Whatever a leader does, the masses follow; whatever standards he sets, his followers emulate them. This mass psychology applies to all facets of life.'[5]

Credible leaders are perceived as trustworthy; their intentions, words and actions carry weight; and their teams are more likely to follow their guidance and direction. This makes it easier for them to convey information, inspire others and foster collaboration to get positive business outcomes. Without leadership credibility, employees may merely comply with rules but won't actively work towards common goals or give their best effort. Needless to say, this invariably results in low morale and poor customer service, thereby causing depletion and stagnancy in business.

CEOs without integrity end up destroying businesses, as illustrated by cases like Enron, WorldCom and Satyam, where they misled their shareholders and brought about the demise of their companies.

Credibility is the most fragile of all leadership characteristics. A single act can risk the credibility of even the most celebrated leaders. Dominique Strauss-Kahn, the International Monetary Fund chief, had to resign over allegations of raping a hotel maid in New York in 2011.[6] Rajat Gupta, the former global head of McKinsey & Co., was jailed for two years over charges of insider trading. These are typical examples of indiscreet acts causing major upheavals in the reputations of individuals.[7]

Table 12.1: Characteristics of Credible Leaders

• Can be trusted to deliver on promises (walk the talk).
• Maintain high ethical standards with zero tolerance for unacceptable behaviour.
• Reflect on their thoughts and actions.
• Set an example through conduct, behaviour, courtesies and conversations.
• Are courageous enough to call a spade a spade.
• Are not afraid of losing position and power in defence of what is right.

Factors That Undermine Credibility

Certain negative tendencies such as incongruence (between words and actions), unethical behaviour, unfairness, poor self-management, risk-averse behaviour, fixed mindset and being unreliable or opaque can severely undermine our credibility.

The true measure of credibility for an individual as well as an organization would be meeting the best ethical values. That is when leaders are mindful of their behaviour and constantly reflect on it.

A Workout for Building Credibility

Credibility is undermined when we don't walk the talk, violate ethical standards or suffer from a serious behavioural dysfunction that affects our ability to solve problems objectively. Any aspiring leader must work very consciously to build credibility and reputation, even though sometimes it may not bring immediate or tangible outcomes. Following principles in a complex environment may require some well-intentioned compromises for the greater interest. However, leaders must navigate turbulent waters with great tact and understanding of the context. What's important is to build a reputation by constantly reflecting on your actions and taking responsibility when things go wrong.

1. **Discover Yourself**

    To be credible as a leader, you must be clear about the values and standards by which you choose to live your life. Your values guide your feelings, thoughts, words and the way decisions are made and acted upon. Discovering yourself requires intense work, a most difficult task (see Chapter 1 on Self-Awareness). Sometimes, it requires us to give up some of our most cherished notions about ourselves to discover the person we can become. This inner work should help align your values and actions, as well as alert you in case of any dissonance. Once you are clear about your values, translate them into a set of guiding principles, a credo that you can communicate to the people you lead.

    After all this hard work comes the real test. A leadership philosophy is not enough; you must have the competence to deliver on your promises, the will and the skill to prevail over adversity. Test your confidence against the realities of the challenge. **'To be a credible leader, you must have a character whose essential ingredients are credo, competence and confidence.'**[8]

2. **Lead by Example**

    Leaders succeed in achieving organizational goals by mobilizing and engaging the people who work for them and with them. They achieve this by providing substantive empowerment and support. Merely giving motivational talks while ignoring concerns or underplaying problems does not deliver results.

    One of the key factors that helped me effect a major turnaround for the bank was connecting with the field managers, their teams and the customers and listening intently to their concerns. I would discuss all the issues raised in my interactions with the top executive team and the functional heads to make appropriate decisions and implement them.

We all endeavoured to take decisive action and set right the internal management processes to fix problems without loss of time. This helped improve trust between the corporate office and the operating units, giving us superb business results and enhanced management credibility. Eventually, we could execute a host of technological initiatives to build customer and employee centricity. Finally, it helped us build an ecosystem for business innovation. The management's credibility and the high level of mutual trust among stakeholders enabled us to drive change and achieve extraordinary business outcomes.

3. **Deny Instant Gratification, Fulfil Promises**

Instant gratification may put you in the limelight temporarily and make you appear credible, but it can become stressful and impractical if everyone expects it all the time. Avoid the temptation to make promises out of excitement or to please others. Always consider the demands or requests others make, and say 'no' gracefully when necessary. Make sure to fulfil the promises made after careful consideration, and avoid coming up with excuses not to carry them out.

A busy CEO or leader can maintain a diary of assurances or promises made in order to initiate actions on the same.

My Experience Fulfilling a Promise

Sometime in 1996, I visited Agra in my capacity as zonal manager, Uttar Pradesh, and, in a customer meet,

I agreed to open a heritage branch near the Taj Mahal. Ten years later, about four months before my retirement, I visited Agra again. The customers reminded me of my promise. Although we had considered the suggestion at that time, we did not pursue it for operational reasons. I realized that the customers expected me to make good on that assurance now that I was CEO and had all the authority to make it happen.

In the last 100 days of my tenure, we managed to pull off this nearly impossible task. Four days before my retirement, I inaugurated the heritage branch at Agra as promised, because it was important for me to live up to my customers' expectations. It gave me and my team tremendous satisfaction to fulfil our customers' expectations.

Keeping promises helps uphold our credibility far more than we realize.

4. Develop Personal Discipline

Practise personal discipline, as it is critical to building credibility, whether in punctuality or being responsive. Leaders are expected to be role models, and if their actions, behaviours and decisions are at variance with their expected roles, it does not set the right tone or inspire others. Credible leaders must be sensitive to and reflective of their personal discipline (see Chapter 5 on Self-Discipline).

I remember working with a leader who was otherwise competent but was a very poor time manager, making people wait for hours, including customers. Despite many good qualities, he faced reputational loss on this count.

Experiencing a Very High Level of Credibility

In 2008, while on a short assignment with the Asian Institute of Management in Manila, Philippines, I sought an appointment to meet its then chairman, Washington SyCip. I reached his office and found the gentleman, then in his mid-eighties, waiting to receive me at 8 a.m. sharp. I later learnt that he had returned from New York at 2 a.m. that very morning.

I was amazed at that level of personal discipline, particularly at that age. Such leaders who lead from the front have the moral authority to head great organizations with credibility and charisma.

5. **Listen Before You Act**

Credible leaders lead with a sense of accountability. Listening is one of the most important aspects of developing one's own reputation. Listen to everyone around you, including those who may disagree, in an honest and open manner. Participate in dialogue-based conversations and decision-making processes (see Chapter 18 on Dialogue). Credible leaders actively listen before implementing the necessary changes. Listening well is invaluable for managing potential conflicts, swift problem-solving, improving teamwork, making tough decisions and abiding by principles. The enduring lesson here is to ensure that we are listening to our stakeholders, giving them space to air their challenges and taking appropriate actions expeditiously.

6. **Be Accountable for Problem-Solving**

Acknowledging errors, prompt problem-solving and responsiveness build or restore, as the case may be, trustworthiness and credibility. In their book *Credibility*, James M. Kouzes and Barry Z. Posner suggest the **Six As of Leadership Accountability** to build credibility: Accept, Admit, Apologize, Act, Amend and Attend.

Some years ago, we had gone for a family dinner in a restaurant at a leading five-star hotel in Mumbai. While placing the order, we requested a portion of vegetables without onions for my sister-in-law. When the food arrived, this dish was missing. When we pointed this out, the chef himself came to our table and accepted the mistake, apologized and then ensured that we got that dish quickly. As compensation, we were given dessert for the table at no additional cost. We left with a deeper sense of appreciation for this restaurant.

In this case, the chef practised the **Six As of leadership accountability**. He **accepted** and **admitted** his mistake, **apologized** and **acted** in the right manner to make **amends** and **attend** to us. This greatly enhanced the reputation of the restaurant and its staff. No wonder this restaurant is so popular.

Senior managers and leaders must have the fortitude to acknowledge their errors. Regardless of the hierarchy, owning up to mistakes always strengthens a leader's credibility. Credible leaders make the requisite systemic and procedural corrections and respond quickly. **It is absolutely necessary for senior management to demonstrate exemplary behaviour before it demands accountability from executives down below.** As per a famous quote attributed to Peter Drucker, 'The bottleneck is always at the top of the bottle.'[9]

If you take a principled position, your credibility not only gets enhanced before your seniors but, more importantly, before your subordinates. On issues of principles, if you are pliable or ever pleasing to authorities that matter, the chances are that you will lose credibility.

7. **Build Competence and Character**
   Finally, one must relentlessly work on building character and competencies, both behavioural and professional, because these are the keystones for credibility. Character, for instance, manifests in courageous initiatives to change the culture of the organization. To develop character, one must uphold a high standard of ethical behaviour and personal integrity, remain responsible by setting an example and operate within the broad contours of fairness and inclusivity (see Chapter 14 on Fairness). When Warren Buffett makes an investment decision, he looks for character over IQ, energy or initiative.

The other traits are important but without character, as Buffett would say, it's not a value investment.[10]

—Daaji—

To sum up, building credibility requires conducting your life in an ethical and transparent manner. It will also help build and sustain your personal and professional reputation. As you build your credibility, you will also be able to facilitate the credibility of your organization. Thus, credibility in leadership is a great responsibility and a great service to people.

Questions for Reflection

1. What are your key learnings from this chapter?
2. Create an action plan to develop and improve your credibility using the questions below.

3. How critical is credibility to leadership? What do you do to maintain it?
4. What are the areas where you expect your bosses and colleagues to be dependable?
5. Are you able to hold yourself accountable in those areas? What holds you back?

Chapter 13

Humility: A Differentiator for Leadership Effectiveness

A leader is best when people barely know he exists,
when his work is done, his aim fulfilled, they
will say, we did it ourselves.[1]

—Lao Tzu—

I remember the time, in the late 1980s, when I signed up for my PhD under N.R. Sheth, professor, IIM Ahmedabad. About a year after my registration, he assumed charge as director of the institute. Thereafter, I restricted my visits to him, assuming that he would not have time considering his new responsibilities, but how wrong I was! One day, I received a call from his secretary to meet him at 6 p.m. in his office.

I met him at the appointed time, and he walked to his campus bungalow with me. On the way, he inquired about the progress of my thesis and I shared my hesitation to meet him considering how busy he was. Hearing this, he stopped walking, put his arm on my shoulder and said, 'Anil, the day you registered for your PhD with me, I became a co-student in your research. Never hesitate; you can meet me whenever necessary to share the progress of your work and we can evaluate the same.' Hearing this, I was simply amazed at his humility and realized how wrong I was. Here was a director of India's most prestigious management institute, busy as he was, speaking to me in such a reassuring way. Being accustomed to a 'command-and-control' culture in my own organization, this experience impacted me for life, shaping my own leadership and interactions with people.

We live in a highly specialized, interdependent and ever-changing world, so what you may know today may become irrelevant tomorrow. In such a scenario, hierarchies have only marginal importance, so we need leaders to lead with humility and empathy, acknowledge their limitations and seek support from whoever knows best, without one-upmanship, condescension or insolence. It's in the best interests of the organization and of the leaders themselves. Arrogance can have no place in modern organizations, even though it may bring short-term results; over time, it is bound to be counterproductive to institution-building. Therefore, adopting a humble mindset can help leaders foster a culture of learning and growth and also bring out the best in their employees.

What Is Humility?

Humility is often misunderstood as being weak, ineffectual, meek or a pushover. But that's far from the truth. Humility is actually the state of being free from arrogance or pride; thus, it requires a mature world view and awareness of one's place in the larger scheme of things.

Humble leadership is characterized by a tendency to admit a mistake or not know something and a willingness to learn from others as well as share credit for others' contributions. That makes humility and courage complementary rather than contradictory qualities. As the famous quote goes, 'Humility is not thinking less of yourself, it's thinking of yourself less.' **The humble leadership style is shaped by self-awareness, respect for others and a focus on team spirit.**

Such leaders do not pretend, operate from an inflated sense of ego or abuse their authority to disparage. They openly ask for help, are willing to learn and genuinely reflect on feedback. Humility is a pathway to personal growth and, therefore, that of the organization.

Humility or its absence is always revealed by one's behaviour towards others, particularly our subordinates. Do you have a tendency to order them around or use threats to get work done?—'Do this!', 'Do that!' and 'Why isn't this done?' Or are you considerate and make them feel comfortable working for you—'I need your help; are you busy?', 'Can you please do this, too?', 'I know I am pressing you to do this, but feel free to reach out if you face problems', 'Do you need any additional help?' Humility is thus a sign of a good leader, while arrogance and narcissism (the biggest repellents of good ideas) are ingredients for hubris that can bring down an entire organization.

What Humility Is Not

Now that we've examined the idea of humility and the various ways it exhibits itself, it becomes a simple enough matter to consider what it is not:

- Treatment of a person based on their place in the hierarchy.
- A desire to push through one's own ideas.
- Refusal to consider others' views or feedback.
- Intolerance of mistakes.

To put it succinctly, those who do not value humility invariably appear to be self-important know-it-alls who consider positional power to be their authority to do as they will and exercise it unhesitatingly regardless of context. As in all areas of life, such people may end up occupying leadership positions, but they do themselves and their organizations great harm in the long run. Sooner or later, the truth will emerge.

Humility Is a Great Leadership Quality

In top roles, where the pressure to show business outcomes is high, there is a natural tendency among leaders to be aggressive and arrogant show-offs—qualities that are incompatible with humility.

However, in path-breaking research, Jim Collins, an author and mentor for leaders and CEOs, discovered that one of the leadership features of companies that become good to great over a long period of fifteen years was 'firm resolve and humility'.[2] He considers people with these traits to be **Level 5 Leaders**.

According to Collins, humble leaders are those who:

- Demonstrate a compelling modesty, shun public adulation and are never boastful.
- Act with a quiet, calm determination, primarily relying on inspired standards rather than charisma to motivate.
- Channel ambition into the company, not the self, and set up successors for even greater success.
- Look out the window to attribute credit for the company's success to other people, external factors and good luck.
- Look in the mirror and take full responsibility when things go poorly.

I would add the following: humble leaders **do not dismiss good ideas proposed by others** simply because they did not come up with them themselves. They also **encourage their subordinates to share adverse news** without hesitation or anxiety.

Clinical psychologist June Tangney has identified six intrapersonal aspects of humility: a willingness to see oneself truthfully, an accurate perception of one's place in the world, an ability to acknowledge one's mistakes and limitations, openness, low self-focus and appreciation of the value of all things.[3]

The greatest quality of a humble leader is to treat others with respect regardless of their hierarchical position. I remember way back in 1986, when my boss L.B. Bhide (four levels above me) and I co-authored a book, *Industrial Relations in Banks*.[4] One day, he called me to say, 'Anil, as my co-author, you have as much right as I have to change the drafts of chapters written by me.' This brought me a great deal of relief from the tension of working as a co-author with a top boss.

We come nearest to the great when we are great in humility.[5]

—Rabindranath Tagore—

Kinds of Humility

In my experience, humility shows itself in two ways: intellectual and behavioural.

Intellectual Humility involves recognizing one's intellectual limitations, including gaps and inaccuracies in knowledge. Leaders need to build intellectual humility and be willing to learn from anyone. Today, the youth, especially in the technological arena, have much to teach their seniors, who find it difficult to keep pace with changing technologies.

Behavioural Humility means treating every person with great respect and showing compassion in our behaviour. It is critical for fostering employee motivation. A leader's behaviour must manifest in attentive listening, manners and etiquette, empathy, and emotional intelligence. This absence can be fatal for building effective relationships.

In his book, *Humble Inquiry: The Gentle Art of Asking Instead of Telling*, Edgar H. Schein observed: 'All cultures dictate a minimum amount of respect required or the expected politeness and acknowledgement that adults owe to each other. We all acknowledge that as human beings we owe each other some basic respect. This is what is basic humility.'[6] The essence of Schein's observation is that it should be the **minimum expectation of every leader to be humble and respectful in his dealings** with employees and others—'the kind of question we ask, the way we ask, our tone, our gestures all put together'. Thus, **basic humility must be mandated in the organizational conduct rules**.

Care Health Insurance, with a consistent compound annual growth rate (CAGR) of 30 per cent despite tough competition, has a unique approach towards slow-performing branches. The founding MD and CEO, Anuj Gulati, shared with me his style of dealing with non-performing/slow-performing branches: 'I will go to a slow-performing branch, sit and work from there for a couple of days. Through my own style of working, I will demonstrate an alternative model for engaging people, both staff and customers, and how a climate for business growth can be created. I will put my arms around the manager and ask, How can I help?' His philosophy is manifested in his statement, 'Give respect and security to people. The brand is irrelevant without people. They are the ambassadors of my brand.' It is this conviction that drives his behavioural humility, one that realizes the value that the team brings to the business. His attrition level is 5 per cent compared to 30 per cent in the industry.

Table 13.1: Benefits of Humility in the Workplace

• Fosters a culture of collaboration and mutual respect.
• Builds a psychologically safe environment.
• Encourages a learning environment.
• Improves social cohesion and professional relationships.
• Increases overall psychological well-being.
• Improves relationships at work.
• Improves team performance and employee engagement.

Are Humility and Toughness Contradictory?

There is a misconception that humble leaders may not possess the mental fortitude to get work done and that employees may not listen to them. Humility and toughness are not opposite qualities; they can go hand in hand. As noted earlier, humility is being self-aware enough to know where you lack. However, excessive civility and/or humility are sometimes **misunderstood as meekness.**

In fact, there are occasions or contexts when tough actions are demanded from CEOs. Between 2002 and 2005, Bank of Baroda (a large public-sector bank) slid from its No. 1 position to No. 4. The board gave me the mandate to be tough in arresting the bank's slide and restoring it to its prime position without loss of time. Interestingly, the others in management and employees too volunteered to take up the challenge and took the pressure of work with enthusiasm. I had to be ruthless in ridding the bank of the influence of militant trade unions, who resisted the introduction of technology and created many hurdles. This was certainly not the time for humility, but for toughness. Even in those challenging times, we ensured our toughness lacked arrogance and vengeful intent.

Those who build up others without worrying that it makes them look weak are the real institution builders. Their down-to-earth attitude, their willingness to listen to others and to share credit, and their respect for others are all hallmarks of humility. Such leaders are highly valued, for they place the greater good of the organization above themselves.

A Workout for Developing Humility

Can humility be developed? The answer is YES. In fact, managers can be trained in humility. Many Indian companies, especially in the hospitality and service industries, make use of psychometric testing to measure the humility index of their new entrants and work on developing positive interpersonal skills, including humility.

In fact, humble behaviour in hospitality and service has a strategic advantage because it is critical for business sustenance. Many other industries are slowly realizing the importance of having humble individuals who represent the company and are beginning to invest in training their people to become humbler.

Humility, like any other skill, can be developed with determined effort. Here are some steps to build humility:

1. **Deflate Your Ego**

   Don't allow a sense of superiority or power to influence you. Instead, reflect on your weaknesses and be honest about them.

   Former US Navy SEAL Jocko Willink discusses how young troopers are often assigned tasks that exceed their expertise or experience, leading to their inevitable failure, especially if they act with overconfidence.[7] Failure humbles them, deflating their egos and a false sense of power at having received the assignment. At this point, they become more willing to learn. This process not only teaches them humility but also fosters resilience in the troopers.

2. **Practise Etiquette and Display a Learning Attitude**

   Being dignified, courteous and respectful towards everyone, irrespective of their hierarchical position, and acknowledging and thanking others for a job well done are all examples of humility in practice. It demonstrates to others that we respect them, which can boost their self-esteem.

   Always show a willingness to listen, learn, acknowledge mistakes, ask others for help and respect others' viewpoints. Accept feedback on how you can improve yourself. Humility is not just admitting your shortcomings but actively seeking to overcome them. It is about a general readiness to learn best practices from others and from your own failures. Therefore, it is intrinsically related to learning and teachability—a way of being that embraces constant self-correction and self-improvement.

3. Tame Your Temper

Competence, skills or seniority should not become the source of impulsiveness, arrogance and ill temper. In meetings and professional interactions, avoid being the first to contribute, and instead listen with respect, gain new perspectives and be a part of problem-solving; engage in dialogues instead of debates and be respectful towards all.

Ill temper is the biggest stumbling block in building any worthwhile relationship on the job and is a huge barrier to building motivation and engagement among team members. It shuts the door to any creative contribution by the people we work with.

The high-profile CEO of a major global consulting firm lost out on being re-elected purely on account of his mercurial behaviour, arrogance and rage in dealing with colleagues. Instead, the partners chose a person known to be even-tempered and humble to lead them.

4. Share the Glory

This ensures the team is put first during times of success and gives credit where it is due, but it also means taking the fall and defending the team for failures. A simple act of appreciation in a public forum can do wonders for the team's morale, and they will love the leader for it.

Humble leaders do not grab the limelight; rather, they lead from behind. They graciously acknowledge the team's contribution to their success. As Isaac Newton famously said, 'If I have seen further, it is because I have stood on the shoulders of giants.'[8]

5. Find a Mentor

In the case of severe problems that inhibit humble behaviour, it is a good idea to seek expert help. Find a professional or speak to a mentor who will be honest enough to help you sort out your problems and understand what you need to change to set off on a journey of personal growth. Even a trusted friend with experience and maturity can help.

In summary, we can say that humility is not a sign of weakness but of strength. Great leaders often share their own vulnerabilities and mistakes, thus creating teachable moments. Such open sharing can make us more authentic and enable genuine interactions. This can facilitate a similar culture across the organization. Finally, the practice of humility will put us on guard against aggrandizement and hubris.

Let me end this chapter with these lines from Nelson Mandela's autobiography, *Long Walk to Freedom*, which show that leading from behind requires supreme humility: 'It is better to lead from behind and to put others in front, especially when you celebrate victory. You take the front line when there is danger. Then people will appreciate your leadership.'[9]

Questions for Reflection

1. What are your key learnings from this chapter?
2. Create an action plan to develop and improve your humility using the questions below.
3. Is humility a skill relevant in the workplace?
4. How critical is humility as a leadership skill to you?
5. Reflect on an episode of rudeness and arrogance that you experienced. How did it impact you and what have you learnt from it?

6. Has there been an occasion where somebody's humility impacted you? What aspect of their humility has inspired you?
7. What are the ways in which you can express humility and promote it among your team members?

Chapter 14

Fairness: Exercising Sensitivity in Delivering Organizational Justice

---

Being good is easy, what is difficult is being just.[1]

—Victor Hugo—

Fairness is the fulcrum of good leadership. Leaders who are perceived as fair can inspire loyalty, trust and commitment in employees. A leader who is considered unfair will have their decisions constantly scrutinized, and may end up with a disgruntled and disengaged workforce, which, in extreme cases, can lead to conflicts. A leader's fairness is manifested both in their day-to-day decisions about work allocation, recognition and assigning of enhanced responsibility, as well as in decisions regarding developmental opportunities and promotions for employees. The core of fairness lies in an unbiased and transparent approach in these areas.

In all human processes, however, crafted in a meritocratic system, there is always an element of subjectivity. Therefore, it's the leader's sensitivity and wise judgement that would be a real test of judging any process as fair or unfair.

The human tendency to act unilaterally, without accountability or using discretion inconsistently, often inflicts deep wounds and pain on those who are on the receiving end of this in the workplace, eventually resulting in resentment, bitterness, a lack of motivation and productivity and finally, changing jobs.

Sometimes, even with the best of intentions, leaders face situations where the organization is not fair to its employees. So, they must come up with creative solutions to steer the organization back on course. Take the case of a CEO who was trying to build a fair and transparent culture of performance evaluation and feedback. As part of this exercise, she encouraged leaders at all levels to adhere to a carefully designed and instituted process for quarterly performance feedback sessions with all their direct reports, arranging safe spaces in the office for such conversations. However, despite several appeals, the process was not being followed with the necessary rigour and discipline. As a result, the CEO received regular feedback from the frontlines that the performance evaluation was unfair. This continued for a few quarters.

Eventually, in consultation with a behavioural science expert, she hit upon an idea. She put together a data analytics and visualization team that would work on the communications given by the leaders after their conversations with their team members and work groups every quarter to create a two-item survey for the whole organization.

The first question asked if their leaders/managers had a performance feedback conversation with them, and the second question was whether they considered the performance evaluation fair. The survey data was then published within the organization in the form of heat maps. Initially, there were a lot of red zones across the organization, but when the leaders saw this data being published every quarter, the majority of them altered their behaviour.

In less than a year, the CEO saw a significant part of the organization's heat map change from red to amber to green and began to receive more favourable feedback from the frontlines about the fairness of the performance evaluation system.

This is such an ingenious way of problem-solving and institutionalizing fairness and transparency across the organization. The heatmap conveys the message loud and clear—the importance of due process and the fairness of the leaders—resulting in an improvement over time. In fact, the publicization of the heatmap begins to serve as a mechanism for accountability as it affects the reputation of team leaders. This is an exemplary way to demonstrate leadership; the CEO did not lose sight of the core issue of fairness, thought outside the box for a solution to a persistent problem, and even managed to tackle the behavioural aspect of the team leaders in one move without any apparent conflict or bad blood.

What Is Fairness?

The concept of fairness has been debated across centuries and civilizations. Generally speaking, it is about treating everyone the same way, with impartiality and without discrimination. Philosophers from the time of Plato have described the different kinds of fairness that arise from different qualities or situations (see Table 14.1).

Table 14.1: Types of Fairness

Types of Fairness	Examples
Fairness based on acceptable standards	The same system of justice or an acceptable standard of what is considered right and wrong.

Types of Fairness	Examples
Fairness based on equal opportunity	Opportunity for employees to work on different jobs.
Fairness based on merit	Hard-working individuals succeed, while lazy ones lag behind.
Fairness based on need	A compassionate approach in special circumstances.

(Adapted from philosophers, Aristotle and Rawls, 1971)[2]

In the context of organizations, the concept of fairness for leadership relates to treating people **equally and with equity**.

Equality means treating everyone the same and giving them all the same level of opportunity, resources and support. Equality may not take into account people's circumstances or needs.

Equity recognizes that different individuals may require different kinds of opportunities, resources and support and offers them what they need so that everyone is dealt with fairly.

For example,

- Equality means that all employees get an opportunity for promotion. Equity means providing candidates from socially disadvantaged backgrounds with additional preparatory training for promotion.
- Equality means that the teacher teaches a subject to the entire class in the same way. Equity means that she holds extra classes for children with difficulty learning the subject.
- Equality means that an NGO provides basic farming equipment to each family. Equity means the NGO gives extra money or support to purchase seeds, fertilizers, etc. for families below the poverty line.

Although equality and equity are both important aspects of fairness, equality helps to give the message that everyone is equally important, whereas equity helps to create a level playing field by providing a helping hand to the disadvantaged. Thus, a leader may choose to relax some of the rules in the most extraordinary circumstances—a measure of compassion.

How Do We Know if We Are Fair Leaders?

A simple way to validate the fairness of our actions or decisions is to ask ourselves, 'If I were the employee, how would my work, my progress, my morale and my well-being be affected by such actions and decisions?'

Leadership expert Liane Davey mentions four factors—**outcomes, processes, equality and equity**—that a leader can consider while making decisions that affect his or her team.

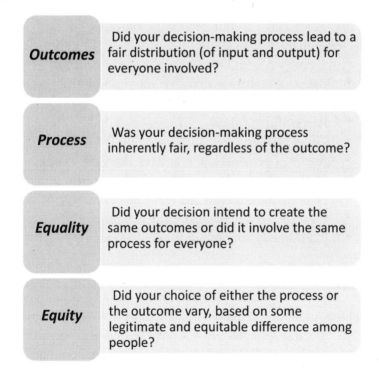

Outcomes	Did your decision-making process lead to a fair distribution (of input and output) for everyone involved?
Process	Was your decision-making process inherently fair, regardless of the outcome?
Equality	Did your decision intend to create the same outcomes or did it involve the same process for everyone?
Equity	Did your choice of either the process or the outcome vary, based on some legitimate and equitable difference among people?

Figure 14.1: Four Factors for Fairness

Davey adds,

> In addition to the fairness of the outcome, your team will
> be judging the fairness of your process . . . For example, if
> you were evaluating performance, did you include the right
> factors (such as measuring salespeople on both the total
> revenue and the profitability . . .). Was your assessment of
> the variables in your decision objective and unbiased (e.g., did
> you get input from multiple sources to reduce the likelihood
> of favouritism)? How you arrive at your decision will carry as
> much weight in how you are perceived as the decision you
> ultimately end up making.[3]

**The key insight here is that transparency always helps correct
perception biases.**
In my experience, a fair leader is expected to have the
following characteristics:

- Balances severity with discretion (proportionate action).
- Reflective about their own actions.
- Respectful to others.
- Good listener.
- Aware of personal biases and blind spots.
- Open to feedback, suggestions and corrective measures.
- Is disciplined, ethical and compassionate.
- Provides a psychologically safe environment.
- Concerned about the well-being of employees.

It is important to note that, in the name of fairness, leaders do
not lower the standards of performance or behaviour, tolerate
mistakes or insubordination, or be excessively nice. Instead, it
means that the workplace is not anxiety-ridden or stressful to
the extent that it takes a toll on the work or even the personal
well-being of employees. Fairness in the workplace has a

positive effect on employees' behaviour and is reflected in their attitudes, commitment, performance, personal motivation and job satisfaction. It improves the organization's reputation as well as team cohesion and productivity, leading to fewer conflicts.

Fairness is not just an attitude.
It's a professional skill that must be developed and exercised.[4]

—Brit Hume, American Journalist—

Process Fairness

While all four pillars of fairness—equity, equality, outcomes and processes—are important, people are less concerned with the outcomes of decisions than the process followed in the decision-making.

Process Fairness is concerned with the way decisions are taken or policies are framed. This is because the process itself should accommodate equity and equality. Process fairness also relates to employees' perceptions of how they are treated by their superiors, whether the culture in the organization is task-obsessive or exploitative, whether it considers the well-being of employees, and whether policies are made after considering people's opinions. Practising a **fair process also means creating a culture of listening, providing a decent work environment and being empathetic while dealing with employee problems.**

The concept of 'Fair process' was developed by Chan Kim and Renée Mauborgne, professors of strategy at INSEAD.[5] It converts execution into strategy by creating people's engagement upfront. People's trust and cooperation improve when a fair process is exercised during the strategy formulation phase. Employees trust that a level playing field exists, inspiring voluntary cooperation during the execution phase (the three principles of fair process).

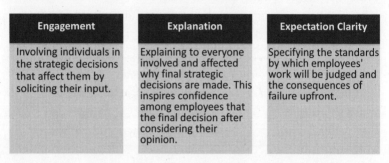

Engagement	Explanation	Expectation Clarity
Involving individuals in the strategic decisions that affect them by soliciting their input.	Explaining to everyone involved and affected why final strategic decisions are made. This inspires confidence among employees that the final decision after considering their opinion.	Specifying the standards by which employees' work will be judged and the consequences of failure upfront.

Figure 14.2: Principles of Fair Process

All executives across levels and functions must implement process fairness; they cannot expect HR alone to implement it. When managers and leaders realize this and implement it, their organizations will take a turn for the better.

Organizations benefit when employees perceive process fairness.

> When employees believe they are being treated fairly— when they feel heard, when they understand how and why important decisions are made, and when they believe they are respected—their companies will benefit. Research shows that practising 'process fairness' reduces legal costs from wrongful-termination suits, lowers employee turnover, helps generate support for new strategic initiatives, and fosters a culture that promotes innovation. What's more, it costs little financially to implement. Yet few companies practise it consistently.[6]

Process Fairness encompasses several distinct aspects of our organizational life. These include:

1. **Procedural Fairness:** Deals with the fairness of the procedures or processes used to make decisions.

When employees feel that decision-making processes are transparent, consistent and unbiased, they perceive procedural fairness. When a leader is perceived to be biased, it can be very demoralizing for employees and affect their productivity.

2. **Interpersonal Fairness:** Relates to how people are treated by others during interactions. It includes respectful communication, consideration and empathy. When individuals feel respected and heard, they experience interpersonal fairness and feel encouraged and motivated.

3. **Informational Fairness:** Focuses on the clarity and completeness of the information provided during decision-making. People perceive informational fairness when they understand the reasons behind decisions and their impact.

4. **Distributive Fairness:** Pertains to the fairness of outcomes or results. If the outcomes are perceived as unjust, even if the process is fair, overall fairness may be compromised.

Rajesh Srivastava, former CEO of J.K. Helene Curtis, shared with me his experience of ensuring process fairness:

'As head of a company, I would regularly visit the market to gain first-hand insights on how to grow the business. During these visits, I realized that our frontline staff had outstanding ideas. To benefit from this previously untapped source of ideas, I instituted a system inviting employees to share their ideas on how to grow the business. They responded enthusiastically.

'Their best ideas were shared with me after evaluation. However, I noticed that all the ideas were from the company's senior members and none from the frontline staff. This puzzled me because I believe that good ideas are not the monopoly of senior managers.

'A few months later, I once again invited ideas from employees, making some changes in the process this time. The ideas were to be sent directly to me. I had the name and gender of all contributors removed and used the letters of the alphabet to save the files instead. This would ensure that the panel would judge the pitches on the strength of the idea rather than the contributor's rank.

'What a significant change this made! In this round, the top two ideas were from frontline staff, the third from a female employee, and the next two ideas were from me and a member of senior management. When the results were made public, employees realized that the system in the company was fair and transparent and everyone's idea was evaluated on its own merit.'

Bottom line: Employees perceive a company as fair when it introduces a system to reduce, if not entirely eliminate, biases and prejudices. This also energizes them to work with renewed vigour and energy.

Creating a Psychologically Safe Workplace

Another dimension of creating a culture of fairness would be to provide a psychologically safe environment where employees and teams feel free to propose their ideas or contest a particular viewpoint in the greater interest of the organization. Such a culture can help unleash creativity in a greater number of people and mobilize their collective genius.

Creating a psychologically safe environment is sine qua non* in creating an ecosystem of fairness. An environment of psychological safety would mean that teams believe that it is okay to take risks, express their ideas and concerns, speak up with questions and admit to mistakes—all without fear of negative consequences. In short, it is the promotion of a culture of candour within communication in the organization. As organizations experience disruptions almost constantly, rapid transformation is the need of the hour. It is therefore critical to address the anxieties of employees in an open and supportive manner. In fact, employees should be encouraged to speak up about their apprehensions, and their concerns should be addressed with alacrity. Such a psychologically safe environment will enhance the team's performance, creativity, innovation and learning and facilitate the successful transformation of organizations.

Sustaining psychological safety would require consistent effort and a willingness to adapt. Regular assessments and surveys can provide insights into the effectiveness of psychological safety initiatives. Actively seeking feedback from employees and using it to refine practices can help the organization pursue its objectives in our ever-changing world.

Barriers to Fairness

While all leaders may aspire to be fair and believe they are, it may not be possible for them to do so at all times. According to the leadership experts at the US-based coaching company FranklinCovey, the reason for this is that human beings have created **stereotypes** and **unconscious biases,** whether known or unknown.[7]

---

* Something that is essential before you can achieve something else.

A **stereotype** is an assumption that everyone belonging to the group will behave the same way. It can be based on religion or caste, home town, upbringing, social status, the time when they were born, profession, etc. **Unconscious biases**, deeply ingrained in the subconscious mind, often stem from personal experiences. When we like or dislike a person in the first meeting without any logical reason, it is most likely rooted in some past experience, which created the subconscious bias in our mind.

Some commonly observed barriers are:

- Favouritism in employee career decisions and biases in assessment.
- Decision-making process is opaque and lacks transparency.
- Wrongful use of discretionary power and inconsistent application of rules.
- Absence of machinery to address issues of unfairness.
- Ambiguity about the accountability of individual behaviours in practising unfair styles.
- Lack of sensitivity and training for practising fairness.

All leaders are expected to follow the principles of fairness in dealing with employees, customers, business partners and others. They set the tone for their teams to practise fairness in their own interactions. The notion of power has to be understood in terms of the judicious and fair use of authority in the interest of the organization.

One good example of an institutionalized culture of fairness is seen in the way Ratan Tata handled investors with great sensitivity towards fair treatment after the famous scam by Dilip Pendse, CEO of Tata Finance (A Tata Group company). Pendse indulged in illegal transactions using investors' money for personal profits. Soon, the investments came crashing down, and many investors believed it was the end of the line for them. Ratan Tata, known for being trustworthy and ethical, decided to protect the interests of every depositor at Tata Finance. He arranged for nearly Rs 600 crore overnight and instructed his team to ensure that every depositor was compensated and their trust was maintained.[8]

A Workout for Developing Fairness

As with other qualities, consistent practice is key to developing fairness.

1. Practise Emotional Sensitivity

Leaders need to be perceptive to understand the anxieties of people who work with them. They must develop emotional sensitivity to make employees feel heard and understood. Take concrete steps to seek employees' opinions and suggestions before developing any major policy.

They must also develop an empathetic understanding of the problems faced by employees and take immediate steps to resolve them. Two key areas of HR policy—promotion and placement—often create major anxiety. Thus, the process of policy formulation and decision-making in these areas should be open, transparent and, wherever possible, consultative (in terms of seeking ideas).

In August 1995, I was appointed zonal manager of the Bank of Baroda (UP Western Zone), Meerut. This was my maiden assignment in operations after being in the HR and training function for around twenty-five years. I had 200 branches under my charge, and I had to supervise their business development and overall administration. The zone's growth had stagnated. Although short on operational experience, my strength was my human process sensitivity and an intense commitment to engage with the people in designing and pursuing a new future for the zone.

One of the main problems hindering growth in the big centres was the placement of managers in an ad hoc manner and the failure to link it with their performance or potential. I, therefore, undertook a selection exercise for thirty identified branches by interviewing the prospective candidates, and after considering their experience, past records and future, I appointed them to the identified branches. In these face-to-face interactions, I could assess their potential and communicate my expectations and support. All the identified managers were emotionally moved by my consulting them for their placement, which helped me make a very balanced decision. My belief in the power of an empathetic and consultative approach to the matter of decisions affecting managers was vindicated.

2. Own Your Biases

As human beings, we all have our biases. But as leaders, we need to reflect on our biases, own them and make sure not to let them cloud our judgement. This ensures that our decisions are more objective.

While considering the promotion of an executive who, in his earlier avatar as an activist for the officers' association, had actively opposed my policies, I had to consciously set aside that past experience and focus on his performance. This allowed me to be objective and sign off on his promotion. Many of my colleagues were surprised by my decision, including the candidate, who later revealed to me that he himself did not expect it because of our history.

3. Ensure Transparent Communication

Whenever there are any changes in policies, appraisal exercises, relocations, transfers or reassignment of roles or resources, we can make our intentions known, get ideas from people and integrate them into policies before implementing them. This will ensure that different viewpoints are considered to make the policy inclusive, equitable and fair to employees. Transparency in communications is key to building leadership; it displays authenticity and credibility (see Chapter 11 on Authenticity and Chapter 12 on Credibility).

4. Be a Fair Role Model

Leaders must be fair and equitable in their decisions, be open to feedback, initiate corrective steps and be accountable in their roles. Discretionary powers must be exercised prudently and responsibly rather than recklessly, as it creates perceptions of unfairness.

Institutionalizing Fairness

Leaders need to initiate several measures in their quest to build a culture of fairness, proactively manage the organizational fairness agenda and embed it into the policy framework. A CEO or a top-level functionary has the responsibility and power to do so.

Special provisions for the growth and representation of the disadvantaged, for instance, minorities, the handicapped, women, etc., demonstrate fairness. The government, from time to time, has formed commissions to protect the rights of such groups. For effective corporate governance, it is mandatory to have at least one woman as an independent director. At the organizational level, fairness can manifest in encompassing policies and practices like a transparent decision-making process, equitable compensation, inclusive policies, conflict-resolution procedures, mechanisms for employee voice, employee-support programmes, diversity, inclusion initiatives, corporate social responsibility, etc.

Institutionalized fairness helps build systemic reforms to bring about qualitative changes. At the organizational level, such a role is to be performed by the board and CEO. Frequent audits of the company culture and assessments of managers for fairness in their decisions help build a culture of fairness. Organizations should also install mechanisms for dealing with grievances relating to unfairness. There are statutory mechanisms in place, such as the Sexual Harassment at Workplace Act, 2013, the whistle-blower mechanism, the National Commission on Women, the National Commission on Scheduled Castes, the National Commission on Scheduled Tribes, etc. At the organizational level, a suitable mechanism for grievance redressal, especially to deal with cases of workplace unfairness, can help mitigate the issues relating to unfairness.

An Example of Institutionalized Fairness

In 2016, the Government of India launched several initiatives to reform the banking sector. One of the key initiatives to improve the CEO selection process in public-sector banks was to form the Banks Board Bureau (BBB). It comprised a representative of the Department of Financial Services (Secretary), a representative of the RBI (Deputy Governor), a representative of the Department of Public Enterprises (Secretary) and three independent members with expertise in banking and HR. The BBB was chaired by the former Comptroller and Auditor General (CAG) of India. I had the privilege of serving as an HR expert. To tackle the mounting criticism of perceived unfairness and political influencing in the CEO selection process, one of BBB's first decisions was to announce the list of successful candidates for CEO positions on its website immediately after the interviews were over. This decision restored confidence in the transparency of the selection process, thereby improving its credibility. Since then, this system has been maintained. This is an example of institutionalized fairness. **Likewise, there may be many areas where transparency in the decision-making process can help ensure a fair process.**

Here are some ways organizations can foster a culture of fairness.

1. **Diagnose the Current Culture**

    I have found that the starting point for any organization to build fairness is to first diagnose the current perceptions of fairness in the organization. Speaking to employees and customers can significantly help with this exercise. Such interactions not only help you connect with them on a more personal level, but they also help you identify the policies and styles contributing to such perceptions. They can reveal interesting and insightful data about the relevance of policies in the current context of multi-generational employees at the workplace, such as gaps in implementation, violations and audits of how discretions are used, and whether such discretions are applied with fair thought processes or through biases. Diagnosis should aid in the policy change process.

2. **Build an Ecosystem for Psychological Safety**

    It is possible to create a psychologically safe environment through good management practices. These include establishing clear norms of accountability at various levels to avoid attribution of blame at the lower levels in a hierarchical organization, encouraging open communication, actively listening to employees and ensuring that operating managers are supported and encouraged to speak in meetings and internal conferences about the problems they face. Overall, it should be clear that their voice is important and that asking questions is not impolite.

3. **Build Process Fairness**

    Maintaining clarity about processes and tying up their loose ends is critical to building process fairness.

Table 14.2: How Organizations Can Practise Process Fairness

1. **Clear communication:** Ensure that all processes, rules and criteria for decision-making are clearly communicated to all those involved.
2. **Consistency:** Consistently apply the same procedure and standards across all situations and individuals. Inconsistencies can lead to resentment and conflict.
3. **Inclusion:** Involve relevant stakeholders in the decision-making process whenever possible.
4. **Objective criteria:** Make decisions based on objective criteria rather than personal biases or favouritism, and establish clear metrics to evaluate the same.
5. **Appeal mechanisms:** Provide mechanisms for individuals to appeal decisions or raise concerns about perceived unfairness. This will help resolve issues in a constructive manner.
6. **Regular evaluation:** Periodically review and assess organizational processes to identify areas that need improvement.
7. **Lead by example:** As a leader, demonstrate fairness and integrity in your own actions and decisions.

By prioritizing process fairness, leaders can create a culture of trust, respect and collaboration within their organizations, leading to higher employee satisfaction, engagement and, ultimately, improved performance.

4. Train Managers in Process Sensitivity

Operating managers have a general tendency to blame their superiors for all their failures, despite their own contributions to problems. Every manager needs training in **Process Sensitivity** to understand their own role in improving the current processes.

Process sensitivity cannot be improved by a lecture; it requires a bouquet of training exposures, such as sensitivity training (popularly known as T-group),[9] role-play-based training and, in some cases, even counselling.[10] Sensitivity training can help us understand how we contribute to problems and learn about our biases, stereotypes, etc. It is highly recommended that HR staff give special focus to developing a culture of fairness in the organization and helping operating managers deal with such issues.

Process fairness can be a corporate value proposition. It needs cooperation and training from different verticals to ensure that managers and executives at all levels are not only sensitized but also made accountable for contributing to a culture of fairness.

5. **Promote Diversity and Inclusion**
   Organizations should take effective measures to build and support diversity and inclusion in the workplace. They must also create an environment where people from all backgrounds feel valued and respected by providing equal opportunities to everyone for promotions, transfers and placement policies. Organizations must establish strict policies against gender stereotyping and sexual harassment.

6. **Customer and Community Service**
   Fair treatment should be extended to customers as well. Corporates that prioritize customer care in their policy go out of their way to resolve customers' problems in a hassle-free way. They ensure this through suitable internal policies such as training, a zero-tolerance policy for delaying decisions and lack of responsiveness, inviting

customers' concerns and considering their views to catalyse major business changes. Corporates should also, as a matter of principle, demonstrate their commitment to fairness by actively engaging with local communities for social development. The Tata Group provides a fine example of fair practice in this area.

7. Maintain Management Credibility

Make sure to consistently implement the rules of behaviour and conduct to prevent accusations of unfairness. There cannot be two sets of rules for the same situation unless they account for specific exceptions in special circumstances. Rule violations by employees should be dealt with in the same manner, regardless of their place in the hierarchy.

In a large public-sector corporation where I served as an independent director, the association of officers complained to the board that the company refused them the use of the training college for their central committee meeting. However, the company allowed the use of the same facility for the engagement ceremony of the daughter of a senior HR executive. Such practices can create problems in building management credibility about fairness in implementing any policy.

In summary, being fair is one of the burdens of leadership. It is a legitimate expectation from those who steer the organization. A system that ensures fair treatment and dealings for all should be a cherished goal. The leadership must communicate transparently, learn from employee feedback, take corrective action, continuously train managers and, in extreme cases, take strict action against the delinquent, irrespective of their rank. This will help build a culture of fairness, which needs to be a critical corporate mission.

Questions for Reflection

1. What are your key learnings from this chapter?
2. Create an action plan to develop and improve your fairness using the questions below.
3. Reflect on occasions when you felt unfairly treated at work:
    a. What lessons did you draw from that experience?
    b. What steps have you taken to protect yourself/your interests?
4. Take some time to reflect on your own prejudices at work. Do you think they stop you from acting fairly?
5. What barriers do you face in practising fairness?
6. Does unfair treatment of your colleagues upset you? How do you respond?

Section 4

Communication and Conversation

Section 4

Communication and Computation

Chapter 15

Communication: A Keystone for Impactful Leadership

---

*The single biggest problem in communication
is the illusion that it has taken place.*[1]

—George Bernard Shaw—

Communication is the **reason** and **essence** of our existence. As we essay various roles in our personal and professional lives—children, parents, siblings, friends, colleagues, juniors, seniors, leaders or 'freshers'—we constantly communicate to articulate our desires and aspirations, values and principles, as well as our emotions, whether our sense of fulfilment and joy or our frustration, worries and concerns. Effective leaders must excel at communicating up and down, horizontally and laterally across the hierarchical ladder, with bosses, colleagues, employees, customers, vendors, investors, regulators and a wide range of other stakeholders. **While traits such as a strong intellectual foundation and credibility are crucial for leaders, it is communication skills that hold the key to a leader's**

success. Poor communicators cannot become effective leaders because they are unable to connect with the people they lead.

What Is Communication?

Communication is the way we express ourselves to build understanding and engagement. It is as important for mental and emotional make-up as nourishment is for the physical body. In *Humble Inquiry*, Edgar H. Schein explains the ways in which we communicate, '. . . we communicate not only through the spoken and written word but through facial expressions, gestures, physical posture, tone of voice, timing of when we speak, what we do not say, and so on . . . there are deeper and less observable processes.'[2]

Effective communication can boost morale and encourage goodwill and cooperation. It can be the single most effective skill to harmonize, enhance and extend the life of relationships. It is one of the most critical skills for leaders to strengthen their connection with their teams, colleagues and bosses. Leaders with good communication skills invariably impress, inspire and persuade their team members to achieve common goals. At a personal level, it can win hearts, uplift sentiments, mobilize people, promote initiatives and encourage people to engage with higher-order purposes.

Communication is the driving force behind professional success and the well-being of the organization and its stakeholders. It is therefore imperative that leaders—in fact, all employees—acquire extraordinary communication skills to promote understanding and motivation. Effective communication leads to a whole bouquet of important professional outcomes.

Effective Communication	Ineffective Communication
• Invites attention and action • Encourages and mobilizes employees • Counsels and coaches team members • Promotes initiative • Persuades and seeks engagement	• Repels attention and action • Discourages and paralyses employees • Misguides and diminishes team members • Kills the spirit of initiative • Diminishes the spirit and creates disinterest

Figure 15.1: The Impact of Communication on Stakeholders

Communication is not just the exchange or transfer of information from one person to another or smart oratory; it is an integrated effort to foster understanding, engagement and inclusion, and align the vision of leaders and their teams. And it goes far beyond the style and craft of speaking; it is, in fact, a kind of intelligence about yourself, your context and your audience. The process of effective communication is anything but simple.

Yet, most people have a very narrow idea of what communication is. Communication is not

- smart talking
- sermonizing, condescending, nitpicking or criticizing
- a monologue that gives the other persons no space to express themselves
- 'telling' or creating compulsions of 'should do/must do'
- glib talking or manipulation
- making empty promises just to impress others

Communicating in this manner can have an absolutely negative impact on leaders' relationships, cast them in an adverse light and lead to much pain and mayhem for them as well as the organization. On the other hand, good communication has far-reaching impacts on the leader and the organization (see Figure 15.2), and we can see that when used effectively, such communication can generate very valuable outcomes. Therefore, we must use communication with care and sensitivity, as it is an extremely powerful tool.

It is for this reason that communication skills are globally emphasized, and one can see numerous executive development programmes by leading business schools on developing communication skills.

Figure 15.2: Impact of Effective Communication
on the Organization

(Adapted from behaviour experts, Schein [1983][3] and Rosenberg [2015][4])

Communication Is the Salt of Leadership Effectiveness

Winston Churchill noted that 'the difference between mere management and leadership is communication'. I doubt if there are truer words about the connection between the two. Competence without good communication skills has little utility, as it fails to inspire, motivate or connect us with the people we work with. Leaders need to be great communicators because that is how they articulate and execute their vision.

It is imperative that leaders build shared understanding with their team members in such a manner that their precise purpose and goals are understood at various levels. This is true for any leader, whether a surgeon performing an operation with a team of doctors and nurses, a coach of any sport or a teacher.

I remember some great teachers not only for their knowledge but also for their teaching skills, which were essentially a combination of effective communication (delivery), persuasion, encouragement, passion, empathy and feedback that made sure that each student in the class learnt well. I remember one of my teachers always saying, 'If the student has not learnt, I have failed to teach.'

In my corporate experience, I came to realize that in 90 per cent of cases of conflicts and misunderstandings, the main issue has been deficit communication. How many times have we heard bosses who are in the habit of insulting their subordinates say, 'But I never meant it!' Obviously, such bosses are insensitive to others and driven by their positional power. In such cases, there is a breakdown of communication, and they fail to inspire and lead their people.

Proper communication and action can save many situations from taking an ugly turn and can contribute to substantially improving the motivation and morale of individuals or groups. That's why communication is the responsibility of every manager and leader.

'**Effective communication provides a glue to create alignment between management and employees, and its importance can never be underrated.**'[5]

Great leaders use effective communication to drive change, resolve issues and mobilize people to achieve organizational purposes and goals. Over the centuries, such leaders have uplifted spirits, inspiring their teams and other stakeholders through their communication skills. They have transmitted their ideas, ideologies and lofty visions through powerful words. Great revolutions and reforms of the past and even the present have been propelled by how leaders communicate. Take, for instance, figures such as Swami Vivekananda, Mahatma Gandhi, Martin Luther King Jr, Winston Churchill and Abraham Lincoln, who mobilized the masses through effective communication skills laced with authenticity and courage. In more recent times, Apple's Steve Jobs and Microsoft's Satya Nadella have been effective communicators in the corporate sector.

Why Managers Fail to Communicate

Research has revealed that communication fails mostly because of personality flaws. One of *Harvard Business Review's* classic article 'Barriers and Gateways to Communication' by American psychologist Carl R. Rogers and social scientist and management theorist F.J. Roethlisberger deals with the following:[6]

1. **The natural urge to judge, evaluate and approve (or disapprove) another person's statement** from a personal viewpoint blocks interpersonal communication. Real communication is about avoiding this evaluative tendency and listening with understanding.
2. **Emotional states (anger, fear, sadness) and attitudes (being right all the time, egoistic orientation)** create biases in our minds about others.

3. **Lack of respect for the other person,** particularly towards adversaries and authority figures.

Thus, it is clear that one's emotions, behaviour and personality flaws influence the effectiveness of communication.

Effective communication is also crucial in two related aspects. What makes communication impactful is the **context, the situation and the people involved**. Sometimes, even the best speakers fail to deliver as they stray into domains other than the immediate context.

I remember attending a book release in which the chief guest, instead of speaking about the book—the immediate context—discussed at great length the international economic scenario, frustrating the author and the audience, both of whom expected the book to be discussed.

The other aspect to remember is that your **communication style** must be flexible and adaptable to the group. For close relationships, such as family, the communication style would be reassuring, supportive, comforting, problem-solving and hands-on, requiring attentive listening. For friends, it can be easy, casual, warm and authentic. For professional circles and social media, the style will be different based on desired outcomes (see Table 15.1).

Table 15.1: Appropriate Patterns of Communication

Context	Communication Style
Bosses	<ul><li>Articulating for goal achievement</li><li>Seeking support for positive outcomes</li><li>Giving assurance for results</li><li>Building confidence and trust</li></ul>

Context	Communication Style
Subordinates	• Persuasive, reassuring and supportive • Building credibility and trust • Tough love • Listening
Customers	• Listening • Exploring • Empathetic • Problem-solving
Social media	• Maintaining gravitas, sobriety • Sense of proportion • Avoiding controversies • Mature and dignified response

A Workout for Developing Communication Skills

Leadership and effective communication skills are inseparable. Impactful communication can build and strengthen relationships, revive morale, provide motivation, improve engagement, and accelerate change and transformation for the general good. Considering the strategic role of communication in leadership, it is essential for leaders to be sensitive to contexts and exercise a variety of suitable communication styles.

There are two broad dimensions of impactful communication that must work synergistically. The first is the **emotional** aspect, which relates to your self-awareness, self-management and reflection. The second is **cognitive,** which relates to skills in communication, such as linguistic ability, public speaking, oratory style and impact-making ability.

Communication works for those who work on it.[7]

—John Powell—

---

1. **Articulate Purpose through an Emotional Call**
    Communication is impactful when leaders are able to articulate the larger purpose of architecting change and transformation that will benefit all their stakeholders and contribute to improvement in organizational health. To create such an impact, communication has to be clear, precise and focused; it cannot be confusing or ambiguous. Such skills require a very strong emotional self and its expression in situations of dilemma, confusion and crisis. Thus, such a skill goes **beyond mere linguistic capability;** rather, its **foundations are deeply embedded in your effort towards personal growth**. In other words, it relies heavily on the following traits of your personality:
    *   **Values and principles:** Whether and how you adhere to your personal code of conduct.
    *   **Self-awareness and emotional regulation:** Whether you can put your emotions aside to make decisions or if they play a part in your decision-making process.
    *   **Understanding:** Whether you listen actively and empathetically, and ask questions from your ego or with humility.

- **Authenticity and credibility:** Whether you practise openness and transparency, whether you try to reduce the 'saying–doing' gap.

2. Work on Your Language Skills

The cognitive skills have two aspects, or dimensions: **linguistic command** and **conversational competence**. The topic of conversational competence is elaborately dealt with in Chapters 17 and 18. In the description below, we are mainly discussing aspects relating to building linguistic excellence.

a. Read

Reading helps improve comprehension and eventually your communication style. Do you read? If yes, what do you read? How do you retain the knowledge gained from reading books or articles and how do you put it to use? Pay attention to the presentation of the reading material; it can help teach different styles of communication and thus shape your own communication style. Reading books and articles beyond your area of specialization will broaden your perspective on various issues. I hugely benefit from reading bestsellers on leadership and technology, as well as autobiographies of great political and business leaders. It sharpens my thought process and challenges me to examine issues from different perspectives.

Even during my busy executive days, I always spared time to visit bookshops on a Sunday afternoon to check out the new arrivals in management, turnaround and transformational leadership and books on the future.

I also subscribed to *Harvard Business Review*. All this significantly helped shape my world view and improve my communication skills. I believe that the depth of our knowledge enhances our communication and conversational skills.

b. Listen

Language is a powerful tool through which leaders can effectively articulate their vision to motivate and engage others. Today, we can connect with a variety of channels of learning, from podcasts and audiobooks to blogs, webzines and apps. We have an entire library on our mobile phones. Google Search alone offers the best articles, speeches and ideas across the globe from top experts. As with reading, pay attention to not only the content but also the manner. Listen not just to *what* they say but also to *how* they say it, how they present their arguments and how they persuade people of their point of view. This has greatly improved my linguistic ability. It has also helped me understand the nuances of words, as well as the appropriate contextual and cultural usage.

c. Review Your Communication Style

Write down your experiences with communication throughout the day and return to them later to see if you were able to communicate effectively. Identify what needs to be improved and work on it. You can reflect on the communication style you use in different contexts and its effectiveness. You can review, reflect and discern the deviations from the appropriate patterns and work on improving them. Disciplined ways of learning can help improve one's communication skills.

d. Build Conversational Skills

Great conversationalists show sensitivity to the context, the audience and the subject. (Of course, they also need to know their subject well.) They express their point of view with grace and candour, and they listen respectfully to others' viewpoints. They aren't domineering, aggressively assertive or dismissive of other points of view—such behaviour can lead to destructive outcomes. We can learn a lot by observing good conversationalists and then working on ourselves. Another way is to talk with peers or mentors with good command over language.

My Experiments with Building Communication Skills

We did not speak English at home, and I learnt the English alphabet at the age of ten, in the sixth grade. It was tough, but I managed to navigate the language through determination and discipline. As a child, I made it a habit early on to highlight new words or a well-articulated story and immediately copy them in a diary. The practice has continued to this day, and I now have a cupboard full of such notebooks and diaries. I love reading books on psychology and leadership by some great authors like Doris Goodwin, Warren Bennis, Edgar Schein, Daniel Goleman, Peter Senge, etc. and pay close attention to their skilful presentation of ideas. I also carefully follow editorials and insightful articles in newspapers and magazines. And while writing my own notes, speeches and letters, I always have a dictionary and a thesaurus at hand to check the appropriateness of a word. This lifelong habit has helped me build a reasonably good vocabulary.

Over the years, I have, through trial and error, learnt to communicate confidently. I can speak with ease, in professional or personal contexts to small and large audiences, including Indians and foreigners. I've also developed my own communication style by liberally using appropriate metaphors to articulate a certain point. My tendency to link an issue with the relevant context and build a connection with ground realities through metaphors has earned me the sobriquet 'One-liner expert on everything'. For example, I often describe an Indian customer as someone 'dying of pain' (कस्ट-मर - जो कष्ट से मर रहा है).

3   Speak Up and Be Responsive

A leader must develop the habit of speaking up in the right forum at the right time and expressing their viewpoints and ideas with great clarity, even if they may not be appreciated.

Similarly, respond to all communication, whether oral or written. Responsiveness is integral to good communication and the hallmark of great leaders. A lack of responsiveness indicates an uncaring attitude and is a bad communication practice.

4.   Appreciate and Respect Good Work

Effective leaders respect and recognize good work liberally, but also genuinely show their appreciation. This boosts morale and motivates employees to raise the performance bar. Leaders who are parsimonious in their appreciation of good work struggle to build motivated teams. Moreover, unappreciated employees can feel undervalued and withdraw their commitment.

Small gestures of appreciation, such as a handwritten note or public acknowledgement, go a long way in building a highly motivated team. A smile, an appreciative nod, a firm handshake or a pat on the back extend the impact of communication beyond words.

Being courteous at all times—thanking people when they help us and apologizing when we are wrong or have hurt others—can help make communication genuine. How often do we thank a lift attendant or domestic helper? Or, for that matter, any person who facilitates smooth daily living.

5. **Communicate Effectively and Safely on Social Media**
Social media can be a powerful way to reach out to people. You can use it to network, build relationships with customers and stakeholders, acquire talent, manage crises, build reputations, share knowledge, etc. Your options are endless! Using social media as a communication tool with employees can offer several benefits, such as fostering better internal communication, engagement and collaboration.

However, indiscriminate and undisciplined use of social media can waste time and even put you at risk. Be particularly mindful of your actions here, as they can have strong, real-world repercussions! Posting anything on social media can potentially have a lasting impact on your reputation and personal or professional life. Be cautious, considerate and proactive, and you can navigate social media with confidence while minimizing risks.

Here are a few guidelines:

- Moderate your involvement and temper your responses at all times, but especially so in times of social or political crisis. Try to avoid extreme opinions, excessive criticism, offensive language and arguments, as these usually backfire.
- Always respond to negative feedback and comments with professionalism and empathy. Avoid being defensive and confrontational.
- Fact-check and verify the content before posting it, as misinformation can have damaging effects.
- Do some research to determine the frequency of your posts and tags. Posting and tagging in the hope of achieving a wider reach can annoy people and be counterproductive.
- To ensure safety, check privacy settings, verify profiles and intentions before accepting friend requests, and avoid clicking unverified links claiming to give you rewards and offers. This is particularly important if you're managing official handles.
- Finally, before venting your frustrations against your company or the government, check your company's policy on social media use.

Red Flags That Derail Communication

Being unresponsive, inconsistent, defensive, unfair, toxic, condescending and procrastinating in the communication process can result in disruptions in interpersonal relations, team spirit, engagement and collaborative working. To communicate effectively, we must be open, responsive, engaging, empathetic and positive even when there are problems; we don't need to be disagreeable to disagree.

Building a Culture of Communication

Leaders, especially at the higher levels, must nurture a culture of positive communication across the organization to encourage creative contribution and teamwork. They should set an example in this regard through symbolic actions such as acknowledging the new ideas and suggestions received from them during town hall meetings or through direct interactions. For example, at Bank of Baroda, we had an internal portal—ideaonline@bankofbaroda.com to facilitate the flow of creative ideas from employees at all levels. The employees got an immediate response based on how far the idea was found fit for implementation. It created an environment in which, irrespective of hierarchical level, the employees were listened to, and feedback from top management created a culture of communication across the organization.

The red flags discussed earlier can create an unfavourable environment for healthy communication. It is important that leaders institute measures to eliminate such dysfunctionality from the organizational culture.

One of the key roles of a leader is to create a facilitative culture at work to engage stakeholders. More particularly, The employees are the main lever for delivering positive business outcomes. This can be best achieved by building a positive communication culture that promotes openness, transparency, collaboration, autonomy and entrepreneurship.

1. **Build a Culture of Responsiveness and Accountability**
   Responsiveness is an amazing way to build authentic and credible interpersonal relationships. Unresponsive people (and organizations) come across as lackadaisical, arrogant

and uncaring. Only if we are responsive can we expect the same from others. A culture of responsiveness helps stakeholders engage with the organization and contribute to its success. Suggestions and feedback put leaders and organizations in touch with reality and help us review and rework our habitual mode of operating. This is why responsiveness is essential.

Leaders should therefore place a clear and unambiguous emphasis on responding to stakeholders' concerns as a matter of duty. More importantly, they should respond in a timely manner and help resolve the issues rather than pass the buck. They should also set up an institutionalized culture of responsiveness and assign accountability for it. A good way would be to develop a measurement mechanism, such as a responsiveness audit.

2. Create an Empathetic Ecosystem

Communicate with empathy, especially when dealing with feelings of hurt and let-down as a result of organizational policies. This can be a game changer, fostering better morale and engagement. Here's a famous example. Sudha Murty, chairperson of Infosys Foundation, describes that while applying for a technical job at TELCO in Pune, she was frustrated by this stipulation, 'lady candidates need not apply', in the job advertisement. Disturbed by this, she dashed off a postcard to none other than J.R.D. Tata. She received a telegram in less than ten days asking her to attend the job interview. Mrs Murty secured the job, and to this day, she describes the experience of working at TELCO and interacting with Tata with great fondness. This is a beautiful example of how a great leader like Tata responded with humility to a job applicant and took decisive action for policy change.[8]

3. Be Responsive

As much as possible, try to address communications directly addressed to you. Often, we receive letters from employees and customers that express hurt, disappointment, feel discrimination or accuse us of wrongful behaviour. When we ignore such communication, our team members may feel disregarded and thus disengaged. Paying equal attention to such communication alongside business matters yields remarkable results.

Employees of Bank of Baroda still recall my timely responses to every single letter, email or call I received from them, as it made them feel heard and cared for. When you respond to employees' concerns, they positively reciprocate in a variety of ways and their commitment to the organization is reinforced.

My Experience Responding Personally with Empathy

Every appraisal and promotion exercise brings some degree of frustration to those who are not able to make the grade. During one such instance, a senior manager wrote to me about his dejection over not being promoted despite his good performance. As per my working style, I decided to respond to this communication instead of marking it for HR. In my email response, I empathized with his feelings by sharing how I felt the same way on an occasion when I was not promoted. I also mentioned that while I acknowledged his good performance, the interview panel assessed the performance of each candidate among the competing basket of candidates and a fair judgement was made.

To this, he replied, 'Sir, your prompt response has reassured me of my capabilities and greatly boosted my morale. In the first place, I just offloaded my emotions without expecting a response to an emotive issue. Your communication has dissolved my frustration and I assure you of my unflinching commitment to the organization. In fact, it will help me work harder.'

Responding to employees' and customers' problems with empathy builds trust and understanding.

4. Use Informal Communication

A powerful way to reach out to people is through informal communication. Stiff formality with our own people does not help. Set a tone for being accessible and keep the hierarchy barriers to a minimum. My boss, the late S.P. Talwar, former chairman, Bank of Baroda, charmed and motivated everyone through his informal communication style. He showed a sense of urgency, not through official memos but through face-to-face communication. He reached out directly to operating managers, even several levels below him, to inquire about the business potential of the areas under their charge and to solve the problems. I once received a thank you note signed by him appreciating my contribution to building the management information system (MIS) for executives. This electrified me and boosted my morale.

In summary, effective communication ability means knowing what to say, when to say it and how to say it with grace and dignity. The essence of communication is developing understanding and acting with empathy. It would also mean being responsive all the time, listening actively and removing bottlenecks in the way of an open and transparent culture for communication. It remains the main lever for reaching out to people and attaining organizational goals.

Questions for Reflection

1. What are your key learnings from this chapter?
2. Create an action plan to develop and improve your communication skills using the questions below.
3. Think of a boss or a colleague you consider a good communicator. What do you appreciate about their communication skills?
4. Think of a boss or a colleague you consider a poor communicator. How did it impact you and the workplace?
5. What are the things you care about most in communication?

Chapter 16

Listening to Attend, Absorb and Act

Listen a hundred times, ponder a thousand times, speak once.[1]

—Kurdish Proverb—

It's a story we have all heard before, over and over. Parents complain that their children do not listen, while children have the same complaint about their parents; bosses complain about their subordinates, and subordinates complain about their bosses. We often hear the disgruntled public complaining about civil servants and politicians not listening. Nobody seems to listen. Our problems fall on deaf ears. It's a problem that besets society at large.

In my executive life, interacting with customers, employees and other stakeholders and participating in meetings took up nearly 80 per cent of my time. The success of these interactions depended heavily on whether I was as engaged with listening attentively as I was with speaking. Whenever I listened more than I spoke, I received positive outcomes; the opposite held true as well.

Let me add that it is not easy to listen, especially when we are in a senior position with so many pressures and unannounced distractions. It requires utmost self-control, self-awareness, emotional regulation, empathy and disciplined practice to listen actively. The challenge, therefore, for leaders is to be conscious of these distractions and deal with them.

Listening by itself is a value that reveals a mind free of any prejudice or bias and shows respect for the other person. This does not mean that every person can be listened to every time they want to be heard. However, managers and leaders at all levels must make a sincere attempt to listen to individuals or groups (like town hall) and, whenever possible, seek their ideas and suggestions, listen to their grievances and show an open mind to take their feedback seriously.

Hearing versus Listening

The problem lies in the general understanding that listening is an act of hearing. Listening is not an empty formality but a fairly complex process, which noted psychologist Howard E. Gardner explains as a four-stage activity.

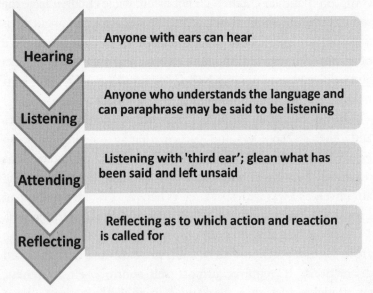

Figure 16.1: Decoding Listening

(Based on Howard Gardner's process of listening, Bennis)[2]

Listening, as a four-step process, involves making meaning of deeper messages behind the superficial ones and then acting on them. A leader must distinguish between the messages that require attention and those that can be ignored. According to Gardner, the essence of listening lies in Steps 3 and 4.

Step 3—Attending, requires the listener to go beyond Step 2 of what has been heard and paraphrased. It requires listening with the 'third ear', which means also hearing what was left unsaid. Peter Drucker notes, 'The most important thing about communication is hearing what isn't said.'[3] That is to say, we need to note the subtleties of body language, gestures, expressions and even silences to see the entire picture.

The last step in the process is to dwell on all you've learnt. It's not enough for a leader to be excellent at being attentive or present. To be truly effective, it is imperative to **reflect** on the messages they've received and think of the appropriate steps (words or actions) (see Chapter 2 on Reflection). What lends credibility to listening **is the action we take thereafter.**

Let's consider a situation where, in a departmental meeting, the manager is a bit taken aback when, one after another, the members talk about the problems hindering their work. For instance, lack of secretarial help, a culture of unequal workloads, overworking, procrastinating on key decisions and an unrelenting emphasis on meeting deadlines.

What is the underlying message? The message is that the employees are experiencing frustration because they feel no one listens to their problems, which has become a big bottleneck in achieving performance deadlines. As a manager, one needs to integrate **Step 3—Attending** and **Step 4—Reflecting,** to get to the root of the issue and create a suitable solution.

Experts in organizational behaviour, Robin Abrahams and Boris Groysberg, in their article 'How to Become a Better Listener', bring out **three aspects of listening** (see Figure 16.2) that support Gardner's four-stage process.[4]

COGNITIVE	EMOTIONAL	BEHAVIOURAL
Gather all information, explicit and implicit. Then understand and integrate it.	Stay calm and compassionate during the conversation. Do not let emotions drive the response.	Convey interest in and understanding of the situation verbally and non-verbally.

Figure 16.2: Three Aspects of Listening

Active or Attentive Listening is the biggest facilitator of building understanding and achieving common goals. It is all about deep involvement, dispassionate listening and truly understanding the listener. I'd like to add a critical dimension to this process: **taking action after listening**.

Why Listening Is Critical for Leaders

Strong listening skills are invaluable in both personal and professional contexts. By actively listening, we demonstrate respect, empathy and a willingness to truly comprehend others' perspectives. Developing and honing our listening skills can enhance our ability to collaborate, problem-solve and connect with others on a deeper level. It is a process that requires practice, patience and a commitment to continuous improvement. By prioritizing and cultivating our listening skills, we can become better communicators and contribute to more meaningful and fulfilling interactions in all aspects of our lives.

Listening is critical for every leader, as it impacts their effectiveness. **When leaders listen, their team feels valued, acknowledged and respected.** A listening leader inspires confidence in employees and creates passion, which invariably leads to exponential results. Throughout my career, I have come across many talented individuals who stunted their professional growth by ignoring sage advice and treading a self-destructive path.

A Lesson in Attentive Listening

The late Udai Pareek, senior professor at IIM Ahmedabad, is widely recognized as the father of human resource development (HRD) in India and highly regarded for his expertise in organizational behaviour. I had the good fortune to attend one of his programmes and asked several questions to clarify my understanding. He listened to me with great curiosity, as though he genuinely learnt from my questions, and even took notes. Later, during our interaction, he told me that he received new insights based on my executive experience.

This was an uplifting and transformational experience for me. Here was the 'Father of HRD in India', a globally recognized name in his field, listening so intently to my points. I was amazed by his attentive listening. It left me with a strong desire to follow in his footsteps.

Listening is crucial for leaders because it plays a significant role in building strong relationships and effective communication within a team or organization. Considering its impact on performance, we cannot afford to ignore listening.

My Experience with Listening

In 2005, I took over as CEO of Bank of Baroda. At the time, my challenge was to restore the bank to its prime position. But how was I to do it? I sat down with my top team to work out the strategies. I decided to listen to our two main stakeholders, our customers and employees, through several town halls to get to the root of the problems.

I faithfully listened to their concerns at the town halls, then discussed the issues at our corporate office and implemented redressal strategies. The problems were wide-ranging, from concerns over our product designs to delays in the delivery of decisions to issues with HR.

I didn't want this to be a one-time act of listening but a continuous process, so we set up two direct helplines to the CEO—one for employees and the other for customers. The rest is history. We resurrected the tempo and doubled the business in just three years.

How did this happen? We listened and continued to listen empathetically, then initiated corrective measures with alacrity and speed. The experience helped me understand field perspectives and earn the trust of my people.

Based on this experience, I concluded that listening helps corporate leaders in a variety of ways:

1. **Facilitates Insight and Effectiveness:** By listening attentively, leaders gain a deeper understanding of their team members' needs, perspectives and challenges. This helps them make informed decisions, provide appropriate support and effectively address concerns. It also helps leaders tailor their communication and leadership approach to align with individual and team requirements.

2. **Builds Trust:** When leaders actively listen, it demonstrates that they value the opinions, ideas and concerns expressed by the team. This helps build trust and, in turn, enhances collaboration, engagement and productivity.

3. **Improves Relationships:** Listening allows leaders to develop empathy and connect with their team members on a personal level. When leaders listen empathetically, they can identify emotions, concerns and underlying issues. This enables them to provide the necessary support, guidance and encouragement, leading to stronger relationships and increased morale.

4. **Promotes Problem-Solving and Innovation:** Effective listening fosters a collaborative environment that values diverse ideas and perspectives. By actively listening to their team members, leaders can tap into their collective intelligence, leverage their expertise and encourage innovative thinking. This collaborative problem-solving not only strengthens relationships but also enhances the team's ability to overcome challenges and achieve goals.

5. **Resolves Conflicts:** Listening plays a critical role in resolving conflicts and managing disagreements within a team. By actively listening to all parties involved, leaders can gain insights into the root causes of conflicts, identify common ground and facilitate constructive dialogue. This helps build understanding, find mutually acceptable solutions and maintain harmonious relationships within the team.

Thus, listening is essential for leaders because it cultivates trust, understanding, empathy and collaboration through effective communication and creates an environment that supports growth and success.

Barriers to Listening

Even with the best of intentions, listening can, on occasion, become challenging for us. These may be the reasons why.

1. **Our preoccupations:** According to communications expert William Isaacs, learning to listen begins with recognizing how we feel in the moment.[5]

    We're often caught in a 'mental traffic jam' and preoccupied by a multitude of thoughts, anxieties and fears. **Such a state is not conducive to listening**. We can truly listen only when we focus, and with disciplined practice, we can listen attentively. How often have you experienced that you predicted or anticipated what the other person would say, even before the meeting, and you started thinking about your responses in advance?

    While there is nothing wrong with preparing in advance in terms of facts and data, especially when the purpose of the meeting is known, this should not stop us from listening. It is critical to provide psychological equality when someone is meeting us. This means treating others with respect and not creating barriers on account of positional power.

2. **Our biases:** When we are obsessed with one right way and close our minds to other ideas, we try to project our opinions, prejudices and beliefs on what is being said. Conversely, when the other party dominates, we stop listening. That is where we stop adding any value. Our assumptions and biases can be a great handicap in problem-solving.

3. **Our inflexibility:** Sometimes our elevated sense of our rank gets in the way of good sense. It makes us stick to our guns even when we are wrong, because we fear that any revision of our position may dilute our power. This hinders the open sharing of grievances or

alternate viewpoints and hampers the manifestation of appropriate solutions to vital issues.

We also fail to listen when we operate with a false sense of entitlement or adopt a rebellious attitude. This creates an unhappy environment, with either incessant arguments or cold silence.

The Hazards of 'Non-Listening'

There is a general tendency among executives to avoid listening to those who ask some inconvenient questions, have contrary opinions or are more competent and have better ideas. Such executives, under the cover of hierarchical positions, find ways to skirt the questions that challenge their decisions or reveal their inconsistent decision-making. Leaders, on the other hand, cannot ignore these voices; instead, we must listen to them intently because they may carry a lot of wisdom. Listening to counterarguments is essential for leaders.

As former US President Barack Obama said in his acceptance speech:

I will listen to you, especially when we disagree. And to those Americans whose support I have yet to earn, I may not have won your vote tonight, but I hear your voices. I need your help.

Ignoring issues— 'non-listening'— can

- Cause misunderstandings and conflicts
- Damage relationships
- Create a toxic environment
- Lead to a loss of productivity
- Distract focus away from constructive work
- Demotivate

A Personal Experience with Non-Listening

I had the experience of working with a CEO who did not listen to anyone. If anyone so much as tried to offer a suggestion on any official matter, his pet retort was, 'Who knows more than me on this?'

I learnt more about the value of listening from this negative experience than from any other time in my career. I experienced the ill effects of non-listening on our motivation. The value of listening and its positive impact was a tangible reality.

Organizations would benefit if they could identify non-listening, arrogant and abusive managers, even if they have a great performance record, and put them on notice to reform (offering help in doing so) or else give them marching orders. Accountability for decent behaviour, including listening to others, should be a criterion for designing any appraisal system, especially for senior executives.

A Workout for Developing Listening Skills

Leaders are normally trained for speaking but rarely for listening. The following section will guide you in building this critical skill, but it will take practice, patience and perseverance.

As with everything else we have discussed, the journey begins with oneself. We need to improve our listening habits instead of expecting others to change.

Listening requires a state of attention and silence, and, more importantly, suspending our prejudices, anger and judgement about people and situations. This requires some deliberate work to create the space that fosters listening. It is very important to pay close attention to the person we are dealing with and listen to them fully.

People become disinterested and switch off from listening when the conversation becomes unproductive, on account of extreme ideological views, political alignments or biases due to gender, race, etc. On the other hand, listening becomes easier when the parties involved demonstrate maturity and respect for each other's views.

Nine-Step Process to Build Listening Muscles

The key to developing our listening ability is to maintain a state of attention in silence and, more importantly, the following steps.

1. **Seek Feedback**
    Request feedback on your listening patterns from someone you trust so you can take concrete steps to make necessary improvements. Again, this is not a one-time exercise, but one that needs to be carried out periodically.

2. **Concentrate**
    Listening requires discipline. We can only listen attentively when we are attentive and silent. When listening, we should consciously control our opinions, ideas, prejudices and impulses so they do not interfere with the process of listening. Emotional regulation (see Chapter

7 on Emotional Regulation and Anger Management) helps with this greatly. The key is to simply become aware of this tendency and practise concentrating on the silence, blocking out all the noise. Silence holds **enormous power. Wise people know when and when not to speak.** Maintaining a cordial environment and controlling emotions during listening are absolutely essential for positive outcomes.

3. Meditate

Philosopher and author J. Krishnamurti noted that 'One listens and therefore learns, only in a state of attention, a state of silence, in which this whole background* is in abeyance, is quiet; then it seems to me, it is possible to communicate.'[6] It is important to have an empty and quiet mind so that we can listen without accumulating prejudices. Meditation and mindfulness practices can help achieve this quietness.*

4. Be Prepared

Only a prepared mind can listen and engage with the other person authentically. If we do not prepare, it may be a waste of an opportunity. The preparation will depend on the issue at hand. For example, in my role as a banker, whenever a customer approached me with a request for a concession, such as an interest rate reduction in their loan account, I prepared myself with a thorough study of the cost-benefit of acceding to the request, checked their track record, their annual income, etc. Whenever possible, I would listen and make a prompt decision rather than procrastinate.

---

* Projecting our opinions, our prejudices, our impulses and our inclinations.

5. Analyse and Reflect to Listen Better

Understanding our current behavioural pattern is the first step in learning to listen. Generally, we are not so conscious of how we listen. We can begin by observing ourselves and our reactions. Once we observe and know our patterns, we can practise listening attentively without interrupting the other person and we can respond only after having understood their point of view.

Hence, we need to observe or reflect at ease with an open mind on the following:

*   Do I listen respectfully and make the other person comfortable? Or do I interrupt and challenge the speaker?
*   Am I prepared to accept a different point of view?
*   Am I prepared to modify my perspective?
*   Am I open to changing my position on an issue?

6. Journal

One way to improve listening is to keep a daily diary of your listening style during the day. This can help you assess your progress. I have personally benefited from this practice. For example, in order to focus more on listening, my executive secretary was advised to maintain a log of my speaking time, especially in the morning meeting with my top executives, which I reflected on every week. As a measure to improve my listening, I observed a 'speaking fast' for the first fifteen minutes in these meetings and paid focused attention to what others said. Over a period of time, it helped me in developing sensitivity to my listening style.

7. **Seek Professional Help**

   Some individuals experience a pathological obsession to speak; they might benefit from professional help. At some initial stage of executive life, the organization can help such executives, but in our culture of avoidance, authentic feedback often goes unnoticed and the negative behaviour stays uncorrected.

8. **Keep Emotions in Check**

   In addition, when engaging in a conversation, especially to resolve issues, a few key habits such as politeness, keeping emotions in check and avoiding tendencies to blame others, digressing or rushing through will help you express genuine interest and aid in listening better (see Chapter 7 on Emotional Regulation and Anger Management and Chapter 18 on Dialogue).

9. **Understand the Agenda**

   Listening is a serious exercise that requires focused attention and involves both intellectual and emotional attention. It doesn't mean that everything said should be taken seriously, especially when the other party may have a hidden agenda. In such situations, one could apply Socrates' Triple Filter Test.

The Triple Filter Test

One day, an acquaintance approached the great Greek philosopher Socrates with some information.

Acquaintance: I just heard something about your friend that I thought you should know . . .

Socrates: Wait a minute. Before you say anything, I'd like this information to go through the **Triple**

Filter Test. Let us take a moment and filter this information. The first filter is **Truth**. Can you say with certainty that this information is true?

Acquaintance: No, I am not sure. I heard it from . . .

Socrates: Okay, so you are not sure if this information is true. Let's use the second filter, which is **Goodness**. Is this information about my friend something good?

Acquaintance: No. In fact, it is something bad.

Socrates: So, the information is bad, and you are not sure if it is true. Now, let's use the third filter—**Usefulness**. Will this information be useful to me?

Acquaintance: No, I don't think so.

Socrates: When you cannot confirm if this information is true and is neither good nor useful, I don't want to listen to it.

(Adapted from the book *Leading Wisely* by Manfred F.R. Kets de Vries[7])

In summary, listening is the bedrock of effectiveness both in our personal and professional lives, even though it's a difficult skill to develop. As we have seen, we need to recognize that listening involves erasing our own biases and moving into a state of mental quietness to discern the difficulties of others and engage in the concrete problem-solving process. Listening can multiply our capacity to learn and be creative in many ways. Training in public speaking can be dangerous without equal skills in listening.

Questions for Reflection

1. What are your key learnings from this chapter?
2. Create an action plan to develop and improve your listening skills using the questions below.

3. Think of a boss who was a good listener. How did it impact the teams and their performance?
4. Recollect an interaction that made you unhappy because you were not listened to. What did you learn from it?
5. Do you consider yourself a good listener? What are the ways in which you could improve your listening skills even more?
6. What can you do so that your team members can become better listeners?

Chapter 17

Detoxifying Communication: Becoming Accountable for Your Behaviour

---

There is no such thing as a failed relationship,
only failed communication.

—Anonymous—

While I was on a research project at my bank's corporate office in Mumbai in the mid-1980s, a particular communication became the subject matter for lunchtime discussions. The general manager (legal), who was known to be very autocratic and egoistic, had issued a circular about guidelines on an operational issue that had a legal angle. One regional manager sought clarifications on a particular aspect of the said communication, concluding his letter with, 'Please enlighten on this matter.' The general manager's response: 'My communication is abundantly clear, and therefore you read and reread till you are enlightened on the matter.'

This was a classic example of **toxic communication.** It did not serve any purpose except to demoralize the receiver, and it sent the wrong signal across the hierarchy. The regional manager did not get the clarification that he sought, and the words of his superior lacked courtesy, sensitivity and empathy. It created fear and animosity between the two levels of hierarchy. Is that appropriate conduct by anyone, let alone a top functionary?

Toxic communication is always de-energizing, frustrating and destructive to any relationship. It tends to bring down self-esteem and self-worth by hitting morale, eventually affecting productivity.

Although the main purpose of communication is to build understanding, such communications often lead to a major derailment in relationships and morale. Many bosses use communication as an opportunity to wield their power over juniors, to intimidate and demotivate them. No wonder the style of communication in many cases smacks of arrogance, egoism or sermonizing. The main purpose is forgotten, and it blocks future communication.

Youngsters often tell me how some of their superiors lack basic decency in their communication and that they lack the dignity and decorum expected of corporate behaviour. I have witnessed such behaviour myself and also heard about such bosses from others over the years. Table 17.1 lists the traits of toxic and non-toxic bosses, as described by participants in my training programmes over the years. Broadly speaking, toxic bosses exercise the power of their rank at the expense of their juniors (but are generally deferential to their seniors).

Table 17.1: Toxic Bosses versus Non-Toxic Bosses*

Toxic Bosses	Non-Toxic Bosses
Moody and unpredictable in interactions	Treat people with decency and respect
Critical, condescending and insulting	Encourage and appreciate

---

* Compiled after interactions with managers in several training programmes.

Toxic Bosses	Non-Toxic Bosses
Stonewall, shutting the other person out	Facilitate and encourage others
Defensive, place blame and shrug off responsibilities	Feel accountable for actions
Seldom give positive feedback	Give balanced feedback, and convey adverse feedback without being offensive
Judgemental and not interested in listening	Listen with attention and provide resolutions to problems

Communication is a powerful tool. It can create harmony, build relationships and dissolve differences. It can also do the exact opposite and create discord and destroy relationships. It depends on how you use it. **Arrogance and toxicity can never create sustained performance in the long term. It demotivates employees and discourages the chances of making a creative contribution.**

Words Can Build or Demolish Relationships

At the end of the day, people won't remember what you said or did; they will remember how you made them feel.[1]

—Maya Angelou—

It's a rather obvious statement, but it needs to be emphasized nonetheless. Words can build relationships—and they can break them, too. Soothing and encouraging words build lasting bonds, while taunts or sharp words, especially if used often, invariably harm relationships. The delivery of your words, too, has a huge impact.

Professionals can lose business if they are not careful with their communication. A friend of mine recounted his experience with his doctor: 'Whenever I tried to find out a little more about his treatment plan for my wife, he would respond with irritation that he knew his job and I should leave it alone. I did not like his lack of empathy and courtesy, so I am now looking for another doctor.' That doctor lost a patient, even though he was professionally competent, because of his bedside manner. This holds true for all of us; even skilled professionals need to have good communication ability.

Great leaders know exactly what to say, when to say it and how to say it.

In her article 'The Power of Words', Lucy Swedberg, executive editor and senior editorial director at Harvard Business Publishing, notes:

> As Jonah Berger, a Wharton professor and natural-language-processing expert, explains in *Magic Words*, there are specific words that, when used in the right way at the right time, are more impactful than others—at changing minds, engaging audiences, and driving action.[2]
>
> For example, in the workplace, a shared organizational language (such as start-up founders' use of the word 'pivoting,' retailers' use of 'omnichannel,' or entire teams' use of more personal pronouns like 'we' or 'I' instead of the more distanced 'they') 'can facilitate conversation, make people feel connected, and increase their perception that they are part of the same tribe,' Berger writes. This can increase feelings of trust and affiliation—and even the likelihood of promotion.

Berger's book reinforces and should remind us all that there is value in thinking deeply about each word we use; how it expresses a particular concept or nuance and how people from different geographies, cultures and backgrounds might experience it.[3]

While choosing the right words can create magic in relationships and bolster our confidence, choosing the wrong words can be detrimental to building lasting relationships.

I know of a leading management consultant—let's call him Suresh—who is a rare genius, but his tongue is his biggest enemy. A senior adviser with a global consulting firm, Suresh was known to belittle and insult the work that was presented at internal meetings. 'This presentation is worth shit; I will give you two out of ten for it.' 'Who appointed you to this position? It's clear that you need to go back to school to understand the basics!' While everyone recognized his extraordinary talent, his condescending attitude eventually cost him his job, with his contract being cancelled prematurely. This is a clear example of how words can wreak havoc in one's career and business.

As an antidote to the above, the CEO of the same firm was always encouraging, making his observations with sensitivity and straightforwardness. When he found the presentation not up to the mark, he would comment, 'We need to bring some depth to our arguments; the presentation as such is good, but it needs to be reshaped to create an impact; we need to add . . . X portion or Y portion.'

Communication Red Flags

Taunts and harsh words make lasting dents in relationships. It's important for a leader to cultivate a better inner and outer environment for communication.

Be wary of using words that are cruel, hostile or discriminatory. Language that diminishes people causes emotional harm, creates an uncomfortable environment, breeds resentment and erodes trust.

Generally speaking, toxic language includes

- Insults about a person's character, appearance, intelligence or sexual orientation
- Insults that target race, ethnicity or gender
- Insults that belittle people
- Excessive use of profanity
- Gossip and rumours
- Passive-aggressive language
- Excessive or biting sarcasm

A Workout to Overcome Toxic Behaviour

Successful leaders constantly reflect on their behavioural patterns in an attempt to overcome their flaws. They understand that such behaviour could be detrimental to building and sustaining relationships.

Such reflection requires a deep and unflinching understanding of ourselves—our motives, biases, listening patterns, emotional states, power orientations and ego states. Practising skilled communication and thoughtful responses in different situations can help us design responses that are sensitive, direct, unambiguous and balanced.

Chapter 2 (Reflection) discusses how one can reflect, identify patterns and develop a more personable style of communication.

If you ever experience toxic behaviour, here are a few things that could help:

- **Regulate your emotions:** This is the first thing to do, as that will shape your response to the situation.
- **Do not get into an argument:** Take care not to fall into the argument trap, as it might turn out to be futile and extremely upsetting.
- **Ignore the negative comments:** Refuse to react to the negative comments, and try to change the focus of the conversation to something that is productive.
- **Discourage backbiting:** If someone speaks negatively about others behind their back, ask them to stop and resolve their differences among themselves. A boss of mine followed the practice of putting his phone on speaker mode if any colleague indulged in criticizing the other colleague and would invite them to join the call.
- **Set boundaries:** Let someone know if they have crossed the line; it will make them think twice about their behaviour.
- **Confront toxic behaviour:** If nothing else works, confront them head-on about their toxic behaviour and express discomfort. Take care to be polite and courteous. A good policy is to first acknowledge their

positive traits and then point out the problems along with appropriate suggestions for corrective action. As a policy, I aligned the toxic executives with jobs that had minimum human interaction.

- **Escalate the matter:** In case you are not able to resolve things on your own, consider escalating the matter to a senior or to HR.
- **Be respectful and decent:** Shun arrogance of any kind in behaviour and action; be respectful and humble in dealing with everyone, irrespective of their hierarchical position.

Early Home Gym

It may be interesting to note how toxic behaviour can pass on from generation to generation in certain families and cultures when the elders in the family sometimes unconsciously indulge in backbiting or use derogatory language.

Children growing up in such households may assume that such behaviour is normal and begin doing the same. Hence, it is prudent that we watch what we are saying about relatives, neighbours and friends while being conscious of our tone and body language.

Role of Leaders in Developing a Non-toxic Culture

Leaders at every level must reflect and enact policies to control such toxic behaviours. While there is no magic antidote, here are some strategies that can help managers mitigate the toxic behaviours of leaders across the hierarchy and promote a healthier work environment:

- Foster open communication
- Lead by example
- Provide leadership development
- Encourage a supportive culture
- Establish clear expectations and accountability
- Prioritize employee well-being

Ironically, words are an effective way to overcome and overpower toxic communication styles, whether our own or someone else's. We can realign toxic communication so that it becomes harmonious by using the right words in the right context and tone.

Words often communicate our personalities and can either be facilitative or obstructive in attaining outcomes. Words, whether good or bad, stick with us for life. The wrong use of words can break great friendships and relationships. Persuasive words can bring positive results.

Here are a few golden rules and dos and don'ts to create a healthy and positive culture of communication.

Table 17.2: Golden Rules for Words

Use Words to	Dos	Don'ts
Inspire and encourage, do not criticize or discourage	Always show appreciation for good work; give gentle and constructive feedback and empathetic responses to problems.	Avoid criticizing in an intemperate way and passing value judgements. It is not only unproductive but also hugely demotivating.

Use Words to	Dos	Don'ts
Mobilize, not paralyse	Encourage teamwork and reward team performance.	Do not play one person against the other and do not set unrealistic targets and impossible deadlines.
Create passion, not indifference	Communicate problems with genuineness and transparency; share the larger vision and a possible new future to seek engagement.	Avoid centralizing ideas and withholding critical information.
Show empathy, not apathy	Be supportive at all times, especially during adversity. Stand by your team.	Avoid indifference to problems.
Improve, repair and harmonize. Don't damage, confuse or embarrass	Encourage through counselling and mentoring. Provide perspective in a conflict situation; encourage mutually acceptable solutions.	Avoid inappropriate and hurtful communication in case of below-par performance. Do not divide and rule.
Teach, don't sermonize	Provide a teachable point of view from organizational episodes.	Avoid ambiguity.

Use Words to	Dos	Don'ts
Look for solutions, do not point fingers	Make the solution the priority—for the current problem and to avoid such a situation in the future.	Avoid playing the blame game.

None of the rules and guidelines can work unless we show some amount of self-control and self-restraint while reacting to people and situations. Here are a few safeguards that can serve as a reminder to mind our words.

Table 17.3: Safeguards for Minding Words

1. Control your emotions and words. Do not get provoked.
2. Train yourself to be civil, even in difficult circumstances.
3. Choose the right words, not ones that hurt. Work on your vocabulary for this.
4. Be respectful regardless of people's positions on the hierarchical ladder.
5. If you cross the line, apologize right away.

It is important to choose our words carefully and be mindful of how they might impact others. Building and maintaining healthy relationships requires open and respectful communication, where words are used to uplift, support and foster understanding rather than to harm or damage. It is imperative that, as we work on developing our leadership and communication skills, we cultivate the right use of words. This entails mastering the language and knowing when to withhold words and when to use them with force. Only with moderation and mastery over our words can we become effective communicators and leaders.

Better to trip with the feet
than with the tongue.[4]

—Zeno—

Questions for Reflection

1. What are your key learnings from this chapter?
2. Create an action plan to overcome your toxic behaviour using the questions below.
3. Recall your bosses who were often toxic. In what ways did it affect you? What did you learn from such experiences?
4. Would you counsel a colleague who is toxic in their communication?
5. How can you nurture a non-toxic culture in your team/ organization?

Chapter 18

Dialogue: The Most Effective Tool for Problem-Solving

In true dialogue, both sides are willing to change.[1]

—Thích Nhất Hạnh—

Dialogue is the key mechanism of an effective and serious conversation. In our day-to-day lives, we often encounter situations that can lead to conflicts if left unresolved. In such situations, a serious attempt at conversation through dialogue holds the potential to break the logjam and resolve the issues.

I managed industrial relations for a large chunk of my career, during which I observed that a breakdown in dialogue between management and trade unions invariably led to conflict. It was through dialogue that an understanding was reached.

As the saying goes, a stitch in time saves nine. Failure to deal with developing issues in a timely manner usually results in a bigger problem. This is because the involved parties tend to procrastinate out of fear that discussions may open a can of worms or the hope that the problem will resolve over time. On the contrary, **I dare say with confidence that avoiding dialogue is tantamount to an invitation to a conflict.**

What Is Dialogue?

Dialogue is an intense engagement between people to overcome differences, build meaning and purpose, develop new insights and perspectives and thus improve understanding and resolve problems.

In his book *The Fifth Discipline*, Peter Senge explains dialogue in this way: 'Dialogue can be understood as the art of thinking together. It involves joint exploration of ideas, perspectives and assumptions with the goal of reaching a deeper understanding and shared meaning.'[2]

Through the process of dialogue and conversations, people can challenge existing mental models, co-create new possibilities and align their efforts with common goals. It is a transformative tool for understanding diverse perspectives, suspending assumptions and focusing on shared learning, problem-solving and conflict management.

Dialogue can effect a mind shift, turning combatants engaged in one-upmanship into collaborators who work together to resolve problems. It is often a relentless, long-term process involving reviews and feedback, requiring a commitment to the process so as to resolve the issues. It is a democratic process that respects the perspectives of the parties involved.

Failure to engage in dialogue to resolve differences is attributed to falling into the ego trap of 'why should I?' Another strong reason is the fear that it might put us on the back foot.

Such reservations are counterproductive, eventually causing an impasse and, sometimes, irreparable damage to relationships.

The Dialoguing Process

Dialogue is a process in which people suspend their initial opinions and collaborate to examine new avenues of working together. The process can harness **collective intelligence** to create new opportunities and capacities for creative collaboration.

William Isaacs, of the MIT Sloan School of Management and a long-time researcher on dialogue, observes that the process of dialogue takes us through these four stages:[3]

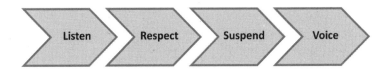

Figure 18.1: Four Stages of Dialogue

Listen: Listening is the essence of any dialogue process and is the first step towards making a dialogue purposeful and productive. It requires a lot of effort and is one of leadership's biggest challenges. Our listening can lead to new perspectives from new awareness and sensibilities, which can eventually dispel our assumptions about the issues (see Chapter 16 on Listening).

Respect: Another important process is respect for the core issue and for the other party—to see them as sincerely as we see ourselves, as human beings with our own views, experiences, orientations and standings. When we respect someone, we accept that they have things to teach us.

Suspend: When we go for dialogue, there is always a context, a situation in the background, a pile of information and, in some sense, a strategic framework or bias in our minds regarding the problem or issues. We also carry labels or stereotypes in our heads, such as unions, management, communists, socialists, rightists, etc. These labels can hinder conflict resolution. The solution is to suspend our judgement and prejudices and quiet the mind. Only through unbiased listening can we accept others for who they are and build mutual trust and understanding.

Voice: Finally, one of the biggest challenges in the dialogue is our authenticity in speaking up about the issue. We might be tempted to be politically correct or diplomatic in the name of maintaining relationships. This is inauthentic.

Here lies the opportunity to display the courage to voice concerns, point out inconsistencies and the consequences of maintaining the status quo, defend fixated stands and protect ideologies. This is where we need the courage to drive change.

Voicing creates huge possibilities—it can create an emotional climate for change and a new paradigm of trust. Voicing can invite multiple views from the participants and facilitate the creation of an accommodative space for learning and internalizing.

How I Used Tough Conversations

At a time when our organization was sliding and there was general apathy and low morale, I had tough conversations with the employees through several town halls. While I listened to their concerns and promised to address them, I authentically shared my own concerns about the general complacent attitude and its impact on the bank's progress and their own careers. Without mincing words, I told them about my policy of zero tolerance for ineffective customer service and announced a charter in this regard.

Thus, tough conversations are a part of both personal and organizational life, and managers and leaders are expected to use them when required.

The Importance of Listening

By its very nature, **a dialogue is a two-way process.** Imagine a dialogue between a husband and a wife, a father and a son, a boss and a subordinate, a government secretary and a corporate CEO, a board chairperson and the CEO. In each of these, there is as much potential for success as for failure. It all depends on how intellectually and emotionally committed each actor is to seeking positive outcomes, as well as how willing they are to invest in their commitment to the dialogue process for sorting out issues.

What makes a dialogue successful? It is when the involved parties listen, have the courage to own their mistakes or inadequacies and initiate prompt corrective action. Conversely, the failure of dialogue occurs when we become prisoners of a fixed mindset, and in our egotistic fixation with our thoughts, we are unwilling to listen to the other person. **Dialogue fails when we experience barriers to listening.**

Why Dialogue Is Critical for Leaders

Conversation and dialogue can shape our relationships. These are important mechanisms to develop understanding, resolve problem areas, crystallize our thinking, negotiate a new order and lay the foundation for relationships.

The basic intent and purpose of initiating any serious dialogue is to build trust through mutual learning and to convey that we care.

While engaging in dialogue, we need to ensure that conversations stay on track and do not deviate or digress too much on account of emotional turmoil. As leadership expert Alec Grimsley says in his book *Vital Conversations*:

> When you're engaged in a vital yet difficult conversation, the stress levels encountered by both parties will be significantly higher than in everyday conversations, and if there is historical baggage the tension will be even more acute. Selecting

what you say and how you say it is critical to keeping the conversation on the rails.[4]

Dialogue Process at the Institutional Level

I have personally experienced a breakthrough from a deeply distrustful situation to a more collaborative understanding through a series of unrelenting dialogues.

In 1997, I was posted as general manager, overseeing the Eastern Zone in Kolkata. This zone had a history of union–management problems, which manifested in poor work culture, frequent work stoppages, restrictive practices, defiance of official discipline, poor customer service and stagnant business. The indulgence of senior and top management in the zone was suboptimal, and trade unions always complained that they were not heard. Top management initiatives in engaging with the zone were minimal on account of the union's coercive tactics to get their demands agreed to. There was a stalemate on both sides. No wonder that a posting in this zone as head of operations was perceived as a 'punishment posting'.

When I took over, I wanted to break this impasse and initiated a problem-resolution process, mainly through several rounds of dialogue. In the first few weeks, I met groups of operating managers and representatives of three workmen's unions separately to understand the pain points. One of the dominant concerns of the union representatives was that management did not listen to their issues. They provided data in support of their arguments. I listened to them day after day, engaged with them and initiated many confidence-building measures through quick problem-solving of pending issues. I allowed catharsis to take place from both sides, the union and management, and after a series of dialogues, I began on an emotionally clean slate to carve out a new vision for growth and development with excellent outcomes. Faith in dialogue-based conversations opened new opportunities for building trust.

The level of trust started building up, and soon we engaged the trade unions in improving the ecosystem of business development and customer service. Our deep conversations through the process of dialoguing, accompanied by positive actions, led to many reforms, such as the introduction of computerization, which the union had resisted tooth and nail, the opening of new branches, the extending of service for customers, improvements in attendance, punctuality and job rotation, all of which had been hamstrung for two decades! The business took off, staff morale improved and the zone showed good performance, giving hope for the future. My belief in the process of dialogue-based conversations, even in the most strained and difficult situations, yielded many positive results. (For details, see Chapter 6 in *Dare to Lead*, 2023)[5]

Four Success Factors for an Effective Dialogue

Figure 18.2: Four Success Factors for Effective Dialogue

Learning from my Kolkata experience and other postings, I have observed that the process of dialogue by itself is never adequate in turning around a relationship unless parties to dialogue are committed to

1. **Shunning Defensiveness:** There must be a willingness to listen intently to the issues and points raised by the other party or the group with openness, without erecting walls of defensiveness. Any dialogue process is likely to fail if there is no acknowledgement of real issues or owning up to our part in the problem.

2. **Confidence-building Measures:** Dialogues succeed when both parties engage in confidence building. This sets the stage for building mutual trust. Let's say, in a dialogue, a subordinate points out to the boss that several communications on a particular subject have gone unanswered by the HR department. It may be useful to look into this problem organizationally and set up a response mechanism without loss of time. Such quick actions are more likely to reinforce trust rather than offering explanations for the lack of response.

3. **Seeking Engagement:** After the ice is broken, the parties can move on to serious problem-solving engagement. Going back to the example of my Kolkata experience with dialogue, after the initial confidence-building measures by the management and continuing the process of dialogue, we involved trade unions in improving staff discipline and customer service on the ground.

    Furthermore, I needed to address the three major mental and emotional hurdles among the staff and unions of the Kolkata Zone. These were **fixed perceptions** and **emotional baggage** that the Kolkata staff and union carried due to years of neglect, as well as the **flawed intentions and actions** of the top management, which failed to address those issues.

I knew I had to work on creating the right intentions and actions to outweigh the years of damage. Going forward, I deployed the parties involved in conversations and dialogues to 'diagnose the issues, build bridges with the union and staff, understand them and . . . most importantly, exercise patience in a suspicion-filled, high-voltage arena where sparks flew at the slightest provocation!'[6]

4. **Perception Change:** Our culture and value systems influence our perceptions. The dialogue process must aim to change perceptions through quick actions and set in motion a newly agreed-upon way of working and managing problems. The Kolkata experience taught me that if we see others through the lens of our existing perceptions and emotions, then we are most likely to go wrong in understanding them. Maybe the other side is just stating facts, but we often doubt their intentions and feel hurt.

One of the key factors in the success of conversation on difficult issues is to assume that the other party is equally invested in problem-solving rather than doubting their intentions. Both parties must initiate the conversation with a fresh perspective and demonstrate their genuine intentions through tangible actions.

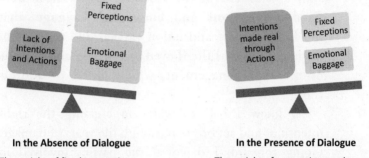

In the Absence of Dialogue	In the Presence of Dialogue
The weight of fixed perceptions and emotional baggage is heavy, as they remain unresolved due to a lack of intentions and actions.	The weight of perceptions and emotional baggage is less, as the intentions to resolve the issues are made real through the right actions.

Figure 18.3: Importance of Dialogue Process

Emotional Baggage—Often the Biggest Hurdle to Initiating Conversations

Painful memories of the past, let-downs and acts of disloyalty, infidelity or discrimination can accumulate huge emotional baggage and block any initiatives for dialogue and conversation. Every time someone groans about the past, it can be a major hindrance to conflict resolution. Being excessively emotional can override our ability to think and listen clearly. Often, the guilt or need to blame others for our plight takes over the logical flow of a conversation.

While it is quite natural to be deeply upset about some scars of the past, it would be injurious to carry the past into the present and future and thereby spend our lives nurturing such scars. It is, therefore, necessary to own up to and deal with such emotional cholesterol that blocks our energy. If the parties involved are closely connected, like parents and children, spouses and close kin, it becomes all the more necessary to give expression to such feelings with a view to understanding the other person and also accept their apology and a promise of changed behaviour. Sometimes emotional catharsis and its expression act as catalysts to restore the relationship. In short, it may be worthwhile to examine how our lack of sharing of our deepest feelings may damage us emotionally, and how the expression of hidden feelings and an approach to understanding the other person can help build the ruptured relationship. The larger issue is this: Do we want to keep ourselves in a permanent state of moaning and groaning or do we want to break free of that trap?

A Workout for Building Dialoguing Skills

Dialogue is not casual talk on serious issues, nor is it a one-shot affair. It may require several sessions, depending on the issue. Dialogue requires a desire to resolve an issue, serious preparation and deep emotional engagement by the parties concerned. It is a negotiation process where the parties build a bridge of understanding through openness and honesty to create better outcomes. It is important to remember that conversations can fail miserably if any of the parties operate from a power base or have a hidden agenda.

Seek first to understand, then to be understood.[7]

—Stephen R. Covey—

The dialogue process can be difficult because of power imbalances among the concerned actors. Therefore, the actor in the higher position needs to be very sensitive to this aspect and understand its impact on the outcomes. Effectively deploying our listening skills is one of the key levers of successful conversations and dialogue (previously discussed in Chapter 16 on Listening).

1. Take initiative and extend an invitation for such conversations and dialogues; choose a neutral venue and be under no time pressure.
2. Take charge of your emotions, keep your nerves in control, be civil all through and avoid hurried, short-tempered or temperamental reactions.
3. Use open-ended questions to encourage the other person to provide detailed responses. This can lead to deeper and more meaningful dialogue. Avoid asking questions that can be answered with a simple 'yes' or 'no'.
4. Engage in constructive discussions based on facts and evidence and not merely on opinions. Be open to others' perspectives. Remember, a good conversation may not always result in a consensus, but it is necessary to attempt it with sincerity.
5. Be mindful of the language you use and avoid the blame game. Use 'I' instead of 'you' in expressing your feelings. For example, say, 'I felt let down' rather than 'You let me

down'. Similarly, do not provoke fear or anxiety during sensitive conversations.

6. Aim for a balanced conversation, with both parties having the opportunity to speak and be heard. Do not monopolize the conversation. Engage actively, offer thought-out responses, contribute relevant ideas and ask follow-up questions.

7. Be objective and thorough in discussing the issue logically with facts; avoid ambiguity; validate the information being provided and seek clarifications, if any, politely.

8. Use silence as a catalyst to facilitate conversations, especially when there is tension around. Tactical silence and pauses can help ease the environment. It can have a calming effect when tempers run high during a meeting.

9. Avoid digression and indecision. Equally, do not make promises that cannot be fulfilled. Keep the focus on problem-solving and avoid one-upmanship.

10. Avoid rushing to close the dialogue. Each side may take time to think about the rationale and usefulness of the proposals and continue the process with sincerity until understanding is reached.

11. Be authentic and genuine; authenticity fosters trust and builds stronger relationships with others. Avoid trying to impress or be someone you're not, as it can hinder genuine conversation.

A final word, even at the cost of repetition: **Any successful dialogue or conversation requires us to suspend our opinions and set aside knee-jerk or emotional reactions to respectfully listen to others with a sincere attempt at issue resolution.**

Finally, after perusing the four chapters, here is the essence of the entire section on communication:

Effective Communication Is

1. **Clear:** Factual and data-based; no beating around the bush, excessive use of jargon or leaving open to many interpretations.
2. **Decent:** Respectful and considerate in dealing with others; no sarcasm, innuendoes, personal attacks, hurtful words or blame games.
3. **Complete:** Covers responses to all issues raised or intended to communicate; not selective.
4. **End to end:** Covers the entire chain of people or departments who are involved in the matter; no discrimination or omission.
5. **Timely:** Prioritized and timely responses to important communication; no unnecessary delays.
6. **Emotive:** Appreciative and empathetic; uses the power of gestures, gratitude and personal touch in interactions; honest and expressive of feelings of exhilaration as well as pain.
7. **Hierarchical sensitivity:** Decency, grace and dignity in communications; respects the decision sought and respects everyone.
8. **Respectful:** Courteous and considerate to all stakeholders, regardless of rank.
9. **Unbiased:** Study an issue from multiple perspectives before forming opinions; no judgement, no denial or digression.

10. **Authentic:** Honest, persuasive and builds trust.
11. **Credible:** Consistent, connecting the dots and acknowledging the efforts of others.
12. **Action-oriented:** Quick decisions and actions that display responsibility and accountability and are supportive of others in the process of implementing the decisions.

It also requires the leader to

13. **Focus on context:** Stay on the issue; analyse it from multiple perspectives before forming opinions; do not be judgemental.
14. **Listen deeply:** Listen with an intent to act; be respectful and considerate of others; do not give false hopes.
15. **Use the right words:** Use caution in choosing the right words for different situations; avoid toxic words that can derail reputations and relationships.
16. **Use analogies and images:** Analogies, metaphors, parables or images communicate the message far more effectively than a lengthy write-up.
17. **Use the dialogue process:** Take responsibility, make an effort and avoid one-upmanship; use the dialogue process to sort out even the most difficult problems.

Questions for Reflection

1. What are your key learnings from this chapter?
2. Create an action plan to develop and improve your conversation and dialogue skills using the questions below.

3. In what situations have you effectively used dialogue-based conversations? What were the outcomes? What would you do differently now?
4. When it comes to resolving conflicts, what immediate measures do you take?
5. What kind of issues do you think can be resolved through conversations and dialogue?
6. What are your strengths in making conversations productive? What areas would you like to improve?

Acknowledgements

Sometime in the mid-1990s, I boarded a flight from Jaipur to Kolkata in an old 737 Indian Airlines aircraft. The aircraft made three unsuccessful attempts to take off, and I was scared. It finally took off on its fourth attempt. Writing this book has been a somewhat similar experience. It was conceptualized about eight years ago, but for some reason or another, it did not begin. In the interim, I authored two books and revised another one. Finally, this book took off in 2023.

Writing a book is never a solo process—it wasn't for me, at least. Your ideas and thoughts require validation from various people, including subject experts, other writers, senior leaders, colleagues, etc.

I am lucky to have such a group of well-wishers and friends who have always helped me in my writing endeavours. My special appreciation goes out to:

- Rajen Gupta, former professor at IIM Lucknow and MDI Gurgaon, and my go-to person for conceptual clarity whenever I feel stuck with an idea.
- Rajesh Srivastava, an author and a former CEO, for his valuable comments on some of the chapters and for sharing two stories, which are part of this book.
- Prasenjit Bhattacharya, CEO, Great Managers Institute, and his associate Basuri Dutta, for helping me with some

excellent real-life stories to strengthen the power of certain concepts.

- T.V. Rao, former professor at IIM Ahmedabad, for his encouraging comments on the manuscript.
- B.P. Vijayendra, former principal chief general manager, RBI, for his excellent eye for detail and valuable input.

I am extremely grateful to all the professionals, both in India and abroad, who have generously spent time in going through the manuscript and offered their endorsement for the book.

I also thank Ashwini Doreswamy, who helped me with the research, developing visuals and overall organization of the chapters. After she joined, the project of writing this book took off in a real sense. Her commitment has been immensely valuable in completing this book.

Seetha Natesh, our freelance editor, has been of immense help in providing perspective and strategic review of the content to enhance the overall utility of the book to its readers. Her help has been valuable in presenting this book in the shape that you see now.

I also appreciate Nirmala, Sandeep, Ganesh and Washid Ali, mid- and senior-level managers of different companies and participants of my session at IIM Calcutta, who volunteered to read some of the chapters and offer their feedback from the perspective of the utility of contents for aspiring leaders. Their input has been really beneficial.

My wife Vandana, has always been a model of emotional intelligence and loving kindness. She has been a great support in all my academic endeavours, including this one.

A special appreciation goes to our house help Manoj, who enthusiastically nourished us with his culinary skills.

Finally, I thank Manish Khurana, senior commissioning editor, and Aparna Abhijit, copy editor, at Penguin Random House India, who have been a great support for this book from conceptualization to completion.

Notes

Preface

1 Michael Useem, *The Leadership Moment: Nine True Stories of Triumph and Disaster and Their Lessons for Us All* (New York: Crown Currency, 1999).
2 Warren G. Bennis and Robert J. Thomas, *Geeks and Geezers* (Massachusetts: Harvard Business Review Press, 2002).
3 Robert J. Thomas, *Crucibles of Leadership* (Massachusetts: Harvard Business Review Press, 2008).
4 Anil K. Khandelwal, *Dare to Lead: The Transformation of the Bank of Baroda* (Gurgaon: PRHI, 2023).
5 Warren Bennis, *On Becoming a Leader* (USA: Basic Books, 2003).

Introduction

1 Warren Bennis, *On Becoming a Leader*.
2 Carol S. Dweck, *Mindset* (USA: Robinson, 2017).
3 Jeffrey Pfeffer, *Leadership BS: Fixing Workplaces and Careers One Truth at a Time* (USA: HarperBusiness, 2015).
4 Abinash Panda, 'Experience-centric Leadership Development Process: Challenges and the Way Forward for Organisations in India', *International Journal of Indian Culture and Business Management* 16 (1) (2018): 99–116.

5   Warren Bennis, *On Becoming a Leader*.
6   Edgar H. Schein, *Humble Inquiry: The Gentle Art of Asking Instead of Telling (The Humble Leadership Series)* (USA: Berrett-Koehler Publishers, 2013).
7   Morgan W. McCall, Jr, 'Recasting Leadership Development', *Industrial and Organizational Psychology* 3 (2010).
8   David V. Day, 'The Difficulties of Learning from Experience and the Need for Deliberate Practice', *Industrial and Organizational Psychology* 3(1) (2010): 41–44.
9   Jeffrey Pfeffer, *Leadership BS: Fixing Workplaces and Careers One Truth at a Time* (USA: HarperBusiness, 2015).

Chapter 1: Self-Awareness: Knowing Thyself Is the First Step

1   Lao Tzu, *Tao Te Ching* (UK: Penguin Books, 2021).
2   'T-Group Programs', *ISABS*, https://www.isabs.org/t-group.html (last accessed 4 July 2024).
3   Bernie Swain, 'Successful Leaders Know What Made Them Who They Are', *Harvard Business Review*, September 2018, https://hbr.org/2016/09/successful-leaders-know-what-made-them-who-they-are (last accessed 14 January 2024).
4   Tasha Eurich, 'What Self-Awareness Really Is (and How to Cultivate It)', *Harvard Business Review*, 4 January, 2018, www.hbr.org/2018/01/what-self-awareness-really-is-and-how-to-cultivate-it (last accessed 20 November 2023).
5   Ibid.
6   Michael Bunting, *The Mindful Leader: 7 Practices for Transforming Your Leadership, Your Organisation and Your Life* (UK: Wiley, 2016).
7   Susan David and Christina Congleton, 'Emotional Agility', *Harvard Business Review*, November 2013, https://hbr.

org/2013/11/emotional-agility (last accessed 21 November 2023).

8   James Wilson, 'You, By the Numbers', *Harvard Business Review*, September 2012, www.hbr.org/2012/09/you-by-the-numbers (last accessed 22 December 2023).

9   'The Johari Window: Building Self-Awareness and Trust', MindTools, www.mindtools.com/au7v71d/the-johari-window (last accessed 20 December 2023); 'Understanding the Johari Window model', SelfAwareness, www.selfawareness.org.uk/2022/09/25/understandingthe-johari-window-model (last accessed 22 December 2023).

10 'Fundamental Interpersonal Results Orientation-Behaviour Assessment (FIRO-B)', Psychometrics, www.psychometrics.com/assessments/firo-b (last accessed 22 December 2023) (also see www.thehumanelement.com/firo-theory/ [last accessed 22 December 2023]).

11 '360 Degree Feedback: Encouraging Teamwork and Improving Performance', MindTools, www.mindtools.com/a78j7m1/360-degree-feedback (last accessed 13 March 2024).

Chapter 2: Reflection: Diving Deep into the Self

1   Peter F. Drucker, 'Quotable Quote', Goodreads, https://www.goodreads.com/quotes/7346041-follow-effective-action-with-quiet-reflection-from-the-quiet-reflection (last accessed 5 July 2024).

2   Clayton Christensen, *How Will You Measure Your Life?* (USA: Harper Business, 2012).

3   Jumana Shah and Soumitra Trivedi, 'This IIM Grad Sells Idlis', DNA, 21 November 2013, www.dnaindia.com/india/report-this-iim-grad-sells-idlis-1041294 (last accessed 30 November 2023).

4   Jennifer Porter, 'Why You Should Make Time for Self-Reflection (Even if You Hate Doing It)', *Harvard Business Review*, March 2017, www.hbr.org/2017/03/why-you-should-make-time-for-self-reflection-even-if-you-hate-doing-it (last accessed 21 November 2023).

5   Donald A. Schon, *The Reflective Practitioner: How Professionals Think in Action* (USA: Basic Books, 1983).

6   'Famous Quotes on Reflection and Well-Being', George Mason University, https://wellbeing.gmu.edu/famous-quotes-on-reflection-and-well-being/ (last accessed 10 July 2024).

7   James R. Bailey and Scheherazade Rehman, 'Don't Underestimate the Power of Self-Reflection', *Harvard Business Review*, 4 March 2022, www.hbr.org/2022/03/dont-underestimate-the-power-of-self-reflection_(last accessed 21 November 2023).

8   Warren Bennis, *On Becoming a Leader* (USA: Basic Books, 2003); Warren Bennis with Patricia Ward Biederman et al., *The Essential Bennis* (USA: Jossey–Bass, 2009).

9   Graham Gibbs, *Learning by Doing: A Guide to Teaching and Learning Methods* (Oxford Polytechnic: Further Education Unit, 1988).

10 Manfred F.R. Kets de Vries, 'Why It's So Hard to Ask for Help', *Harvard Business Review*, July–August 2023, www.hbr.org/2023/07/why-its-so-hard-to-ask-for-help (last accessed 8 March 2024).

11 Jeff Haden, 'Expert Opinion', INC, 7 September 2023, www.inc.com/jeff-haden/while-warren-buffett-says-i-just-sit-in-my-office-read-all-day-this-lifelong-habit-is-just-as-crucial-to-his-success.html (last accessed 11 January 2024).

12 Tasha Eurich, 'What Self-Awareness Really Is (and How to Cultivate It)', *Harvard Business Review*, 4 January 2018, www.hbr.org/2018/01/what-self-awareness-really-is-and-how-to-cultivate-it (last accessed 20 November 2023).

13 Anil K. Khandelwal, *Dare to Lead: Actionable Insights Drawn from the Transformation of Bank of Baroda* (Gurgaon: PRHI, 2023).

Chapter 3: Self-Management: Building Your Strengths

1 Peter F. Drucker, 'Managing Oneself', Goodreads, https://www.goodreads.com/quotes/9616762-you-should-not-change-yourself-but-create-yourself-that-mean (last accessed 5 July 2024).
2 Peter F. Drucker, 'Quotable Quote', Goodreads, https://www.goodreads.com/quotes/16406-the-best-way-to-predict-your-future-is-to-create (last accessed 5 July 2024).
3 *Sarala Gita* (Gorakhpur: Gita Press, 2018).
4 Daniel Goleman, 'What Makes a Leader', *Harvard Business Review*, January 2004, www.hbr.org/2004/01/what-makes-a-leader (last accessed 3 April 2024).
5 Peter F. Drucker, 'Managing Oneself', *Harvard Business Review*, January 2005, https://hbr.org/2005/01/managing-oneself (last accessed 6 May 2024).
6 Nick Lovegrove, *The Mosaic Principle: The Six Dimensions of a Successful Life and Career* (UK: Profile Books, 2017).

Chapter 4: Self-Discipline: Fuel for Personal Growth

1 Daaji (Kamlesh Patel), *The Wisdom Bridge: Nine Principles to a Life* (Gurgaon: PRHI, 2022).
2 Rajesh Srivastava, *The 10 New Life-Changing Skills: Get Them and Get Ahead!* (Gurgaon: PRHI, 2022).
3 Daaji (Kamlesh Patel), *The Wisdom Bridge: Nine Principles to a Life.*
4 Peter Senge, *The Fifth Discipline: The Art & Practice of the Learning Organization* (New York, USA: Currency Double Day, 1990).

5   Kerima Greene, 'Manchester United's Sir Alex Ferguson on the secret to his success', CNBC, October 2015, www.cnbc.com/2015/10/16/manchester-uniteds-sir-alex-ferguson-on-the-secret-to-his-success.html (last accessed 5 January 2024).

6   Ram Charan, 'The Discipline of Listening', *Harvard Business Review*, 21 June 2012, www.hbr.org/2012/06/the-discipline-of-listening (last accessed 22 March 2024).

7   Aditya Gajanan Kukalyekar, 'How much time does Virat Kohli spend in gym?', CrickTracker, November 2017, www.cricktracker.com/much-time-virat-kohli-spend-gym/ (last accessed 22 March 2024).

8   Devendra Pandey, 'Hardik Pandya's fitness secret', *Indian Express*, November 2022, www.indianexpress.com/article/sports/cricket/hardik-pandyas-fitness-secret-moong-dal-khichdi-tempered-just-right-by-his-travelling-chef-8259407/ (last accessed 4 April 2024).

9   Wilhelm Hofmann et al., 'Yes, But Are They Happy? Effects of Trait Self-Control on Affective Well-Being and Life Satisfaction', *Journal of Personality*, June 2013, https://pubmed.ncbi.nlm.nih.gov/23750741/ (last accessed 22 January 2024).

10   Dalai Lama and Howard C. Cutler, *The Art of Happiness* (UK: Hodder Paperbacks, 1999).

11   Acharya Buddharakkhita, trans., *The Dhammapada: The Buddha's Path of Wisdom*, Access to Insight (BCBS Edition), 30 November 2013, https://www.accesstoinsight.org/tipitaka/kn/dhp/dhp.12.budd.html (last accessed November 2023).

12   James Clear, *Atomic Habits: An Easy & Proven Way to Build Good Habits & Break Bad Ones* (USA: Random House Business Books, 2018).

13   Isaac Chanakira, '3 Practical and Effective Stoic Exercises from Marcus Aurelius, Seneca and Epictetus', Daily Stoic, www.dailystoic.com/practical-stoic-exercises/ (last accessed 15 January 2024).

14 Ryan Holiday, *Discipline Is Destiny: The Power of Self-Control* (UK: Profile Books, 2022).

15 Trina Paulus, *Hope for the Flowers* (USA: Paulist Press International, 1986).

Chapter 5: Time Management: How to Work Smarter with Your Time

1 Brene Brown, *Dare to Lead* (London: Vermilion, 2018).

2 William Oncken Jr., Donald L. Wass and Stephen R. Covey, 'Who's Got the Monkey?', *Harvard Business Review*, November 1999, www.hbr.org/1999/11/management-time-whos-got-the-monkey (last accessed 3 April 2024).

3 Ray Dalio, *Principles* (USA: Simon & Schuster, 2017).

4 Stephen R. Covey, *The 7 Habits of Highly Effective People* (USA: Free Press, 1989).

5 Julian Birkinshaw and Jordan Cohen, 'Make Time for the Work That Matters', *Harvard Business Review*, September 2013, www.hbr.org/2013/09/Make-time-for-the-work-that-matters (last accessed 6 January 2024).

6 Nandan Nilekani and Tanuj Bhojwani, *The Art of Bitfulness* (Gurgaon: PRHI, 2022).

Chapter 6: Resilience: Bouncing Back from Setbacks

1 Nelson Mandela, 'Quotable Quotes', Goodreads, https://www.goodreads.com/quotes/270163-do-not-judge-me-by-my-successes-judge-me-by (last accessed 5 July 2024).

2 Ranjay Gulati, 'Investing in Growth through Uncertainty,' *Harvard Business Review*, July–August 2023, www.hbr.org/2023/07/investing-in-growth-through-uncertainty (last accessed 15 January 2024).

3 Ginni Rometty, *Good Power* (USA: Harvard Business Review Press, 2023).

4　Genie Joseph, *The Act Resilient Method: From Trauma to Transformation* (USA: Eve Publishing, 2017).

5　Andrea Rice, 'What Resilience is and isn't', PsychCentral, January 2022, https://psychcentral.com/lib/what-is-resilience (last accessed 5 April 2024).

6　Dalai Lama, *The Four Noble Truths* (UK: HarperCollins, 2009).

7　Jonas Salzgeber, *The Little Book of Stoicism: Timeless Wisdom to Gain Resilience, Confidence, and Calmness* (USA: Jonas Salzgeber, 2019).

8　'Raising awareness of stress at work in developing countries: advice to employers and worker representatives (A modern hazard in a traditional working environment)', WHO, 1 June 2007, www.who.int/publications-detail-redirect/924159165X (last accessed 21 November 2023).

9　Catherine Walsh, 'Leadership on 9-11: Morgan Stanley's Challenge', Harvard Business School Working Knowledge, December 2001, www.hbswk.hbs.edu/archive/leadership-on-9-11-morgan-stanley-s-challenge (last accessed 4 January 2024).

10　Diane L. Coutu, 'How Resilience Works', *Harvard Business Review*, May 2002, www.hbr.org/2002/05/how-resilience-works (last accessed 4 January 2024).

11　Daniel Goleman, 'Resilience for the Rest of Us', *Harvard Business Review*, 25 April 2011, www.hbr.org/2011/04/resilience-for-the-rest-of-us (last accessed 4 January 2024).

12　Shawn Achor and Michelle Gielan, 'Resilience Is about How You Recharge, Not How You Endure', *Harvard Business Review*, 24 June 2016, www.hbr.org/2016/06/resilience-is-about-how-you-recharge-not-how-you-endure (last accessed 4 January 2023).

13　'Yoga Boosts Mental Health Grades', IIT Bombay Study, *Times of India*, 20 November 2020, www.timesofindia.indiatimes.com/city/mumbai/yoga-boosts-mental-health-grades-iit-bombay-study/articleshow/79314941.cms (last accessed 27 November 2023).

14 Nassim Nicholas Taleb, *The Black Swan: The Impact of the Highly Improbable* (UK: Penguin Books Ltd, 2008).

15 Héctor García, and Francesc Miralles, *Ikigai: The Japanese Secret to a Long and Happy Life* (UK: Random House, 2017).

16 Srikanth Bolla, 'About Srikanth Bolla', www.srikanthbolla. com/about/ (last accessed 10 April 2024).

17 Liz Fosslien and Mollie West Duffy, 'Stop Telling Employees to Be Resilient', *MIT Sloan Management Review*, April 2022, www.sloanreview.mit.edu/article/ stop-telling-employees-to-be-resilient/ (last accessed 27 November 2023).

18 George S. Everly, Jr., 'Building a Resilient Organizational Culture', *Harvard Business Review*, 24 June 2011, www.hbr. org/2011/06/building-a-resilient-organizat (last accessed 27 November 2023).

19 'When a crisis becomes an opportunity', Microsoft Stories Asia, 10 September 2020, https://news.microsoft.com/ apac/features/when-crisis-becomes-an-opportunity/ (last accessed 27 December 2023).

20 'Reinhold Niebuhr Quotes', BrainyQuote, https://www. brainyquote.com/quotes/reinhold_niebuhr_100884 (last accessed 8 July 2024).

Chapter 7: Emotional Regulation and Anger Management: Taming Your Temper

1 Aristotle, 'Quotable Quote', Goodreads, https://www. goodreads.com/quotes/21401-anybody-can-become- angry-that-is-easy-but-to (last accessed 5 July 2024).

2 Daniel M. Wegner, Ralph Erber and Sophia Zanakos, 'Ironic processes in the mental control of mood and mood-related thought', *Journal of Personality and Social Psychology*

(1993), www.researchgate.net/publication/14904416_Ironic_Processes_in_the_Mental_Control_of_Mood_and_Mood-Related_Thought (last accessed 5 December 2023).

3 Daniel Goleman, 'What Makes a Leader', *Harvard Business Review*, 1998, reprinted January 2004, www.hbr.org/2004/01/what-makes-a-leader (last accessed 24 January 2024).

4 Dalai Lama, 'Dalai Lama Quotes', BrainyQuote, https://www.brainyquote.com/quotes/dalai_lama_446760 (last accessed 5 July 2024).

5 HH the Dalai Lama and Archbishop Desmond Tutu with Douglas Abrams, *The Book of Joy: Lasting Happiness in a Changing World* (UK: Penguin Random House, 2016).

6 Udai Pareek, *Training Instruments in HRD and OD* (India: Tata McGraw Hill, 1994).

7 M.K. Gandhi, *The Story of My Experiments with Truth* (Delhi: Rupa, 2011).

8 Ram Lochan Yadav, 'Anger; Its Impact On Human Body', *Innovare Journal of Health Sciences* (2017), www.researchgate.net/publication/328065633_ANGER_ITS_IMPACT_ON_HUMAN_BODY (last accessed 7 May 2024).

9 A. Parthasarthy, *Bhagavad Gita: Commentary by Swami Parthasarathy* (India: Vedanta Life Institute, 2014).

10 'Emotional Regulation', Positive Psychology, August 2019, www.positivepsychology.com/emotion-regulation (last accessed 5 February 2024).

11 Amy Morin, '11 Anger Management Strategies to Calm You Down Fast', Verywellmind, November 2023, www.verywellmind.com/anger-management-strategies-4178870 (last accessed 5 February 2024).

12 Dana Sinclair, *Dialed In* (UK: Simon & Schuster, 2024).

13 'Anger management: 10 tips to tame your temper', Mayo Clinic, 14 April 2022, www.mayoclinic.org/healthy-

lifestyle/adult-health/in-depth/anger-management/art-20045434 (last accessed 5 February 2024).

14 HH the Dalai Lama, Archbishop Desmond Tutu with Douglas Abrams, *The Book of Joy: Lasting Happiness in a Changing World.*

15 Adam Grant, *Originals: How Non-conformists Change the World* (UK: W.H. Allen, 2017).

16 Andrew Brodsky, Joshua D. Margolis and Joel Brockner, 'Speaking Truth to Power: A Full Cycle Approach', Working paper (2015).

17 Justin Brown, 'The Dalai Lama explains the most effective way to deal with your anger,' Ideapod, 26 January 2017, www.ideapod.com/dalai-lama-reveals-need-embrace-anger-transform/ (last accessed 15 January 2024).

Chapter 8: Compassion: Empathy in Action

1 Dalai Lama and Archbishop Desmond Tutu, 'The Eight Pillars of Joy', Beliefnet, https://www.beliefnet.com/inspiration/the-eight-pillars-of-joy.aspx (last accessed 10 July 2024).

2 Sangeeta Devi Dundoo, 'Sonu Sood: "Migrant workers built our homes; I couldn't watch them being homeless"', *The Hindu*, 29 May 2020, www.thehindu.com/entertainment/movies/sonu-sood-migrant-workers-built-our-homes-i-couldnt-watch-them-being-homeless/article31685826.ece (last accessed 3 September 2023).

3 Plato, Goodreads, https://www.goodreads.com/quotes/1231-be-kind-for-everyone-you-meet-is-fighting-a-harder (last accessed 5 July 2024).

4 Thupten Jinpa, *A Fearless Heart: How the Courage to Be Compassionate Can Transform Our Lives* (New York: Avery, 2015).

5 Jane E. Dutton, Kristina M. Workman and Ashley E. Hardin, 'Compassion at Work', *Annual Review of Organizational Psychology and Organizational Behavior* (March 2014), www.annualreviews.org/doi/abs/10.1146/annurev-orgpsych-031413-091221 (last accessed 30 January 2024).

6 Tania Singer and Olga Klimecki, 'Empathy and Compassion', *Current Biology* (September 2014), www.researchgate.net/publication/265909916_Empathy_and_Compassion (last accessed 30 January 2024).

7 'The Neuroscience of Compassion', CCARE Press, July 2022, https://ccare.stanford.edu/press_posts/the-neuroscience-of-compassion/ (last accessed 8 May 2024).

8 Lila Lieberman, 'The Neuroscience of Compassion', Uplift, www.uplift.love/the-neuroscience-of-compassion/ (last accessed 30 January 2024).

9 Rasmus Hougaard, Jacqueline Carter and Jason Beck, 'Assessment: Are You a Compassionate Leader?', *Harvard Business Review*, 15 May 2018, www.hbr.org/2018/05/assessment-are-you-a-compassionate-leader (last accessed 8 November 2023).

10 Ian Cook, 'Who Is Driving the Great Resignation?', *Harvard Business Review*, 15 September 2021, www.hbr.org/2021/09/who-is-driving-the-great-resignation (last accessed 8 November 2023).

11 Varun Warrier, 'Study finds that genes play a role in empathy', University of Cambridge Research, March 2018, www.cam.ac.uk/research/news/study-finds-that-genes-play-a-role-in-empathy (last accessed 8 November 2023).

12 'Compassion Cultivation Training', Stanford University, https://med.stanford.edu/psychiatry/education/cme/cct.html (last accessed 8 November 2023).

13 'Rising Phoenix', Tata Group, www.tata.com/newsroom/rising-phoenix-taj-2611 (last accessed 5 February 2024);

'Tata and the Community', Tata Group, www.tata.com/ community (last accessed 5 February 2024).

14 Patu Keswani, 'How a Wedding Invite Changed Lemon Tree's Hiring?', 2015, www.indiainclusionsummit.com/ video/how-a-wedding-invite-changed-lemontrees-hiring-patu-keswani-iis/ (last accessed 5 February 2024); 'About us', Lemon Tree Hotels, www.lemontreehotels.com/ about-us.aspx (last accessed 5 February 2024); 'Lemon Tree Annual Report (2021–2022)', Trendlyne, https://trendlyne. com/fundamentals/documents-annual-reports/81513/ LEMONTREE/lemon-tree-hotels-ltd/#documents.

Chapter 9: Courage: Conquering Your Fears

1 Osho, *Courage: The Joy of Living Dangerously* (USA: St. Martin's Griffin, 1999).

2 Anais Nin, *The Diary of Anais Nin, Volume 3, 1939–1944* (USA: Mariner Books, 1971).

3 Kelly Kuehn, '85 Courage Quotes That Will Inspire You to Face Your Fears', *Reader's Digest*, 8 December 2023, www. rd.com/article/courage-quotes/ (last accessed 23 March 2024).

4 Cooper Woodard and Cynthia Pury, 'The Construct of Courage: Categorization and Measurement', *Consulting Psychology Journal: Practice and Research* (June 2007), www. researchgate.net/publication/232442435 (last accessed 25 October 2023).

5 Prasad Kaipa and Navi Radjou, *From Smart to Wise: Acting and Leading with Wisdom* (Gurgaon: PRHI, 2013).

6 Kathleen Reardon, 'Courage as a Skill', *Harvard Business Review*, January 2007, www.hbr.org/2007/01/courage-as-a-skill (last accessed on 27 March 2024).

7 HH the Dalai Lama and Archbishop Desmond Tutu with Douglas Abrams, *The Book of Joy: Lasting Happiness in a Changing World* (UK: Penguin Random House, 2016).

8　Manfred F.R. Kets de Vries, 'How to Find and Practice Courage' *Harvard Business Review*, May 2020, www.hbr. org/2020/05/how-to-find-and-practice-courage　　(last accessed 10 October 2022).

9　Anil K. Khandelwal, *Dare to Lead: Actionable Insights Drawn from the Transformation of Bank of Baroda* (Gurgaon: PRHI, 2023), Chapter 7.

10　'Sherron Watkins Had Whistle, But Blew It', *Forbes*, 14 February 2002, www.forbes.com/2002/02/14/0214watkins. html?sh=4dd0eba32b98 (last accessed 10 October 2022).

11　Oprah Winfrey, *What I Know for Sure* (USA: Macmillan, 2014).

12　Lucius Annaeus Seneca, Goodreads, https://www. goodreads.com/quotes/731385-it-is-not-because-things-are-difficult-that-we-do (last accessed 5 July 2024).

Chapter 10: Relationships: Making Meaningful Connections

1　Jim Collins and Bill Lazier, *Beyond Entrepreneurship 2.0: Turning Your Business into an Enduring Great Company* (USA: Portfolio, 2020).

2　Robin S. Sharma, BrainyQuote, https://www.brainyquote. com/quotes/robin_s_sharma_531656 (last accessed 5 July 2024).

3　Edgar H. Schein and Peter H. Schein, *Humble Leadership: The Power of Relationships, Openness, and Trust (The Humble Leadership Series)* (USA: Berrett-Koehler Publishers Inc., 2018).

4　Bill George, *Authentic Leadership: Rediscovering the Secrets to Creating Lasting Value* (USA: Jossey–Bass, 2003).

5　Jim Collins and Bill Lazier, *Beyond Entrepreneurship 2.0: Turning Your Business into an Enduring Great Company* (USA: Portfolio, 2020).

6   Udai Pareek, *Training Instruments in HRD & OD* (India: Tata McGraw Hill, 1994).

7   'Fundamental Interpersonal Results Orientation-Behaviour Assessment (FIRO-B)', Psychometrics, www.psychometrics.com/assessments/firo-b (last accessed 22 December 2023) (also see www.thehumanelement.com/firo-theory/ [last accessed 22 December 2023]).

8   'Myers Briggs Type Indicator', The Myers Briggs Company, https://www.themyersbriggs.com/en-US/Products-and-Services/Myers-Briggs (last accessed 9 May 2024).

9   T-Group, www.isabs.org (last accessed 7 March 2024).

Chapter 11: Authenticity: Being Your Real Self

1   Carl Gustav Jung, Goodreads, https://www.goodreads.com/quotes/75948-the-privilege-of-a-lifetime-is-to-become-who-you (last accessed 5 July 2024).

2   Bill George, *Authentic Leadership: Rediscovering the Secrets to Creating Lasting Value* (USA: Jossey–Bass, 2003).

3   Ibid.

4   David Gergen, *Hearts Touched with Fire: How Great Leaders Are Made* (USA: Simon & Schuster, 2022).

5   Herminia Ibarra, 'The Authenticity Paradox', *Harvard Business Review*, January–February 2015, www.hbr.org/2015/01/the-authenticity-paradox (last accessed 3 October 2022).

6   Kolb's Learning Cycle adapted from 'What is Experiential Learning', www.experientiallearninginstitute.org/resources/what-is-experiential-learning/ (last accessed 4 March 2023).

7   Brené Brown, *Dare to Lead* (USA: Vermilion, 2018).

8   Bill George, 'Authentic Leadership Rediscovered', *Harvard Business School Working Knowledge*, November 2015, https://hbswk.hbs.edu/item/authentic-leadership-rediscovered (last accessed 3 October 2022).

Chapter 12: Credibility: Building Trust and Reputation

1   John C. Maxwell, QuoteFancy, https://quotefancy.com/
    quote/841302/John-C-Maxwell-Credibility-is-a-leader-
    s-currency-With-it-he-or-she-is-solvent-without-it   (last
    accessed 5 July 2024).
2   M.K. Gandhi, *The Story of My Experiments with Truth*
    (Delhi: Rupa, 2011).
3   James M. Kouzes and Barry Z. Posner, *Credibility: How
    Leaders Gain and Lose It, Why People Demand It* (USA:
    Jossey–Bass, 2011).
4   Christopher Wolf, 'The Formula for the Perfect Leader', *US
    News*, 12 December 2023, www.usnews.com/news/leaders/
    articles/2023-12-12/survey-americans-want-trustworthy-
    leaders-above-all-else (last accessed 6 February 2024); 'The
    25th Annual Reputation Quotient (RQ®)', The Harris Poll,
    2023, https://theharrispoll.com, (last accessed 6 February
    2024).
5   A. Parthasarthy, *Sarala Gita* (Gorakhpur, India: Gita Press,
    2018).
6   Gerry Mullany, 'Strauss-Kahn Resigns from I.M.F. in
    Wake of His Arrest', *New York Times*, May 2011, www.
    nytimes.com/2011/05/19/business/19imf.html   (last
    accessed 5 December 2022).
7   Walter Pavlo, 'Former McKinsey and Co. Boss, Rajat
    Gupta, Guilty of Insider Trading', *Forbes*, June 2015,
    www.forbes.com/sites/walterpavlo/2012/06/15/former-
    mckinsey-and-co-boss-rajat-gupta-guilty-of-insider-
    trading/ (last accessed 5 December 2022).
8   James M. Kouzes and Barry Z. Posner, *Credibility: How
    Leaders Gain and Lose It, Why People Demand It* (USA:
    Jossey–Bass, 2011).

9   Peter Drucker, AZQuotes, https://www.azquotes.com/
    quote/1371399 (last accessed 1 August 2024).
10 Daaji (Kamlesh Patel), *The Wisdom Bridge: Nine Principles to
    a Life* (Gurgaon: PRHI, 2022).

Chapter 13: Humility: A Differentiator for Leadership Effectiveness

1   Lao Tzu, Goodreads, https://www.goodreads.com/author/
    quotes/2622245.Lao_Tzu?container=bebo&page=48#:~:
    text=A%20leader%20is%20best%20when,%2C%20
    "We%20did%20this%20ourselves (last accessed 5 July
    2024).
2   Jim Collins, 'Level 5 Leadership: The Triumph of Humility
    and Fierce Resolve', *Harvard Business Review*, 1 January 2001,
    www.hbr.org/2001/01/level-5-leadership-the-triumph-
    of-humility-and-fierce-resolve-2 (last accessed 4 January
    2023).
3   J.P. Tangney, 'Humility: Theoretical perspectives, empirical
    findings and directions for future research', *Journal of Social
    and Clinical Psychology* (2000), (last accessed 4 January
    2023).
4   L.B. Bhide and Anil K. Khandelwal, *Industrial Relations
    in Banks: Text and Cases* (India: Om-Ameya Prakashan,
    1986).
5   Rabindranath Tagore, *Stray Birds* (India: Niyogi Books
    Private Limited, 2018).
6   Edgar H. Schein, *Humble Inquiry: The Gentle Art of Asking
    Instead of Telling (The Humble Leadership Series)* (USA:
    Berrett-Koehler Publishers, 2013).
7   Jocko Willink, *Leadership Strategy and Tactics: Field Manual*
    (India: Pan Macmillan, 2020).

8   Isaac Newton, *The Correspondence of Isaac Newton* (USA: Cambridge University Press, 1959).

9   Nelson Mandela, *Long Walk to Freedom* (UK: Abacus, 1995).

Chapter 14: Fairness: Exercising Sensitivity in Delivering Organizational Justice

1   Victor Hugo, Goodreads, https://www.goodreads.com/quotes/369798-being-good-is-easy-what-is-difficult-is-being-just (last accessed 5 July 2024).

2   Aristotle and Roger Crisp, *Nicomachean Ethics* (Cambridge: Cambridge University Press, 2014); John Rawls, *A Theory of Justice* (USA: Harvard University Press, Revised edition 2020); 'About John Rawls and Interpretation of *A Theory of Justice* (1971)', www.plato.stanford.edu/entries/rawls/ (last accessed 22 December 2023).

3   Liane Davey, 'How to Earn a Reputation as a Fair Manager', *Harvard Business Review*, 3 August 2018, www.hbr.org/2018/08/how-to-earn-a-reputation-as-a-fair-manager (last accessed 29 November 2023).

4   Brit Hume, BrainyQuote, https://www.brainyquote.com/quotes/brit_hume_185934 (last accessed 5 July 2024).

5   W. Chan Kim and Renée Mauborgne, 'Fair Process: Managing in the Knowledge Economy', *Harvard Business Review*, January 2003, www.hbr.org/2003/01/fair-process-managing-in-the-knowledge-economy (last accessed 14 March 2024).

6   Joel Brockner, 'Why It's So Hard to Be Fair', *Harvard Business Review*, March 2006, www.hbr.org/2006/03/why-its-so-hard-to-be-fair (last accessed 14 March 2024).

7   Pamela Fuller, Mark Murphy and Anne Chow, *The Leader's Guide to Unconscious Bias* (UK: Simon & Schuster, 2020).

8   'Ratan Tata Story: Stockifi Tweet', Rattibha, https://en.rattibha.com/thread/16421696893620305924737706/ (last accessed 14 March 2024).

9 'About T-Group', T-Group, www.isabs.org (last accessed 7 March 2024).
10 'About Role-Play Training', Indeed.com, www.indeed. com/career-advice/career-development/role-play-training (last accessed 14 March 2024).

Chapter 15: Communication: A Keystone for Impactful Leadership

1 George Bernard Shaw, Goodreads, https://www.goodreads. com/quotes/178425-the-single-biggest-problem-in-communication-is-the-illusion-that (last accessed 5 July 2024).
2 Edgar H. Schein, *Humble Inquiry: The Gentle Art of Asking Instead of Telling (The Humble Leadership Series)* (USA: Berrett-Koehler Publishers, 2013).
3 Edgar H. Schein, *Process Consultation: Its Role in Organization Development, Volume 1* (USA: Addison–Wesley Publishing Company, 1983).
4 Marshall B. Rosenberg, *Nonviolent Communication* (USA: Puddle Dancer Press, 2015).
5 Anil K. Khandelwal, *Dare to Lead: Actionable Insights Drawn from the Transformation of Bank of Baroda* (India: Penguin Random House India, 2023).
6 Carl R. Rogers and F.J. Roethlisberger, 'Barriers and Gateways to Communication', *Harvard Business Review*, November–December 1991 (This article originally appeared in its July–August 1952 issue), www.hbr.org/1991/11/barriers-and-gateways-to-communication (last accessed 12 December 2023).
7 '56 Inspiring Team Communication Quotes to Motivate Your Team', Indeed, 25 June 2022, https://www.indeed.com/career-advice/career-development/team-communication-quotes (last accessed 9 July 2024).

8   Sudha Murty, 'Apro JRD', Tata.com, www.tata.com/
    newsroom/heritage/appro-jrd-tata-sudha-murthy-tribute
    (last accessed 5 February 2024).

Chapter 16: Listening to Attend, Absorb and Act

1   'Kurdish Proverb [17649]', Illustrated World of Proverbs,
    https://www.worldofproverbs.com/2012/04/listen-hundred-
    times-ponder-thousand.html (last accessed 5 July 2024).
2   Warren Bennis with Patricia Ward Biederman et al., *The
    Essential Bennis* (USA: Jossey–Bass, 2009).
3   Quote shared in an interview with Bill Moyers, *A World of
    Ideas, Peter Drucker: Father of Management*, 17 November
    1988, www.billmoyers.com/content/peter-drucker/ (last
    accessed 5 July 2024).
4   Robin Abrahams and Boris Groysberg, 'How to Become a
    Better Listener', *Harvard Business Review*, 21 December 2021,
    www.hbr.org/2021/12/how-to-become-a-better-listener (last
    accessed 5 September 2022).
5   William Isaacs, *Dialogue: The Art Of Thinking Together*
    (USA: Currency, 1999).
6   J. Krishnamurti's 1st Public Talk on 9 July 1967, www.
    jkrishnamurti.org/content/1st-public-talk-9th-july-1967
    (last accessed 4 March 2024).
7   Manfred F.R. Kets de Vries, *Leading Wisely* (UK: Wiley,
    2022).

Chapter 17: Detoxifying Communication: Becoming Accountable for Your Behaviour

1   Maya Angelou, 'Quotable Quote', Goodreads, https://
    www.goodreads.com/quotes/663523-at-the-end-of-the-
    day-people-won-t-remember-what (last accessed 9 July
    2024).

2   Jonah Berger, *Magic Words: What to Say to Get Your Way* (USA: Harper Business, 2023).

3   Lucy Swedberg, 'The Power of Words', *Harvard Business Review*, July–August 2023, www.hbr.org/2023/07/the-power-of-words (last accessed 5 August 2023).

4   Zeno, QuoteFancy, https://quotefancy.com/quote/1652854/ Zeno-of-Citium-Better-to-trip-with-the-feet-than-with-the-tongue (last accessed 5 July 2024).

Chapter 18: Dialogue: The Most Effective Tool for Problem-Solving

1   Thích Nhất Hạnh, *Living Buddha, Living Christ* (Canada: Penguin Random House Canada, 2007).

2   Peter Senge, *The Fifth Discipline: The Art & Practice of the Learning Organization* (USA: Currency Double Day, 1990).

3   William Isaacs, *Dialogue: The Art Of Thinking Together* (USA: Currency, 1999).

4   Alec Grimsley, *Vital Conversations: Making the Impossible Conversation Possible* (UK: Barnes Holland Publishing, 2009).

5   Anil K. Khandelwal, *Dare to Lead: Actionable Insights Drawn from the Transformation of Bank of Baroda* (Gurgaon: PRHI, 2023).

6   Ibid.

7   Stephen R. Covey, 'Habit 5: Seek First to Understand, Then to Be Understood', FranklinCovey, https://www.franklincovey.com/the-7-habits/habit-5/ (last accessed 5 July 2024).

Scan QR code to access the
Penguin Random House India website